THEATER IN THE PLANNED SOCIETY

UNIVERSITY OF NORTH CAROLINA
STUDIES IN THE GERMANIC LANGUAGES
AND LITERATURES

Initiated by RICHARD JENTE (1949–1952), *established by* P. E. COENEN (1952–1968)

SIEGFRIED MEWS, EDITOR

Publication Committee: Department of Germanic Languages

77. J. W. Thomas. TANNHÄUSER: POET AND LEGEND. With Texts and Translations of his Works. 1974. Pp. x, 202. Cloth $10.75.

78. Olga Marx and Ernst Morwitz, trans. THE WORKS OF STEFAN GEORGE. 1974. 2nd rev. and enl. ed. Pp. xxviii, 431. Cloth $12.90.

79. Siegfried Mews and Herbert Knust, eds. ESSAYS ON BRECHT: THEATER AND POLITICS. 1974. Pp. xiv, 241. Cloth $11.95.

80. Donald G. Daviau and George J. Buelow. THE *ARIADNE AUF NAXOS* OF HUGO VON HOFMANNSTHAL AND RICHARD STRAUSS. 1975. Pp. x, 274. Cloth $12.95.

81. Elaine E. Boney. RAINER MARIA RILKE: *DUINESIAN ELEGIES*. German Text with English Translation and Commentary. 1975. 2nd ed. 1977. Pp. xii, 153. Cloth $10.75.

82. Jane K. Brown. GOETHE'S CYCLICAL NARRATIVES: *DIE UNTERHALTUNGEN DEUTSCHER AUSGEWANDERTEN* AND *WILHELM MEISTERS WANDERJAHRE*. 1975. Pp. x, 144. Cloth $10.25.

83. Flora Kimmich. SONNETS OF CATHARINA VON GREIFFENBERG: METHODS OF COMPOSITION. 1975. Pp. x, 132. Cloth $11.50.

84. Herbert W. Reichert. FRIEDRICH NIETZSCHE'S IMPACT ON MODERN GERMAN LITERATURE. FIVE ESSAYS: 1975. Pp. xxii, 129. Cloth $9.90.

85. James C. O'Flaherty, Timothy F. Sellner, Robert M. Helm, eds. STUDIES IN NIETZSCHE AND THE CLASSICAL TRADITION. 1976. Pp. xviii, 278. Cloth $14.95.

86. Alan P. Cottrell. GOETHE'S *FAUST*. SEVEN ESSAYS. 1976. Pp. xvi, 143. Cloth $11.50.

87. Hugo Bekker. FRIEDRICH VON HAUSEN: INQUIRIES INTO HIS POETRY. 1977. Pp. x, 159. Cloth $12.95.

88. H. G. Huettich. THEATER IN THE PLANNED SOCIETY: CONTEMPORARY DRAMA IN THE GERMAN DEMOCRATIC REPUBLIC IN ITS HISTORICAL, POLITICAL, AND CULTURAL CONTEXT. 1978. Pp. xvi, 174. Cloth $11.50.

For other volumes in the "Studies" see pages 172 ff.

Send orders to: (U.S. and Canada)
The University of North Carolina Press, P.O. Box 2288
Chapel Hill, N. C. 27514
(All other countries) Feffer and Simons, Inc., 31 Union Square, New York, N. Y. 10003

NUMBER EIGHTY-EIGHT

UNIVERSITY
OF NORTH CAROLINA
STUDIES IN
THE GERMANIC LANGUAGES
AND LITERATURES

Theater in the Planned Society

Contemporary Drama
in the German Democratic Republic
in its Historical, Political, and Cultural Context

by

H. G. Huettich

CHAPEL HILL
THE UNIVERSITY OF NORTH CAROLINA PRESS
1978

© University of North Carolina
Studies in the Germanic Languages
and Literatures 1978

ᵕ ℮

Library of Congress Cataloging in Publication Data

Huettich, H. G., 1946—
  Theater in the planned society: contemporary drama in
the German Democratic Republic in its historical, political,
and cultural context.

  (University of North Carolina studies in the Germanic
languages and literatures; no. 88)
  Includes index.
  1. German drama—Germany, East—History and criticism. 2. Communism and literature. 3. Literature and state—
Germany, East. I. Title. II. Series: Studies in the Germanic
languages and literatures (Chapel Hill, N. C.); no. 88.

PT3721.H8   832'.9'1409   76-20606
ISBN 0-8078-8088-4

Manufactured in the U.S.A.

FOR MY PARENTS

Contents

Preface

The American reader's exposure to the literature of the German Democratic Republic (GDR), generally known as East Germany, has been minimal. In the area of German studies, however, the study of the culture of the GDR has been the fastest-growing discipline at American universities in recent years.

Today in the United States, public recognition of the GDR is at an all-time high. Since 1969 the attention given to the "other" German state by government agencies, the media, and educational institutions has steadily increased. This achievement of a new "higher profile" in the public mind is partly due to the GDR's recent efforts to improve its international public relations and to relax cold war tensions. But the primary credit for this new focus must be placed where it rightfully belongs: with historical necessity.

For twenty years the GDR was deliberately ignored in sources of public information in the vain hope that it would indeed go away if ignored long enough. By 1969, however, the GDR could no longer be ignored. Economically it had come to rank among the top ten industrial nations of the world: it was the second largest industrial producer of the Warsaw Pact nations. As such, it had forced other nations to recognize its growing importance in international relations: it had become a potential trade partner. These developments culminated in the GDR's admission to the United Nations in 1973 with status equal to that of the other new member, the Federal Republic of Germany (West Germany), and, finally, in the formal diplomatic recognition of the GDR by the United States in the fall of 1974.

Americans who are interested in the cultural life of the GDR must first be prepared to dismiss those preconceived notions of "German Culture" which are usually gained through exposure to German history or to the cultural life of the Western, Americanized Federal Republic.

The GDR, geographically "Middle" rather than "Eastern" Germany, is a "socialist democracy," i.e., a socialist state based upon a governing communist party. In its simplest definition, the GDR is indeed a Communist country. GDR cultural life thus follows a set of rules that do not correspond to the more familiar patterns of West Germany or the United States.

Like all Communist states, the GDR is a centrally planned society. Consequently, its literature is a planned literature. This is nowhere more evident than in the production of drama. Socialist realism, the "historically concrete representation of reality in its revolutionary development," confines the East German theater to the topical representation of contemporary life in the German Democratic Republic. The Socialist Unity Party (SED) envisions the theater, traditionally Germany's "moral institution," as a vehicle for the transmission of a socialist morality. The SED's cultural policy places the contemporary topical drama of the GDR in the vanguard of cultural-political activity; it is at once one of the prime educational tools of the planned society and its most effectively planned literary genre. This politicization of the theater makes the dramatist a political figure, and his work a political phenomenon. A primary task of the present volume is to investigate the strategies used by various dramatists to respond to this social mandate and the way in which their imposed social role affects the nature and quality of their work.

To the liberal West the social-political mandate under which the GDR dramatists must work represents the most fascinating aspect of their literary situation. This study attempts to examine the development of contemporary GDR dramatists and their theater within the framework of the GDR's socialist/Communist system and to trace the reciprocal relationships between the dramatists and their planned society. We could do worse than to take our own drama and dramatists as seriously as the GDR regards hers.

Given these circumstances, a note on the methodology of this study will be of benefit to the reader. The present study has two major objectives: (1) To trace the development of the GDR's contemporary topical drama (GDR drama about the GDR) in its historical context; and (2) to define the sociopolitical function of drama and dramatists in that society. These objectives necessitate an historical approach which I have tried to apply as objectively and consistently as possible. From the very beginning, it was evident to me that to separate politics from literature, art from society, and history from literary history would not only be a thankless endeavor, but a fruitless one as well. I am convinced that the literary artist, and especially the writer of drama, engages in a social function in any society. In the GDR, this function is raised to another degree, to a political function. Necessarily, this implies certain controls and restrictions to which the dramatist must tailor his work, since the primary function of the dramatist's work is not defined by the dramatist, but by the cultural policy of the state which fluctuates with the historical development of the GDR.

Here, the all-important questions of artistic freedom and aesthetic quality become unavoidable. To do full justice to these questions, however, would entail

xii

an incisive ideological critique of the sociopolitical structure of the GDR which I do not presume to present in my historically oriented study of contemporary drama. Furthermore, I am not convinced that "artistic freedom" and "aesthetic quality" are causally related—however these concepts may be defined. Existing definitions of these concepts do not significantly rise above justifications of subjective personal taste tied to personal ideology. In my own subjective taste, I may value the drama of Heiner Müller far above that of Helmut Sakowski. This however only defines my taste as an American middle-class scholar, but says little indeed about the historical function of the theater in the GDR which is my primary object of inquiry.

For those who wish to pursue this question further, within the framework of this study or outside of it, I have carefully and objectively outlined the ideological consistencies and inconsistencies in the cultural policy of the GDR to the extent that available historical evidence permits. Thus the reader may make his own aesthetic and ideological judgments in reference to the cultural-historical processes, the dramatists, and the works encompassed in the present study.

★ ★ ★

A word about the terminology, abbreviations, and translations used: I have studiously tried to avoid the acronym game to which the GDR's bureaucratic jungle lends itself too readily. For obvious convenience, I use only two abbreviations, the English *GDR* for German Democratic Republic, and the German *SED* for Sozialistische Einheitspartei Deutschlands (Socialist Unity Party of Germany). Although this seems inconsistent, it reflects accepted use in the literature. All other organizations are referred to in their non-abbreviated English-translations, again as they are being standardized in the literature: i.e., Free German Youth for Freie Deutsche Jugend, etc. Periodicals are referred to in full and cited with their original title. All quoted passages from German sources, both in the text and annotations, have been translated by the author unless otherwise indicated.

Acknowledgments

I owe a great debt of gratitude to the following people and organizations without whom this project could not have been realized: In Madison, Wisconsin, I thank Wigand Lange, Reinhold Grimm, David Bathrick, and Elisabeth Hermand for their criticism and support. In West Germany and West Berlin, I thank Heinar Kipphardt, Walther Dieckmann, Hans Mayer, and Wolfgang Schivelbusch for their time and information. In the GDR, I thank Heiner Müller, Paul Kanut Schäfer, Karl Mundstock, Paul Herbert Freyer, and Fritz Marquardt for helping me accomplish an almost impossible task in 1971 and 1972. Also in the GDR I received valuable assistance from the staff of the Deutsches Theater, the Henschelverlag, and the Heinrich Heine Buchhandlung.

A special note of gratitude must be given to Jost Hermand, whose critical guidance and support I have enjoyed throughout the various stages of this project. Finally, I am greatly indebted to my former associate Susan Huettich who worked with me from the beginning, but not to the end, and to Judith Ann Jensen and James Orville Smith for their help in revising the final manuscript.

Santa Monica, California   H. G. Huettich
December 1975

Addendum to the Preface

In the last chapter of this study I suggest a hopeful prognosis for the progressive development of significant German drama indigenous to the GDR, albeit "barring any radical shift" in the highly productive liberal cultural policies of the "Honecker era." This view was based on the evidence of open dialogue between the SED's leading theoreticians and dissenting writers who considered, respected, and above all listened to each other in their common quest for the continued qualitative improvement of the GDR's literary production. This peace, however, was not a lasting one. It is depressing to me—as it is to all those involved in the critical study of the GDR, its society and its culture—that my tentative assessment of the future has proven to be illusory during the last few months. It is evident that those of us who have studied GDR literature and cultural policy for many years should have by now learned never to trust any cultural-political peace in that country for too long. Once more, the shift in policy toward a rigid neo-Stalinist line is based on the Soviet model. When Marxist dissenters are expatriated involuntarily, when Marxist intellectuals are threatened in the pursuit of their livelihood, when Marxist authors are rousted in the streets—as has been the case recently with any number of writers treated in this study—then the future of that ostensibly "great Marxist experiment on German soil" is greatly endangered. Let us hope that the dramas resulting from this new policy will be played in the theaters—and not as tragedies in the streets or in the prisons and the asylums.

15 February 1977   H. G. H.

Introduction: Theater in Flux, 1945–1949

1. POLITICS AND LITERATURE

History officially begins for the German Democratic Republic on 7 October 1949, when a new People's Parliament and a new constitution took over the affairs of state from the Soviet Military Administration. But the prehistory of that state, the years between the end of the Second World War in 1945 and the date of obtained sovereignty, cannot be divorced from the historical process. In a span of twenty-nine years, this process has brought one-third of a totally devastated nation from utter economic and cultural prostration to an economic and cultural position within the alliance of Eastern European socialist states second only to that of the Soviet Union. The history of the theater in the German Democratic Republic is an integral part of this cultural, economic and political development. An objective study of East Germany's dramatic literature must necessarily strive for a historical perspective if it is to be fully understood.

In *Theater Bilanz*, an excellent, all-encompassing survey of GDR theater compiled in 1971 under the auspices of the Society of Theater Workers of the GDR, the history of East German theater is viewed as a historically homogeneous and continuous phenomenon:

> The continuity of development of GDR theater is evident in the stages of its manifestation: in building the base for an antifascist, democratic theater (1945–49), in the development of the humanistic people's theater in the new state (1949–55), in the creation of the premises for a socialist national theater of the GDR (1956–62), and in the maturing period of the theater arts in the developed, i.e., fully achieved, socialist society of the GDR.[1]

---

[1] Manfred Nössig and Hans Gerald Otto, "Grundlagen einer Bilanz," in *Theater Bilanz: Bühnen der DDR: Eine Bilddokumentation 1945–1969*, ed. Christoph Funke et al. (Berlin: Henschelverlag, 1971), p. 9. (This and all further quotations from German sources have been translated by the author unless otherwise indicated.)

The authors of the survey go on to quote Walter Ulbricht, First Secretary of the ruling SED from 1949 to 1971, and thus the GDR's most powerful political leader, who stated in 1969: "Our conception, even at that time [1945–49], contained the idea of the socialist national culture of the GDR."[2]

Insofar as Ulbricht's statement reflects official hindsight, it cannot be accepted without considerable reservation. An epoch of theater history has been categorized and incorporated into a historical perspective based upon the current cultural policy. In the German Democratic Republic, as in other Communist societies, theater history is regarded as nothing more than history, and history is always interpreted in accordance with the current requirements of power. Cultural policy in such a socialist society is perhaps one of the most important facets of domestic policy. It is a very serious—at times deadly—issue, and it must be viewed as such. One of the basic premises of the German Democratic Republic is the assumption that its artistic production must be viewed and treated as a socially formative force.

The responsible scholar must assume that the cultural functionaries of planned societies will habitually attempt to make previous history consistent with the current point of view. In 1969, the "socialist national culture" had become a reality in the German Democratic Republic: a socialist perspective in the arts supported national objectives in both the domestic and the foreign spheres. To say that it was planned that way from the beginning, to say that the "prehistorical" epoch 1945–49 formed the basis for a homogeneous, continuous development toward a socialist national culture, is at the very best an attempt to conceal objective historical conflicts under a cloak of nonhistorical rationalization.

The direct influence of history cannot be denied. During the early period prior to 1949 political development in the Soviet Occupation Zone was entirely subject to economic contingencies. For the Soviet Military Administration, economic contingencies meant first, reparations, and second, the channelling of economic output toward Moscow. The concept of a divided Germany, and thus any conception of the future in terms of "socialist national" evolution, had not yet entered into the reckoning because the formation of a separate Communist state had not yet been postulated. For the first two years, 1945–47, the Soviet Military Administration did not have a clear, centralized conception of the future role of the Soviet Occupation Zone or, for that matter, of the rest of Germany. Although it is certain that the Soviet Military Administration informed Ulbricht and other reimported German Communists of its intentions, the fact that these intentions were somewhat contradictory and disorganized made planning difficult. The lack of clear direction on the part of the Soviet Military Administration was obvious in its contradictory actions: dismantling some factories while urging production in others; stripping the railroad system while insisting on improved transport capabilities; and organizing a labor force for the Soviet

2 *Ibid.*

Occupation Zone while deporting a large number of skilled German workers and technicians to Russia. The role of the German Communists at that time must have been extremely frustrating, since their lack of decision-making power and the administrative chaos surrounding them precluded effective planning on their part.

Official planning was out of their hands in any case—as were all other matters of *Realpolitik*—until much later. While in 1945 German civilians were quickly given the responsibility of administering a new democratic order of civil law in the Soviet Occupation Zone, they had no such authority in economic and political planning. Until 1948, there was no single coordinated plan for the Soviet Zone. Plans by the Soviets, plans by the Germans, and all of the various provincial plans were drawn up independently of each other, and the execution of the Soviet plan took precedence over all of the others.[3]

From this perspective, the developments at the German Writers' Conference of 1947 are not surprising. While the "socialist national culture" of the future GDR was supposedly being conceived—a conception presupposing a permanently divided Germany—Marxist critic Alexander Abusch, one of the most important exponents of GDR cultural policy, had a different prognosis. He saw the two streams of German literature since 1933, that of the "emigration" (writers exiled during the Third Reich) and that of the "inner emigration" (writers who remained in Germany), as a basis for a common German literature of the future.[4] A united Germany was certainly a part of most people's conception of the future at that time, and the cultural functionaries of the Soviet Occupation Zone had no reason to think otherwise.

These functionaries were merely trying to maintain an "anti-fascist democratic order." This mission was taken very seriously by all levels of power from the Soviet Military Administration on downward. There is some indication that cultural activity in the Zone was not proceeding to the liking of the German Communists, who had hoped to immediately emulate the Communist model of the Soviet Union. The political establishment of the principles of democratic civil law proceeded quickly enough; but a tendency toward "bourgeois" aesthetic ideals persisted. Political engagement in literary activity was still the exception rather than the rule. This made the situation in 1946–47 somewhat like the "total suspicion of ideology" prevalent in West German society and literature of the time.[5] This suspicion rested, of course, on the horrible experiences of the Hitler era, experiences which had led to a sense that *all* contacts between politics and the

---

[3] Cf. Joseph P. Nettl, *The Eastern Zone and Soviet Policy in Germany 1945–50* (London: Oxford, 1951), p. 65.

[4] Cf. Frank Trommler, "Der zögernde Nachwuchs: Entwicklungsprobleme der Nachkriegsliteratur in West und Ost," in *Tendenzen der deutschen Literatur seit 1945*, ed. Thomas Koebner (Stuttgart: Kröner, 1971), p. 28.

[5] Cf. Hans Mayer, *Deutsche Literatur seit Thomas Mann* (Reinbek bei Hamburg: rororo, 1968), p. 53.

arts must necessarily result in the distortion of both.

Friedrich Wolf, a leading prewar Communist, revolutionary, and play-wright who had spent the war exiled in Russia, expressed the frustration of the German Communists in his own personal way: *"But writing plays—forget it!! Too bad!!!"* [6] This is what Wolf, actually the leading dramatist of Germany's organized left wing since the twenties, wrote to Vsevolod Vishnevsky, the renowned Soviet dramatist, on 10 September 1946. Before Wolf expressed this obviously painful sentiment, he pointed out the missed opportunities for a socialist drama in that period. Wolf saw that both older and newer political plays with prosocialist or anti-fascist content—his own included—were being relegated to the "third and fourth position"[7] in favor of "plays of Anglo-French snob-bism,"[8] such as those by Jean Anouilh and Thornton Wilder which were cur-rently in vogue even on the stages of the Soviet Zone. Wolf was naturally disappointed. As an emigrant returned from exile in Russia, he had hoped for the establishment of a more immediately historical drama, a drama linked to the reality of the postwar situation and analogous to the contemporary Soviet theater of that time.

Wolf further noted that there were indeed good "anti-fascist" plays (those, for example, by Herbert Lommer and Hedda Zinner, both Communists of Wolf's mold), but that they were not staged often enough. The argument pro-ducers used against them was that it was too early to write clearly and analytically about the recent past. Wolf's complaint was that the entire German theatrical scene (inclusive of the Soviet Zone) was in the clutches of an analytical and symbolistic nihilism designed to show that the human situation is hopeless and that there is nothing man can do to alter his fate. He believed he saw this not only in the theater, but also in criticism: "We used to have progressive criticism! *Today*, however, even the 'critics' in our Zone are silent in the face of the unbridled snobbism which furthers symbolistic *l'art pour l'art* plays."[9] Here, indeed, Wolf may be venting the rancor of the neglected artist, but the central point of his protest remained the lack of a consistent cultural policy of the sort he had observed in the Soviet Union. As a Communist Party member, he was committed to the idea that a society must have a cultural program that imposes upon the arts a moral and social didactic role in conformity with the Communist view of history. He saw that the basic theses of the new society he envisioned were slow in manifesting themselves in the realm of German theater.

Wolf expressed understandable concern that in this cultural battle between

[6] *Friedrich Wolf/Wsewolod Wischnewski: Eine Auswahl aus ihrem Briefwechsel*, ed. Gudrun Düwel (Berlin: Deutsche Akademie der Künste, 1965), p. 58.

[7] *Ibid.*, p. 57.

[8] *Ibid.*, p. 56.

[9] *Ibid.*

Communist and capitalist ideals the most important early years could be lost to the American administration and the conservative cultural traditions of Western Europe. Wolf quoted producers who would have staged good Soviet plays, but who had only "six to eight badly translated and miserably reproduced"[10] Russian dramas available to them. In contrast, he noted that the American administration provided "thirty-eight good new American plays, well translated and well printed."[11]

Wolf's letter contradicts the generally held but historically uncritical conception of the actualities of literary production in the first years of today's German Democratic Republic—at least in terms of the drama. Today we are generally led to believe that from the beginning everything went smoothly and according to plan. But the influence of Soviet cultural policy and the incorporation of socialist plays into the repertoire were not immediate, and were by no means considered inevitable. The Americans quickly and incisively comprehended the cultural situation, and thus the first round in the cultural battle for the minds of the "poets and thinkers" went to the Cold Warriors of the West. They had, at least, won the race to provide "good," i.e., playable, texts to producers in sufficient quantities.

On another level, the Soviet Military Administration was quite generous: it licensed no fewer than seventy-five institutions in the Soviet Zone where plays were produced in the first postwar season (1945–46).[12] Theaters even appeared in cities and towns where there had never been any. This rather liberal cultural policy of the Soviet victors remained, for the time being, without the progressive, goal-oriented tendencies which might have been expected. There was, for example, no explicit pressure to give Russian or German socialist drama preferred treatment in the repertoire; censorship restricted only Nazi and militaristic tendencies and was therefore not obviously different from the censorship practiced in the Allied Occupation Zones and West Berlin. The reason for the Soviets' leniency is simple and historically demonstrable. The future role of the Soviet Occupation Zone had not yet become clear to the Soviet Military Administration. The deliberate change of repertoire in favor of socialist plays during the following years corresponds directly to the breakdown of communications between the Soviet Military Administration and its Allied counterparts over the reunification question and the growing Berlin crisis.

The "socialist national culture" that has developed in the GDR is quite different from anything known in the rest of Europe. It is certainly not the result of the quest for an ideal, but is, instead, the cultural reflection of political action

---

[10] *Ibid.*, p. 57.

[11] *Ibid.*

[12] Cf. Heinz Kersten, "Theater und Theaterpolitik in der DDR," in *Theater hinter dem "Eisernen Vorhang,"* ed. Reinhold Grimm et al. (Hamburg: Basilius, 1964), pp. 14–57.

determined by a historical situation. There was, however, a distinct time lag between political developments and their cultural repercussions in the theater. The 1947–48 season of the postwar theater was by far the most important in terms of political events. During this third season, the power play strategies of East and West became more acute with each new development, finally climaxing with the concrete political separation of the two Germanies. The main strategies at this stage of the Cold War were the currency reforms in both East and West Germany, the takeover of Eastern economic planning by Ulbricht and the SED[13] in 1948, the Berlin Blockade by the Soviets, and the outlawing of the Communist Party in the West. Thus the formation of the German Democratic Republic as a sovereign state on 7 October 1949 was at least partly due to the deterioration of the relationship between the Soviet Union and the United States.

The series of determinant actions during those years began on 6 June 1947, when the East German Provincial Ministers walked out of the Conference of German Ministers in Munich. This rejection of the West was followed in the Soviet Occupation Zone on 30 June by the formation of the Society for the Study of the Culture of the Soviet Union. On 23 July, the SED further rejected the West by refusing to participate in the Marshall Plan. In response, the American administration banned the activities of the Cultural League for the Democratic Regeneration of Germany (Kulturbund) in the American Sector of Berlin because of its obvious Communist tendencies. This was followed by similar edicts in the British and French Sectors. The already tense situation deteriorated rapidly as the Fourth Four-Power Conference of Foreign Ministers in London closed without results on the pressing questions of German reunification and the growing Berlin crisis. After the Soviet representative, Marshall Sokolovsky, walked out on the Control Commission, rendering it useless, on 28 March 1948, it was only a small step to the start of the Berlin Blockade on 24 June 1948.

2. THE STATE OF THE THEATER

The history of socialist drama in the German Democratic Republic starts in the immediate postwar years, but in its early stages it is not as extensive as one might suppose. After the Deutsches Theater reopened on 7 September 1945 with Lessing's *Nathan the Wise*, a humanist drama from the height of eighteenth-century German Enlightenment, Gustav von Wangenheim produced a Soviet play, Rakhmanov's *Restless Old Age*. The following season brought a little more "socialist realism," which is now generally defined as the uniform literary theory of the socialist/Communist countries. Its tenets were first set forth by Maxim

---

[13] The SED resulted from the East German fusion of the Communist Party of Germany and the Social Democratic Party of Germany, effective 20 January 1946. Its control was exercised by members of the former Communist Party, and today, although other parties do exist, it is *the party* in the GDR.

Gorki and adopted by the First Soviet Writers' Congress of 1934. "Socialist realism" was supposedly the historical extension of the "critical realism" that characterized the socially critical literature developed by nineteenth-century liberals. The chief difference between the two resulted from the belief that since the adverse prerevolutionary social-political conditions had been rectified in Russia by 1934, contemporary Russian society was not open to criticism. Thus socialist realism began to confine itself to the "positive" literary portrayal of Communist societies. This consistently affirmative form of socialist realism has been, and continues to be, the basis of official cultural policy in Communist states, including, of course, the GDR.

During the second postwar season, Konstantin Simonov's *The Russian Question* and Evgeny Zhvarts's *Shadows* were produced at the Deutsches Theater. The fact that *Shadows* was produced by Gustav Gründgens is in itself an indication of how liberal the climate was, since Gründgens had been one of the more successful actors in the Third Reich. In addition, Alexey Arbuzov's romantically somewhat disjointed but nevertheless socialistically developmental *Tanya* played the Landestheater Dessau, while Boris Lavrenyov's revolutionary drama *The Breach* was produced at the Dresdener Volksbühne. *The Breach* shows not only proletarians but also some levels of the bourgeoisie caught up in agitation for the revolution—appropriate fare for the political education of the predominantly bourgeois Germans in the Soviet Zone. The great theatrical success of 1948, however, took place in the House of Culture of the Soviet Union, which was later to become the Maxim Gorki Theater: there, the Deutsches Theater staged Friedrich Wolf's translation of Vsevolod Vishnevsky's *Optimistic Tragedy*. The impact of these relatively few Soviet plays was considerably amplified, since successful performances in Berlin were naturally followed by similar productions in the "provinces." Until the noticeable alteration of policy in 1950, the repertoire of the German Democratic Republic had a distinctly cosmopolitan flavor; the 1949 season featured works by Maxim Gorki— *The False Money* at the National Theater of Weimar, and *Vassa Zheleznova* at Brecht's brand new Berliner Ensemble. Meanwhile, the newly established Maxim Gorki Theater, under the freshly replanted linden trees of Berlin's main street, presented socialist realism in the form of Anatoly Sofronov's *Lyubov Yarovaya* and Konstantin Trenyov's *Moscow Character*.

A short look at Berlin will serve to illustrate the situation of German theater at that time. Before the blockade, Berlin was the legendary "open city" of cold war and international intrigue—but also of culture. In terms of the theater, this meant that all theatrical activities, East and West, were attended and reviewed by audiences and critics from both sides. This mutual accessibility had the makings of a bona fide cultural class struggle. Since actors and critics depend on good reviews for their livelihood, success, in this context of the budding social systems of East and West Germany, was in part a good review, or simple appreciation, by the opposition.[14] It is easy, then, to understand Friedrich Wolf's lament. He realized quickly and correctly that some directors and producers working in East Berlin had as their objective not the socialist cause, but rather applause from West Berlin.

Up to this time, Berlin had been the theater center of Germany. A great number of actors and other theater workers had settled there to work in the liberal cultural climate that still prevailed. Berlin's fleeting but unique status as an "open city" allowed them to live and work in all of the Sectors without much restriction. But the Soviet Sector was without a doubt the theatrical place to be since most of the best theaters were located there and enjoyed the financial support of the administration. Thus, until the 1949–50 season, when the climate of the theater was altered by the formation of the GDR, an explicit internationalism dominated the theater arts of the Soviet Zone.

Between 1946 and 1949, the repertoire in the Soviet Occupation Zone was largely unregimented. It is not an overstatement to say that all the world was on stage in SOZ theaters during that period; the fare included plays by authors of all four occupation powers as well as the "classics" of various cultures. As important as the Soviet drama was, its impact must undergo some qualitative evaluation. For the effect of Soviet drama during that time was not determinant or exemplary. The Soviet plays must be seen as part of a complex of influences which also contained the "pessimistic nihilistic snobbism" deplored by Friedrich Wolf, as well as such trivial Broadway fare as Chase's *Harvey*.

This is not to underestimate the importance of the Soviet dramatic influence, but only to expand the critical perspective. Socialist realism is necessarily directly related to the concept of a socialist national culture. These concepts, however, were not the sole nor even the greatest determinants of cultural development during those important "prehistoric" years of the German Democratic Republic.

The development of the repertoire continued through the second and third postwar seasons, until finally the Soviet political and cultural machinery moved toward the establishment of a separate socialist state. The repertoire, directly under the influence of the Soviet cultural officers Alexander Dymshits and Ilya Fradkin, the cultural specialist for theater, began to move distinctly away from the prevalent "formalistic" plays by playwrights such as Anouilh, Sartre, and Wilder, toward the didactics, morality, and realism of German and Russian plays with socialist contents. Alexander Dymshits wrote in February of 1950: "In his latest plays, *Dr. Wanner*, *What Man Sows*, and *Like the Animals of the Forest*, Friedrich Wolf, author of the famous drama *Professor Mamlock*, gives a vivid and passionate picture of the national disaster into which fascism plunged Germany.

[14] Hans Mayer, Carl Schurz Professor of German, University of Wisconsin, Interview, Milwaukee, Wisconsin, November 1971.

These plays constitute an epic work of profoundly instructive value for the German people."[15]

By 1950, the situation against which Wolf was declaiming in 1946 had completely reversed itself. Even Wolf, despite his vow never to write plays again, had in fact resumed writing plays.[16] His return to the dramatic pen was obviously related to the open condemnation of "Anglo-French snobbism." Dymshits writes further in the same essay: "The American imperialists in Trizonia [the American, British and French Sectors] are giving every encouragement to a literature that is hostile to the people, a literature that preaches spiritual barbarism and moral degradation."[17] The cultural policy for which Wolf and other German Communists had longed in 1946 was meanwhile, by the fifties, becoming a reality in the East.

But until the concrete historical developments which culminated in the split of 1949 forced a corresponding cultural perspective from the political leaders, there was no clear line of development for the GDR theater. Only when effective cultural planning finally commenced in 1949 were the beginnings of socialist culture in the GDR determined. One of the first cultural elements to exhibit the results of such planning was the drama.

[15] Dymshits, "The Literature of Democratic Germany, *Soviet Literature* (Moscow), XIX/2 (1950), 158.

[16] Wolf, in this letter, renounces only playwriting. It is the situation of the theater which he rejects because he is disillusioned. He does not reject literary activity as such, and expresses high hopes for projects such as novels and film scripts.

[17] Dymshits, "Literature of Democratic Germany," p. 160.

I.

Veterans Into the Breach: Grünberg, Wolf and Wangenheim

The formation of a Provisory People's Parliament in the Soviet Zone on 7 October 1949 officially signaled the birth of the sovereign German Democratic Republic. In modern German literary history, 1945 has generally been regarded as a "point zero." It was seen as a *tabula rasa*, the beginning of an entirely new era. However, some of the latest studies have effectively questioned and essentially disproved the existence of such a "point zero" in 1945.[1] There were, in fact, German literary traditions that had long prevailed, which were built on, and which had never lapsed. They had been overlooked in the general desire of the German populace, critics notwithstanding, to dismiss the immediate past from participation in the formation of the future.

It is nevertheless clear that the date of the formal division of Germany into two republics is also the most significant juncture in the more recent cultural history of the Germans. We may more tenably postulate a "division point 1949" than any "point zero," if we must succumb to the search for a precise inception date for the postwar epoch. The consequences of the German Reich existed as a common experience for all Germans until 1949. We must remember that the ill-fated Reich existed—if only theoretically—until then. But with the division of states in 1949, any common experience, any concept of "the German people" as one nation, was dramatically destroyed. Even the end of the war, the final and terrible prostration of an inherently proud national consciousness, had not been able to do this. Not only did the political split create a national schizophrenia by creating two new identities to cope with, but the point of reference common to each severed part, the remains of the Reich, "the womb which could still spawn evil," as Brecht referred to it, was formally—if only symbolically—removed. This concrete "division point" of national cultural identification having finally

[1] Cf. Frank Trommler, "Der 'Nullpunkt 1945' und seine Verbindlichkeit für die Literaturgeschichte," *Basis: Jahrbuch für deutsche Gegenwartsliteratur*, I (1970), 9–25.

been reached, literary developments East and West began to diverge and to reflect, in their divergence, the radical differences between the liberal West and the Communist East.

The German Writers' Conference of 1947 had brought to light two conflicting strains of literature. At that time, even the leading literary voices of the Soviet Zone were forecasting a fusion of the "bourgeois democratic" strain on the right and the tradition of the "fighting humanists" on the left. In reference to this conference, Alexander Abusch reported that "it was correctly realized that concepts such as 'inner emigration' and 'outer emigration' must be overcome since the objective now is the creation of a unified, truly people-oriented German literature."[2] By 1949, however, as we have seen, the political realities in Germany had progressed to such an extent that consideration of a common development bordered on the absurd. The movement in West Germany was toward cultural internationalism and cosmopolitanism, toward explicit acceptance of the literature of America and Western Europe for the first time since 1933.[3] In contrast, the cultural functionaries of East Berlin, reinforced by the large number of returned left-wing emigrants, grasped at the tradition of pre-1933, proletarian-oriented literature from the German revolutionary movement of the twenties, now officially referred to as "the Way,"[4] and tried to emulate in all cultural affairs the "great" and revolutionary example of the Soviet Union.

The Soviet example implicitly required that the role of literature in East German society be radically changed. All preoccupation with art for its own sake, as well as with dilettantism, form, myth, and mysticism of any kind, had to be negated. Art had simply to be functional, and, as such, supportive of the party and accessible to the intellects and feelings of the majority of the people. Literature was assigned a central role in the social system as a planned, organized and well-integrated part of a cultural policy aimed at solidifying the people behind the party. The central role of cultural activity in the plan was formulated by Abusch in 1948: "The Two-Year Plan is itself a great cultural act, because it is also a great

---

[2] Abusch, "Schriftsteller suchen den gemeinsamen Weg," in *Literatur im Zeitalter des Sozialismus: Beiträge zur Literaturgeschichte 1921–1966* (Berlin: Aufbau, 1967), p. 558.

[3] The critic Franz Schonauer provides a concise summation: "In 1945 the Allied victors occupied Germany and started their program of reeducation. Books and periodicals, printed on bad paper, already appeared during the first few months of the occupation. The literature of the West, at first presented as mandatory reading for these underclassmen of democracy, was comparable to a shock. The following reaction was an unmitigated reception of the new, for most Germans unknown, authors. There were the Americans—Hemingway, Faulkner, Dos Passos, Steinbeck and Thomas Wolfe; the French Existentialists, and the greats of European literature—Valery, Gide, James Joyce, and Eliot" (*Bestandesaufnahme: Eine deutsche Bilanz 1962*, ed. Hans Werner Richter [München: Desch, 1962], p. 480).

[4] The official viewpoint on the historical traditions of the German Democratic Republic cites *Die Straße*, the battles before 1933; *Die Nacht*, the time of fascism; and *Der Aufbau*, the early years of the GDR.

plan for the education of the working people. The fulfillment of this plan is, above all, not a question of technology, but a question of people."[5]

This call for socially responsible cultural activity was made in reference to the first centralized "Plan," the Two-Year Plan for 1949–50 announced by Walter Ulbricht in 1948, before the formal emergence of the German Democratic Republic. The cultural element of the plan was interpreted in various ways by various people working in various genres. The leading authors within the realistic tradition, Johannes R. Becher, Anna Seghers, Hans Marchwitza, and Willi Bredel, seemed mired in epic antifascist treatments of their exile periods. Their failure to focus on the contemporary scene distressed the SED, which was looking for something more immediate from its literary forces.

In December of 1948, not six months after Walter Ulbricht had announced the SED's new plan to the Economic Commission, by which it was summarily adopted, Martin Böttcher, a chief critic on the staff of the official SED daily newspaper, *Neues Deutschland*, went to work against the writers he considered stragglers. His polemic appeared in a literary supplement to *Neues Deutschland* on 12 December. Its title was "Writers in No Man's Land," and it accused contemporary East German literature of floundering between the battle lines of the class struggle without adequate direction and without proper recognition of the realities of the emerging nation.

Undoubtedly Böttcher's sharp words in *Neues Deutschland* were "official" doctrine. The cultural and literary goals of the Two-Year Plan were expressed in a resolution adopted by the First Party Conference of the SED:

> The cultural objective, to educate people by way of a new social insight and a new relationship to work, can only be achieved if all writers and artsits dedicate their entire strength and enthusiasm to the task. The contribution of writers and artists toward the Two-Year Plan consists of the development of realistic art, and the desire to reach the highest artistic achievements in their fields.
>
> Through their works, progressive writers can help to develop the joy of work and optimism of the workers in the factories and the working rural population. Their works can communicate the essence and meaning of the Two-Year Plan and all contingent questions to the entire populace. . . .[6]

The resolution, in effect, called for "literary" support of the reconstruction of the GDR and was the basis of Böttcher's criticism. Alexander Abusch took it upon himself to protect "the great realists" (his friends) from this doctrinaire attack. In "On the Work of Our Writers," a scathing reply to Böttcher's article, Abusch tries to rescue traditional aesthetic precepts of the beleaguered "realists."

---

[5] Abusch, "Die Schriftsteller und der Plan," in *Literatur im Zeitalter des Sozialismus*, p. 575.

[6] Martin Böttcher, "Kulturelle Aufgaben im Rahmen des Zweijahrplanes," in *Kritik in der Zeit: Der Sozialismus—seine Literatur—ihre Entwicklung*, ed. Klaus Jarmatz et al. (Halle: Mitteldeutscher Verlag, 1970), p. 147.

Yet he paraphrases the Party admirably when he acknowledges that "man stands in the center of the plan, which will only be the beginning for more far-reaching plans. The working man, his material and cultural endeavors, his vocational and spiritual development, must also be regarded as the central objective in our cultural endeavor. . . ."[7] He adds that "it is correct to demand that writers write about today's events. But that should not be construed to mean that a writer should no longer write about the past."[8] Abusch erred, however, in his conclusion. The party resolution specifically meant that the artist's natural preoccupation with the past, which Abusch tried to justify, was the element which was to be eliminated, in order that authors might concentrate on the present. Literature's function, in the eyes of the party, would be to generate positive statements in support of the ideology of the new state.

It is plain to see what type of theater was desired when we consider Friedrich Wolf's criticism of Bertolt Brecht's 1949 production of *Mother Courage*. Wolf objected to the fact that Mother Courage has not changed in the end: "And I would have thought that Courage would have been even more effective if her words 'The war be damned!' at the end (as in the case of Kattrin) had resulted in a clear expressive action as a result of that insight."[9] Brecht's answer to this criticism by the more doctrinaire socialist is a brilliant example of his dialectical thinking:

> The play was written in 1938, when the playwright foresaw a great war: He was not convinced that the people would necessarily learn something from the disaster which, according to his view, was about to affect them. Dear Friedrich Wolf, you, especially, will confirm that the playwright was a realist in that case. Even if Courage doesn't learn anything, the audience can, in my opinion, still learn something by watching her.[10]

Three years later, Brecht's view was to be considered "objectivism" by the party, and condemned as such. The party theorized that so-called "objective" treatments of "enemy ideology" implied approval or at least toleration of those ideologies. Thus Wolf's view was quite representative of the official position. This impetus for positive realism in the theater arts comes, without a doubt, from the Soviet Union, and it is no accident that Wolf should represent this view, since his exile was largely spent in that country.

The venerable Communist writer and career revolutionary Otto Gotsche, who was one of the leaders of the German Communists in the Weimar Republic and in the anti-Hitler underground, agreed wholeheartedly with the new task of

---

[7] Abusch, "Die Schriftsteller," p. 576.

[8] *Ibid.*

[9] Brecht, *Gesammelte Werke* (Frankfurt am Main: Suhrkamp, 1967), XVII (*Schriften zum Theater 3*), 1146.

[10] *Ibid.*

literature. Gotsche went on to become a leading figure in the GDR hierarchy as First Secretary of the Council of State in 1960, aided perhaps by his "hard line" on realistic art. "Art means to proclaim. Art, that doesn't just mean to be able to do something, art means to proclaim, to proclaim the fame of work, of activists, of our peaceful reconstruction, of our desire, of our hard and gloriously great epoch."[11] He goes on to state that literature must be created "in the midst, in the glow of the blast furnaces, the rolling mills, the machine shops, the shipyards, the agricultural implement stations, in the great Plan; it is there that our epoch lives, ferments, forges literature and art."[12] Gotsche's enthusiastic call provides us with an accurate perspective on the theater in relation to the other genres of early GDR literature, since contemporary "socialist realism" found its major representation in the theater, while the great prose writers were still busy ruminating on their exile periods.

The previously mentioned impetus from the Soviet Union had been partially reinforced by a Party resolution, "About the Repertory of Drama Theaters and Measures for Its Improvement," adopted on 26 August 1946 by the Central Committee of the Communist Party of the Soviet Union in conjunction with the new policy statements of Andrey Zhdanov, still Stalin's cultural oracle, in favor of party-oriented literature and socialist realism. The resolution reads, in part:

> Dramatic literature and the theaters must reflect in plays and performances the life of Soviet society in its incessant surge forward, and contribute fully to the further development of the best sides of Soviet Man's character, which have been shown so patently during the Great Fatherland War. Playwrights and directors must make Soviet youth spirited, optimistic, devoted to their country, believing in the victory of our cause, unafraid of obstacles, and capable of overcoming any difficulty. The Soviet theater must also show that such qualities belong, not only to a few elect ones or to heroes, but to many millions of Soviet citizens.[13]

This resolution signalled the beginning of the development of realistic theater arts in the German Democratic Republic. It was the theoretical foundation of the achievements of the Weimar Actor's School, which was subsequently transformed into the Maxim Gorki Theater of Berlin. The Gorki Theater was especially active in applying the "Stanislavsky Method" to contemporary theater, since that method had Stalin's official sanction. The resolution was also the cultural-political impetus that propelled such a large number of Soviet plays into the GDR repertoire between 1949 and 1952.

[11] Gotsche, "Diskussion: Wo steht die Gegenwartsliteratur? Der Gegenwart nicht ausweichen," in *Kritik in der Zeit*, p. 216.

[12] *Ibid.*, p. 217.

[13] Quoted in Marc Slonim, *Russian Theater from the Empire to the Soviets* (New York: Collier, 1962), p. 364.

In 1951–52, Zhdanov's cultural doctrine was directly reflected by the actions of the SED functionaries in Berlin. The concept of Berlin as an "open city" was abandoned once and for all. This was the natural cultural result of the power politics of the Berlin Blockade by the Soviets and the ensuing economic embargo by the Western Allies. Concrete manifestations of the restrictive policy were, first, attacks against individual plays and productions, and second, repertoire changes that furthered the most banal socialist realism in the theater. Specifically, Brecht was again a target, as his *Days of the Commune* (*Tage der Kommune*), his adaptation of Gorki's *The Mother*, and the Brecht/Dessau opera *The Interrogation of Lucullus* (*Verhör des Lukullus*) received wrathful criticism from the SED. As a countermove, the number of Soviet plays of the realistic mode were increased greatly. They were held up against the condemned "formalism" as great and shining examples to follow. Thirty-seven Soviet plays were produced in 1951 in the German Democratic Republic, while in 1952 Soviet plays accounted for over 25% of the repertoire, not even counting concurrent performances—the highest in GDR history.

The statistical evidence must again be qualitatively evaluated. The extent of direct Soviet influence on the history of GDR drama cannot be measured in terms of numbers of productions. The regulation of the repertoire in favor of great numbers of plays of Soviet socialist realism was primarily directed at the audience. These plays were a tool (among others) of the political and social reeducation of a public clinging to middle-class values. Since going to the theater had always been a typically middle- and upper-class activity in Germany, the use of this particular tool seemed to make obvious sense. The theatergoer, expecting a traditional activity, would be subjected instead to a radical political lesson. But the effort was not notably successful. The primitive didactics of the more simplistic plays of Soviet realism—in which, for example, a love triangle consists of a boy and a girl and a tractor, and the tractor wins—were naturally most effective in rural areas and smaller towns and cities. But the cosmopolitan, sophisticated atmosphere of the cultural life of Berlin (although Berlin has a great proletarian theater tradition going back to 1890, when Bruno Wille founded the Volksbühne, and more recently to Piscator's innovations in the twenties) still reflected strong strains of traditional "bourgeois aesthetics." Berlin audiences, with their well-developed appreciation of the traditional theater, continued to resist such fare.

Thus the raw masses of Soviet examples were, not surprisingly, without much effect. The only dramatists whose efforts were along the lines of the famous postrevolutionary Soviet dramatists, such as Lavrenyov, Simonov, Korneychuk, and the Tur brothers, were such venerable prewar socialists as Wangenheim, Karl Grünberg, and Friedrich Wolf. It must be remembered that they were writing in correspondence to their own historical tradition, in which Soviet influence was a historical, but hardly immediate, factor. In the twenties and thirties, their works already showed an ideological connection to Soviet realism.

The situation in the drama was thus radically different from the development of prose in the new republic. Such representative Soviet novels of socialist realism as Gladkov's *Cement*, Sholokov's *Newly Plowed Land*, and Ostrovsky's *How the Steel Was Hardened* greatly influenced subsequent novels by GDR authors such as Eduard Claudius (*People at Our Side* [*Menschen an unserer Seite*]), Hans Marchwitza (*Crude Iron* [*Roheisen*]), and Karl Mundstock (*Bright Nights* [*Helle Nächte*]).

Today we can certainly postulate that the socialist peoples' republics, whose social systems are patterned after the model of the Soviet Union, emulate the Soviet model in their theater. Most important here is the concentration on the subject matter of the "here and now," the dramatization of the social and economic contingencies that will make history. We see plays about the redistribution of land, the industrial buildup, inventive socialist workers, class-conscious heroes battling the enemies of the working class, and the progressive activist youth movement throughout contemporary socialist drama. That covers the subject matter of the realistic Soviet drama since 1917 and the "reruns" can naturally be found in the German Democratic Republic. By no means is this solely the result of a direct influence from play to play on an aesthetic level. Instead, it is the cultural manifestation of concrete political influences. It is also the aspect of GDR drama that differentiates it from West German drama. The concentration of the body of this study on the GDR's socialist realist drama, a type of drama that must deal exclusively with the socioeconomic realities of its epoch, is readily justified by its uniqueness in German literary history, if not, more importantly, by its foremost position in the scope of GDR literary concepts.

Zhdanov's policy of socialist realism was also the base for the first new plays in the GDR. Unlike their prose-writing counterparts, experienced prewar Communists dutifully and progressively followed the call and the needs of their party to write contemporary plays in conjunction with the Two-Year Plan. The old adage that the drama is closer to the political realities of any time than any other art form seemed again to be substantiated. George Bernard Shaw's views on theater and art as being the most seductive means of political propaganda were taken to heart by the SED, and found reflection in theater policy under the Two-Year Plan.

Being committed to the ideology of the SED, and convinced of the greatness of its political mandate, Karl Grünberg, Friedrich Wolf and Gustav von Wangenheim filled the need and presented "reconstruction plays" (*Aufbaustücke*). These works were stylistically simple, easy to produce, and easy to understand. To say that they were tendentious, that they were actually nothing more than dramatic representations of the most pressing issues of the Two-Year Plan, is, in terms of this type of drama, not a negative but a positive evaluation. Already, in dealing with the first contemporary plays of the German Democratic Republic, we have touched on their typological element. The orientation toward pressing domestic issues as subject, and party engagement as motivation, may be taken as the least common denominator, as far as GDR theater is concerned.

Karl Grünberg, the veteran proletarian novelist and author of the 1928 workers' novel *Burning Ruhr* (*Brennende Ruhr*), brought a neo-naturalistic treatment of the industrial problems of the day to the stage. Grünberg, born in 1891, had been active as a socialist in the 1919 revolutionary struggle that brought an end to the Wilhelminian era and resulted in the Weimar Republic. In 1920 he joined the German Communist Party and wrote for the party's radical paper *The Red Flag* (*Die rote Fahne*) as an industrial correspondent. He was a frequent visitor to the Soviet Union, a member of the anti-Hitler underground, and subsequently an inmate of the concentration camp Sonnenburg. His lifelong commitment to the Communist cause is evident in his first postwar play, *The Golden Steel* (*Golden fließt der Stahl* [1953]). In this work his vehicle is a weak detective-type fable surrounded by the industrial issues of the time. The play centers on the changeover from private ownership to people's property, the primary economic question of the time. Grünberg also took care to show that his factory had been owned by a Nazi compatriot and war criminal, thus presenting this specific people's property action in accordance with the Plebiscite of Saxony. This decision, limited only to Saxony, by which a general vote of the people determined that the property of Nazi compatriots should become public, was extended however as the legal justification for such action by the party in the takeover of all crucial industry in all provinces of the new state.

Friedrich Wolf's comedy *Mayor Anna* (*Bürgermeister Anna* [1950]) lends character to a typical rural love comedy by setting it in the midst of the revolutionary developments of the Land Reform Policy[14] and the reactionary opposition of a large landowner. Wolf's play, then, is the dramatic treatment of the second most important economic question. It is not surprising that Wolf follows the cultural-political requirements of this time, for they seem to correspond directly to his own ideology as an author. He was born in Neuwied on the Rhine in 1888, and studied medicine in Tübingen. His experiences as an army surgeon in the First World War made him a pacifist. This position took a sharp turn to the left during the revolutionary activity of 1919. During the twenties and thirties he was a prolific dramatist concentrating on social and revolutionary topics. His most significant works in that period were the pro-abortion drama *Cyankali* (1929) and the pro-revolution play *The Sailors of Cattaro* (*Die Matrosen von Cattaro* [1930]), which treated the Austrian naval mutiny in the late stages of

---

[14] "The land reform in the Soviet zone is perhaps the most important post-war measure carried out in Eastern Germany. Its obvious purpose was to destroy the dominant agricultural interests in Eastern Germany, the big farmers and the Junkers. The details of the reform had been planned during the war, and represented the highest point of Russian post-war planning for Germany. In July 1945 one of the chief planners, Hörnle, a German Communist of long standing, was flown to Berlin with instructions to carry out the scheme" (Joseph P. Nettl, *The Eastern Zone and Soviet Policy in Germany 1945–50* [London: Oxford, 1951], p. 85).

World War I. After 1933, Wolf was exiled in France, Scandinavia, the USA, and finally in Russia from 1941 to 1945. In the GDR he became actively involved in the operations of state as Ambassador to Poland in 1950–51. He died in 1953.

Like Grünberg and Wolf, Gustav von Wangenheim was an early German Communist dramatist. He was born in Wiesbaden in 1895. His father was the prominent German actor Eduard von Winterstein. Wangenheim studied with Max Reinhardt before founding the Communist theater company, the Truppe 1931, which toured Germany with revolutionary theater in 1924–25. During his exile in Russia from 1933 to 1945 he wrote drama and film scripts and also directed films. After an unsuccessful stint as general director of the Deutsches Theater from 1945 to 1947, he concentrated on writing for the stage and screen and became active in reestablishing the film industry in the GDR. You're the One (Du bist der Richtige [1950]) is Wangenheim's treatment of GDR youth and their adaptation to the socialist context. It is a glowingly positive representation of the Free German Youth (Freie Deutsche Jugend), the Communist Party's official youth organization,[15] and its role in building national pride and a sense of mission among the younger generation.

GDR critics tend to regard these plays by Grünberg, Wolf, and Wangenheim rather lightly: "They were 'transitional plays,' first steps on a newly paved road, which were soon surpassed; but they have to their credit that they introduced the discussion of the new realities."[16] But, historically, they are more important than that. That they contained transitional elements is clear, but they were also, in effect, models for the further development of the contemporary drama of the German Democratic Republic. They form a solid and unpretentious base in three major ways. First, they solidly establish the use of political-economic crisis issues as subject matter; second, they transfer the heritage of Soviet socialist realism in the theater to the German drama; and third, they establish the dictum that all social elements must be integrated into a plan to further the development of the society—just as plays must be integrated into the cultural policy of the Two-Year Plan.

A closer look at the reconstruction plays of Grünberg, Wolf and Wangenheim will help to clarify their literary-historical importance. Grünberg's play, The Golden Steel, which premiered in Nordhausen in March of 1950, exhibits the struggle of a foundry against the typical 1950 problems of lack of raw materials, qualified technicians, and "progressively" oriented workers. These problems are dealt with energetically and positively, and some characters begin to develop a

<hr>

15 The Free German Youth was founded under the leadership of Erich Honecker on 7 March 1946. It is the official youth organization, and is represented on all levels of life in the GDR. It is in the forefront of SED ideology, and its objective is to educate all young people toward that ideology.

16 Dieter Borkowski, Konrad Hoerning, and Brigitte Thurm, "Dramatik der Deutschen Demokratischen Republik," in Schauspielführer, ed. Karl Heinz Berger et al. (Berlin: Henschelverlag, 1968), II, 661.

sense of a common goal—the reconstruction of their dilapidated factory and an increase in production.

The action unfolds. An engineer disappears, acts of sabotage are discovered, and morale is sinking. Everything is blamed on the missing engineer, Mucha, who, according to a letter discovered by another engineer, has skipped to the West. Actually, this second engineer, Rothkegel, and an accomplice are responsible for the sabotage. Rothkegel has killed Mucha, who had discovered the sabotage, Rothkegel and his crony disposing of the body in a blast furnace about to be tapped.

The discovery of this dastardly act and subsequent ones is made by a team of young activists, one of whom was himself accused of sabotage. Another of their number, a young girl who does laboratory work, caps their efforts by finding traces of gold (Engineer Mucha was distinguished by dental work with an upper bridge of gold) in a qualitative analysis of the steel poured during the night the victim disappeared. The police and party functionaries arrive; the air is cleared; the guilty are exposed and apprehended. Premiums are distributed, and all of the workers vow to redouble their efforts in the struggle to meet the demands of the reconstruction plan.

In the end, Grünberg even approaches the tradition of agitation-propaganda which had been practiced in the German revolutionary theater of the twenties and early thirties; all the characters assemble on the stage in an awesome grand finale, and the youth group of the factory sings. The song's refrain is by now world famous as the hymn of the GDR reconstruction: "Rebuild, rebuild, rebuild, rebuild/ Free German Youth rebuild!/ Rebuild our native land/ For a better future!"[17]

Played first in Dresden on 14 October 1950, Friedrich Wolf's comedy *Mayor Anna* shows Anna, the mayor of a rural village, engaged in building a new school with the help of all the women in the area. There are two major problems. First, the school is not in the construction plan of the district, and thus materials and labor are scarce and must be scavenged. Second, the men of the area are under the influence of Lehmkuhl, a large landowner who is engaged in various clandestine activities. These range from withholding grain from the quota collections and harboring an "illegal" tractor (thus keeping it from collective work) to distilling illegal but extremely palatable spirits. Jupp, a recently repatriated prisoner of war, disapproves of the village's penchant for women's liberation and consequently comes under the influence of Lehmkuhl. Lehmkuhl's Puntila-like virility and generosity have blinded him.

With great wit and energy, Anna and her helpers solve their planning and material procurement problems. A sympathetic party functionary also comes to the rescue. Lehmkuhl sees his hold on the situation diminishing and resorts to

[17] Karl Grünberg, *Golden fließt der Stahl* (Berlin: Neues Leben, 1950), p. 64.

violent acts, including the burning of the almost completed school building. Jupp and the rest of the men see the folly of Lehmkuhl's reactionary fanaticism and become convinced of the need for a "progressive" way of life, which the school represents.

The lovers, separated only by a lack of communication, find each other:

> JUPP (*embracing her*): Anna, girl, Mayor . . . can these go together?
> ANNA: They can.[18]

Their personal future looks promising. But there is also a socioeconomic significance in their union, because Jupp represents technical help, which is much needed to help mechanize the agricultural production of the area.

> JUPP: And today yet, I'm going to drive the tractor, Anna, and—I'll help you with the school.
> ANNA (*fastening his bandage*): Haven't you helped me already?[19]

Certainly Jupp's motivation is primarily personal, but his breakthrough into a collective consciousness shows in his realization of the importance of the school building. Although Wolf's play seems to be the least tendentious of this first wave of plays, it is in fact the most progressive in its basic perspective, since its characters develop both as characters and in direct response to the historical situation.

You're the One was written by Wangenheim for the official Free German Youth theater, the Theater der Freundschaft in Berlin. It was first produced there on 15 June 1950. This play, a simple song of praise for the efforts of the Free German Youth in forming national consciousness and pride in the socialist collective effort, traces the development of a youth who initially lacks collective ideals into a dedicated socialist citizen. Throughout the play, Wangenheim exhibits the "model" young person in all acceptable variations.

The plot rests on an accident: a young man without any collective consciousness or socialist ideology is mistakenly named a youth advisor to the Minister of the new state. Efforts to persuade this "loner" not to accept the position are opposed by the young man who should have been selected. The position changes the "loner" and he develops "progressively." In the end, he is instrumental in capturing the West Berlin *agent saboteur* whose activities were displayed in the first scene. As the captured young agent obstinately proclaims that his captors will never be able to change him, Waldi, the reformed hero, retorts with some justification, that they certainly can, and will.

No doubt "transitional" is a good designation for these plays. They explore the new social, political, and economic realities as subject matter, but it cannot be said that on the whole they show any corresponding exploration of the changes

---

[18] Friedrich Wolf, *Mayor Anna*, in *Gesammelte Werke* (Berlin: Aufbau, 1960), *Dramen* 6, 281.
[19] *Ibid.*

in personal relationships that must have resulted from such a radical change in the system. Reconstruction difficulties are in most cases ascribed to sabotage.

On another level, only the weakest of the plays, *You're the One*, demonstrates a clear perspective on the division of the two Germanies. It would be unfair, however, to view the absence of such a perspective in the other two plays as a defect. The views on the division of Germany expressed by Wolf and Grünberg are historically accurate. The official position still called for peace and reunification. Wangenheim's treatment favors the historically more radical view of the Free German Youth, and is, in that respect, the most openly tendentious of the early plays.

The plays exhibit a definite weakness in characterization, which is easily understandable, since there had not been time for adequate reflection on and development of the psychological complexities that might have been explored even within the new drama's typological constraints. Characters tend to be schematically represented, and are usually reducible to the melodramatic contrast of black—for the evil, reactionary saboteur—with white—for the good, "progressive" socialist and, ideally, for the party member. There is, however, an exception. Friedrich Wolf's experience as one of Germany's most prolific and progressive playwrights precluded an excess of such characterization on his part. His landowner Lehmkuhl is not evil by nature, but rather acts in accordance with the rules of the system that produced him. Much like Brecht's Puntila, he is at times engaging and sympathetic, and always interesting. Wolf's play also differs from other "reconstruction plays" in its relating of action to psychological motivation.[20] In contrast, political theory is the "schematic" motivation of all of the action in the plays by Grünberg and Wangenheim.

Hermann Werner Kubsch's background was similar to that of Wolf and Grünberg. Born in Dresden in 1911, he was an early socialist agitator who had already been arrested by age 14. He later studied at the Bauhaus in Dessau, joined the anti-fascist underground, and was incarcerated in jails and concentration camps from 1933 to 1942. Kubsch's 1950 opus, *The First Steps (Die ersten Schritte)*, and the early plays we have already discussed all seem to have in common a naturalistic dramatic technique. The difference between this early realism of the politically active party members in the theater world of the German Democratic Republic and traditional German naturalism is that the social and political theory that unifies the early GDR dramas was substituted for naturalistic drama's reliance upon adverse biological and environmental forces.

This resulted in the positive portrayal of all of the workers as a unified front—

---

[20] Of the four authors writing contemporary drama—Friedrich Wolf, Karl Grünberg, Hermann Werner Kubsch, and Gustav von Wangenheim—only Wolf was, in fact, primarily a dramatist. The others gained most of their experience writing prose, except for Wangenheim, who was an actor and director.

which was not historically accurate—and a penchant for the socialist activist hero —a figure which, historically, was far from typical. But these departures from the historically actual crystallize the socialist realist aesthetic incorporated in these works. What is shown on the stage is, in theory, reality *as it could be* if Communism's sociopolitical premises were carried to their necessary conclusion. Thus we have a peculiar system of causality in which the cause of an effect need not appear for the effect to be demonstrated.

The "reconstruction plays" were successful in two crucial ways. First, they accomplished their minimal objective, which was to put the present time on the stage quickly and painlessly, thus fulfilling the cultural-political objectives of the Two-Year Plan in the area of theater. Secondly, especially in the case of *The Golden Steel* and *You're the One*, which enjoyed long runs and were "quantitative" successes, the crucial epoch of reconstruction was presented in a heroic manner which may have, at the very least, engaged the imagination of the youthful members of the audience.

Thus it is surprising that the evaluation of the plays of this epoch by GDR critics is generally negative. Certainly these plays will never win any aesthetic contests, but it does seem that aesthetic quality should not be the primary criterion of evaluation in the first place. Historically it was not. A resolution of the Central Committee of the SED of 17 March 1951 reads, in part: "Of the successful attempts to bring contemporary problems to the stage, *You're the One* and *The Golden Steel* must be especially acknowledged."[21]

Thus the first criterion *ex domo* was political. But by 1964 the critical view had changed, and Hermann Kähler, otherwise a competent source of scholarship regarding the theater of the German Democratic Republic, actually expresses embarrassment in having to acknowledge these works. It seems that he has also succumbed to a recently spawned GDR tradition of disowning the humble beginnings, no matter how important they are historically, simply because they are humble. While discussing *The Golden Steel* and *The First Steps* in a footnote— thereby suggesting that they are not important enough to warrant space in his text on contemporary GDR theater—he states:

> In both plays the perspective is insufficiently clear. The new state's power appears only tentatively, as protection of a general concept of justice. The active role of the working class is not exhibited. The impetus is clearly in the hands of agents whose victims would be the workers if the state did not intervene. The historical background and the historical significance are treated only in a tangential manner.[22]

[21] "Der Kampf gegen den Formalismus in Kunst und Literatur, für eine fortschrittliche deutsche Kultur," in *Kritik in der Zeit*, p. 248.

[22] Kähler, *Gegenwart auf der Bühne: Die sozialistische Wirklichkeit in den Bühnenstücken der DDR von 1956–1963/64* (Berlin: Henschelverlag, 1966), p. 194.

This rather tangential approach to literary history is that of a critic who considers himself a historical materialist, i.e., one who, as critic, interprets art from the base of the real political and economic situation in which a work arises.

Kähler basically objects to the plays—in retrospect—because of their transitional elements and their lack of a socialist perspective. His observations are accurate, but he fails to recognize the historical basis of that transitional lack and to note specific instances of the new perspective's incipient development. In Grünberg's play *The Golden Steel*, the saboteur is tracked down through the collective efforts of three young people: Kilian, the activist; Eva Korn, the laboratory analyst; and Fritz of the Free German Youth. Through their quest for the truth, they, as workers, collectively develop a true socialist perspective in an epoch to which such a perspective was still relatively alien. Their conversation as they pick up the first scent of the saboteurs goes as follows:

> FRITZ: Look, Richard, do you think there was a real crime here?
> EVA: That would be horrible. Who would have . . . ? No, that's impossible. You're
> forgetting that he wrote a letter from Düsseldorf.
> FRITZ: The letter, that could have been faked as well.
> KILIAN: And I'm telling you, Korleman and his pals aren't afraid of murder. Don't
> you remember the grenade at the dump?[23]

In the process of solving the mystery they begin to see things from a greater perspective. It is their probing, not the power of the state, that convicts the saboteur. They, as a collective, assume responsibility. What the play actually demonstrates is that the state is essentially weak, a prey to saboteurs, if the workers do not develop a socialist awareness of the value of their role as the base of all power in the socialist state. Engineer Rothkegel can succeed in sabotage only by perpetuating the traditionally "bourgeois" employer-employee relationship between engineers and workers. As soon as the workers exercise their new role, his activities are exposed.

Friedrich Wolf also plumbs the depths of the new order as he demonstrates the changing role of women in its society. An even greater socialist perspective is gained here as the district construction plan is altered when the need for social and educational development is demonstrated. The play clearly delineates and celebrates the "progressive" priorities of the new state and its citizens.

The first wave of contemporary drama in the German Democratic Republic should not be undervalued. From the perspective of planned literature in a planned society—which distinctly places emphasis on dramatic literature about itself—this wave of plays is of epochal significance. The plays meet socialist realism's requirements: they reflect the party emphasis in characterization, subject matter, and cultural-political content, and they positively represent a struggling

---

[23] Grünberg, *Golden fließt der Stahl*, p. 30.

society working, step by step, toward a socialist perspective.

The fact that a fully developed socialist perspective is lacking in these plays, which Kähler negatively notes without considering the historical situation behind it, stems only from the objective treatment by the authors of the real situation. Historically these plays correctly reflect the fact that, at the time of their production, there was no such perspective and no conscious desire for such a perspective. When these plays were conceived and written, for the most part in 1949, the social order was still prevalently "democratic humanistic," with the emphasis more anti-fascist than pro-Communist. The historical events that later led to the general breakthrough to a socialist perspective had not yet occurred.

II.

The Emergence of the Socialist Perspective: 1951–1956

The most critical years in the history of the German Democratic Republic were, without any doubt, the years from 1951 to 1956. These were the years from the beginning of the first Five-Year Plan, the first autonomous plan of the new state, to the Hungarian debacle of 1956. These years also contained prime elements of crisis, including economic failures and the Workers' Putsch of 17 June 1953, which resulted largely from the overly ambitious economic goals.

The primary economic objective of the Five-Year Plan was to double the industrial output of 1950. Special emphasis was placed on the bulwarks of heavy industry: energy sources, steel, and fabrication. The various crises which resulted must be ascribed to the inherent weaknesses of the plan. Its goals were simply too ambitious for the capital resources at hand. These capital deficits were to be overcome by increased productivity, a measure which was naturally unpopular with the labor force. To achieve these objectives of the Five-Year Plan, the SED instigated a major ideological countermove. It was decided that the "anti-fascist democratic order" should be retired in favor of an openly Communist system which required the development of a generally pro-socialist perspective on the part of the GDR populace. Literature was assigned a major role in developing this public feeling.

Walter Ulbricht crystallized the connection of the Five-Year Plan with the development of the socialist perspective, and thus the socialist society:

> After the formation of the German Democratic Republic, the People's Parliament determined the first Five-Year Plan (1951 to 1955). This plan showed that the advance guard of the working class, a part of which was active in various state agencies, had taken up the basic elements of socialist planning during the epoch of the anti-fascist democratic revolution. By the beginning of the fifties, the objective and subjective contingencies for the planned and consequent development of socialism in the German Democratic Republic had matured. Thus, the Second

Party Conference of the Socialist Unity Party resolved the development of social-ism, and founded the basic elements of socialist national policy.[1]

The strict development of socialism in economic matters was accompanied by a correspondingly dogmatic cultural policy emanating from Andrey Zhdanov and the Soviet Central Committee once again. At its Fifth Meeting, the Central Committee of the SED resolved the theoretical basis for the cultural goals of the Five-Year Plan. "The Fight Against Formalism in Art and Literature for a Progressive German Culture" was announced by the Committee on 17 March 1951. In this application, formalism was simply any artistic endeavor which ascribed major importance to the form of a work in the sum total of the artistic effect. The structure of a work of art had become an ideological rather than aesthetic phenomenon. "Formalism means dissipation and destruction of art itself. The formalists deny that the deciding factor of meaning lies in the content, the idea, the thought of the work. . . . In all cases, when the question of form attains independent character, art loses its humanist democratic character."[2]

But it was certainly not the democratic humanist character of art which was at issue; instead, it was the development of a socialist perspective which would enlist the help of literary production to promote the belt-tightening measures of the indispensable Five-Year Plan. A model for emulation was easily found by the Central Committee: "In order to develop realistic art, we orient ourselves to the great example of the socialist Soviet Union, which has created the most progressive culture in the world."[3] This Soviet orientation in cultural affairs was unwavering and dogmatic. Once the line was set, all that fell outside its narrowly defined limits was condemned.

The new plan demanded the greatest commitment and exertion on the part of everyone to build the economic base from which socialism could prosper. In this context, even objective treatments of bourgeois or other "enemy" ideologies became suspect. The SED demanded party-line orientation (*Parteilichkeit*), a specifically engaged engagement, of all artists and intellectuals. At the Third Party Congress of 1950, where the Five-Year Plan was adopted, it was also pro-claimed that any objective presentation of contrary or "enemy" ideologies in speculative writings or works of art was "objectivism," and, as such, implied an inherent approval of them. To combat this danger of "objectivism," the Congress resolved: "Therefore it is the deciding cultural-political task to aim for a radical change in all areas of cultural life and to make an unmitigated end, once and for

---

[1] Ulbricht, *Die historische Mission der Sozialistischen Einheitspartei Deutschlands: Sechs Reden und Aufsätze* (Berlin: Dietz, 1971), p. 100.

[2] "The Fight against Formalism" (Resolution of the Central Committee of the SED, Fifth Meeting, 15–17 March 1951), in *Kritik in der Zeit: Der Sozialismus—seine Literatur—ihre Entwicklung*, ed. Klaus Jarmatz et al. (Halle: Mitteldeutscher Verlag, 1970), p. 250.

[3] *Ibid.*, p. 252.

all, to ideological softness and conciliatory thought."[4]

As could be expected, the heavy artillery of specific criticism was trained on Brecht, who called his dialectic theater "scientific theater," thus implicitly upholding objectivism. Brecht's adaptation of Maxim Gorki's *The Mother* drew wrath from high places. Fred Oelßner, a leading economic planner and a member of the Politbüro and the Central Committee of the SED, struck at Brecht's work for being "bourgeois formalistic" and "left radical" at the same time. Left radicalism was seen as undermining the orderly qualities of Marxism-Leninism upon which socialist states are built. In the Soviet Union in the thirties, the dramatists Meyerhold, Tretiakov, and Mayakovsky had been eliminated as left radical enemies of the state by the Stalin regime. Oelßner followed the Soviet model in his polemic: "But I ask: Is this really realism? Are these typical characters in typical surroundings? I won't even mention form. In my opinion, this is not theater; it is some kind of cross or synthesis of Meyerhold and the Cult of Proletarianism."[5] There was no relief in sight for anything which was not openly tendentious and unidimensionally supportive of a socialist ethic.

In 1951 Brecht's *The Days of the Commune* (*Die Tage der Kommune*), consistent in its promotion of Marxist ideology and objective in its treatment of the historic Paris Commune, was to be produced in honor of the eightieth anniversary of that 1871 proletarian uprising. In its objectivity, this treatment undermined the mythological heights to which this historic event had been elevated in the socialist world. The play was labeled as "objectivistic" and "defeatist" by the Central Committee and the Party College (*Parteihochschule "Karl Marx"*), and, in accordance with the preceding ruling, was not produced.[6] The play did not gain an audience in the GDR until 1956, after a considerable softening of the official GDR cultural-political perspective.

The general outlook for contemporary theater was rather dim in the first few years of the Five-Year Plan. With even Brecht facing political ostracism, conditions for dramatic experimentation were far from ideal. The repressive cultural actions of the SED deprived younger dramatists (and even older ones) of the confidence needed to explore the contemporary scene to a degree that would permit the organic development of the socialist perspective so strongly desired by the party. Consequently there was a dearth of serious dramatic attempts to deal with the problems of the new state. After the first wave of plays by the old guard around 1950, we find no dramatic treatments of contemporary life in the GDR until 1953, when the real political situation had changed drastically. To bridge this domestic production gap, the repertoire of the GDR theaters relied

---

[4] *Neues Deutschland*, 26 July 1950.

[5] Oelßner, *Kampf gegen den Formalismus in Kunst und Literatur* (Berlin: Dietz, 1951), p. 8.

[6] Cf. Jürgen Rühle, *Das gefesselte Theater: Vom Revolutionstheater zum Sozialistischen Realismus* (Köln: Kiepenheuer & Witsch, 1957), pp. 240–41.

heavily on imports from the Soviet Union. It was during the first two years of the Five-Year Plan that more Soviet plays were produced in the GDR than in any subsequent season.

At issue was the development of the socialist perspective, and the immediate problem of the GDR theater was that younger dramatists were slow in coming to terms with reality. But that was not the problem of the theater alone; it was the problem of the society as a whole. Again, the goals of the Five-Year Plan were too ambitious. The bases of any economy, material and labor, had been depleted in the GDR by reparation and deportation. It took superhuman efforts on the part of responsible functionaries and the workers simply to maintain the industrial output reached at the end of the Two-Year Plan (1949–50).[7] Since the standard of living had shown no appreciable signs of improvement in the crucial areas of food and housing, the demands of increased productivity resulted in a restive and disgruntled labor force. Individuals in charge of production were in extremely desperate straits. The Central Committee, however, far from deriving a historical lesson from Lenin's New Economic Policy, which, instituted during a similar crisis in the development of Soviet socialism, had relaxed the stringent Communist economic policy for a time three decades earlier, reasserted the strong economic measures of socialization in industry and agriculture. At the Second Party Conference of 1952, the party, instead of following the successful Soviet model for a similar crisis, went even further along the wrong course by calling for the development of socialism in agriculture through agricultural collectives (*Landwirtschaftliche Produktionsgenossenschaften*).

At this point in the history of the German Democratic Republic, a development of Soviet-American diplomacy came indirectly to the rescue. The Western powers rejected Stalin's serious proposal for the reunification and enforced neutrality of Germany of 10 March 1952. This prompted the Soviet Union to reevaluate its own goals in relation to the German Democratic Republic. Any reunification concepts were cast aside. The decision was made to develop the new state independently as a strong economic, political, and military ally rather than as a protectorate and an economic colony. This decision prompted the cessation of reparations, and the return to GDR control, and thus to the GDR economy, of the many Soviet stock companies (*Sovietische Aktiengesellschaften*) which had been siphoning vital assets off the top of the GDR gross national product. The economic manifestations of that crucial diplomatic move and further subsequent actions by the Soviet Politbüro were instrumental in overcoming the Plan difficulties into which the relatively inexperienced but over-zealous SED had gotten itself by this time.

[7] Because of difficulties of materials procurement, distribution, energy supply, and production facilities which could not be overcome, the Five Year Plan underwent at least four revisions during the time of its implementation. The plan failed to meet its goals in the most crucial areas of electricity, brown coal, iron ore, copper ore, and steel.

But this help from a Soviet shift of policy proved to be, for the time being, too little too late. The SED leaders were to get into even deeper trouble before they learned, or, rather, were forced to learn, that there is a considerable difference between theoretical dreams of a socialist society and the objective reality of running an economy. The strict measures of the Five-Year Plan and the subsequent resolutions of the Second Party Conference of 1952 had actually tried to immediately impose the socialist perspective on all facets of economic, social, and cultural life. But it is impossible to dictate a perspective. If anything more than lip service is the goal, such a perspective, which encompasses all of the elements that determine man's existence, must grow naturally. People can be directed, encouraged, and cajoled toward it, but it must be given a chance to develop organically. Indications are, and by the present state of the German Democratic Republic we are certain, that this perspective developed quite admirably once it received a more benign environment.

In the meantime, the SED sailed blindly along the charted course. On 22 January 1953, agricultural quotas were raised, this time favoring collectives and detrimental to independent farmers. Ignoring a recommendation of 15 April from the Politbüro of the Communist Party of the Soviet Union to soften the line and slacken the pace on the forced march toward socialism, the GDR government on 28 May ordered a general production increase of 10% across the board. The order was based on the resolutions of the thirteenth Meeting of the Central Committee of the SED, which had been held two weeks earlier. This measure was extremely unpopular with the workers and farmers of the "Workers' and Farmers' State." The handwriting of rejection and open violence was on the wall.

But four months after Stalin's death, the Soviet Union saw no need to support a neo-Stalinist economic policy determined mainly by the then still arch-Stalinist Ulbricht—especially when such a policy threatened the precarious potential of such an important ally in its future plans. Consequently, a few days later, on 3 June, the Soviet Politbüro called for a softer line, this time with unmistakable urgency. The SED responded (necessarily), and announced the New Course (*Neuer Kurs*) on 8 June 1953, modeled after the historical New Economic Policy of the Soviet Union. But it was too late. On 17 June 1953, workers found themselves on the streets of Berlin, Leipzig, Dresden, and Jena with rocks in their hands. But they were not alone. They were met by the heavily armed Garrisoned People's Police (*Kasernierte Volkspolizei*) and Soviet tanks and troops. The uprising was, from one point of view, a gallant effort. But it was clearly futile.

The New Course of economic planning in the GDR came about at the urging of the Soviet Union. On the cultural level, a similar impetus came from that direction. Already in October of 1952 the Nineteenth Party Congress of the Soviet Communist Party had indicated a new approach, a move away from the

Stalinist topical realism proclaimed by Zhdanov, especially in the theater. It was Georgi Malenkov who, in anticipation of his later role as prime minister, castigated the dull, lifeless, unimaginative results of the Zhdanovian cultural policy of the postwar era. Malenkov called for a new perspective on Soviet man, and the exploration of satire.[8] The direct effect which this cultural-political move may have had on the development of GDR theater is hard to measure in the light of subsequent political developments. It is certain, however, that this loosening of artistic restrictions in the literary life of Moscow was reflected in the cultural policies of the New Course in East Berlin. In any case, the drought of topical plays, which had lasted almost three years, was suddenly over.

The plays which appeared in the immediate wake of the liberalized New Course were new in two ways. First, they were written by new and younger authors who had developed their craft and gained their experience in the new state; and second, they were firmly committed to the new socialist system. This commitment was directly reflected in the development of a true socialist perspective in dealing with the contemporary problems raised in the plays. In these first dramatic efforts by Erwin Strittmatter, Heinar Kipphardt, Paul Herbert Freyer, and Harald Hauser, there is an innate acceptance of the German Democratic Republic as a national unity, and a healthy appreciation—or at least a realization—of the potential of the historic mission of the Workers' and Farmers' State.

Under the tutelage of Bertolt Brecht, Erwin Strittmatter prepared his *Katzgraben: Scenes from the Farmers' Life*[9] for production by the Berliner Ensemble. Brecht saw the author and the play as the direct results of a new historical process. "Erwin Strittmatter," wrote Brecht in *Notes on Katzgraben* (*Katzgraben Notate*), "belongs to the new writers who have risen not from the proletariat, but with it."[10] Brecht proceeds to the following conclusion: "Without the German Democratic Republic he would not only not have become the writer he is, but probably would not have become a writer at all."[11]

Brecht's evaluation is accurate. Erwin Strittmatter was born in 1912 in Spremberg. His schooling terminated at the age of sixteen when he became a baker's apprentice. Today he deservedly reigns as the dean of GDR writers, although he proclaims himself a simple man. Before becoming a soldier and a deserter in World War II, he earned his living as a waiter, animal caretaker, chauffeur, and laborer. He acquired a piece of farmland in the postwar Land Reform, and still works actively as a member of an agricultural collective. His

---

[8] Cf. Rühle, *Das gefesselte Theater*, p. 425.

[9] The original title of the play is *Katzgraben: Szenen aus dem Bauernleben*.

[10] Brecht, *Gesammelte Werke* (Frankfurt am Main: Suhrkamp, 1967), XVI (*Schriften zum Theater 2*), 775.

[11] *Ibid.*

identification with the land and the common rural people instills his literary work with an organic concept of human nature which is one of the major ingredients of his best works, the novels *Ole Bienkopp* (1963), *Tinko* (1963) and *The Miracle Maker* (*Der Wundertäter* [1966]).

Katzgraben was Strittmatter's first major work; it premiered on 23 May 1953. Although the New Course had not as yet been charted, the political climate was in such an insecure state of flux that the Brechtian deviations from cultural policy evident in the structure of the play went unchallenged by the cultural policy-makers. With the official arrival of the New Course a few days later, the elements in the play that earlier would have caused the party critics to rant against the Ensemble's formalism and objectivism remained unchallenged. This new tolerance was crucial for GDR theater. It indirectly legitimized dialectics and experimentation in the theater in accordance with Brecht's theory as defined in the *Short Organum for Theater* (1948), a development without which the achievements in the following epoch of Peter Hacks, Heiner Müller and Helmut Baierl could not have been realized. This is by no means to imply that *Katzgraben* has revolutionary stature in the development of the GDR drama. The play does, however, show an advanced degree of experimentation and daring in the tentative exploration of new forms within the context of socialist realistic contents. Thus it reflects Brecht's real concern with integrating his dialectic theater into the framework of the cultural policy.

From the point of view of theater of and for a planned society, *Katzgraben*, despite its experimentation, remains ideal. The realism, the content, and the overall ideology of the play strictly reflect the dictates of the Five-Year Plan and the Second Party Conference of 1952, especially in their concern with demonstrating and agitating for the breakthrough of the socialist perspective. Specifically, the plot centers on the efforts of the local party secretary to build a new road, a symbol of the future and the new power structure, from Katzgraben to the city. Großmann, a large landowner who has been exploiting the new farmers in the manner in which he was always accustomed to treating his servants, objects to the road because it will undermine his economic power over the others. What develops is a simple power struggle—on the "people's" side a quest for votes to approve and build the road between the old and the new. Land Reform, Agricultural Implement Stations, Farmers' Cooperatives, and the "leading role of the Socialist Unity Party" are all regarded as axiomatic. They are no longer the concerns of dramatic conflict, however, but are now the accepted bases from which the greater conflict of the play, the struggle between progressive and reactionary ideologies which had to be fought by the people to arrive at the workable socialist perspective, can be shown onstage. In essence, however, there is no real conflict. The deck of historical contingencies is stacked in favor of the progressive development of the socialist perspective. The traditional bourgeois ideology represented and propagated by Großmann is shown to be weak, decayed, and unconvincing in the face of the historical necessity of developing socialism as represented by Steinert, the local party secretary, and his coterie of new farmers, the beneficiaries of the Land Reform.

> STEINERT: Last year you saw no oxen's hair.
> Now oxen are all you see; the party
> Already sees tractors plowing.[12]

The experimental aspect of the play is in the combination of seemingly incongruous elements. Strittmatter presents a strictly "planned" cultural-political content in a loosely structured, episodic form in which the action actually develops noncausally by the juxtaposition of contrasting scenes. Particularly interesting is the fusion of the political and economic guts of the play and the mostly iambic, loose pentameter of the dialogue. Of this Brecht noted: "Perhaps for the first time in German literature we find an iambically elevated folk-diction [*Volkssprache*]. (The farmers in *The Broken Jug* speak the German of their creator, Kleist.)"[13]

Because of Strittmatter's efforts to come to aesthetic terms with progressive elements in his society, his characters, although they speak with force, conviction, and great folk-imagery, remain necessarily schematic because their development is postulated rather than causally demonstrated. The poetic elevation of their picturesque and powerful language has not helped to alleviate the stick-man syndrome which the demand for typical characters in socialist drama has created. Brecht did not see this as a problem, because other elements more than made up for the schematism: "I regard it as a significant achievement that we have our workers and farmers speak like the heroes of Shakespeare and Schiller."[14] Brecht is in accordance with his own idea of the theater in the scientific age when he extols Strittmatter's presentation of economic realities in a poetic form: "Such 'prosaic' things as potatoes, streets and tractors become poetic concepts."[15]

Historically, the play's importance rests in the positive indication that some experimentation was again possible. Furthermore, although the overall tone is positive, adulatory, and even euphoric in its celebration of the breakthrough of the socialist perspective, it is certainly critically objective as well. The play reviews topical concerns and at times "tells it like it is" while also presenting a positive indication of what should be. Even a final highly kitschy tableau complete with a band, tractors, flowers, slogans, and the entire cast announcing the great socialist future cannot cover up such real achievements in the GDR theater of that time: the infusion of spirited, earthy dialogue which remains entertaining

[12] Strittmatter, *Katzgraben/Die Holländerbraut* (Berlin: Aufbau, 1967), p. 56.
[13] Brecht, *Gesammelte Werke*, XVI, 777.
[14] *Ibid.*, p. 779.
[15] *Ibid.*

even though it carries a great load of immediate political content, and the characterization of a party secretary with real human weaknesses. These qualities are, even to this day, rare commodities in GDR drama. For example, the following exchange occurs when Steinert is ready to throw in the towel, and Elli gives him his own medicine:

> STEINERT: I couldn't get exhaust pipes from the council
> for these guys—not to speak of tractors.
> Katzgraben's stench is in my jacket,
> I've got to air it out.
> (ELLI *looks at him amazed.*) Well.
> ELLI: I wouldn't leave.
> STEINERT: Why not?
> ELLI: 'Cause Katzgraben
> isn't good enough to leave behind.
> (STEINERT *looks at her amazed.*)
> Try plowing deeper where nothing grows—
> it's that simple.
> STEINERT: Damn it, I can almost learn things from myself.[16]

Finally, Strittmatter also excellently motivates the development of the socialist perspective in the lives of his characters. A case in point is the awakening of the collective awareness in Bäuerin Kleinschmidt. Having just worked for an entire day for Großmann as repayment for the loan of his horses, she finds out that she may even have to work harder in the future since her daughter intends to go away to agricultural school. At first she objects, but when she realizes that education is what will in the long run break the power of the Großmanns in the society, she suddenly reverses her position.

> ELLI: I won't go to school. I'll never leave you to
> suffer in this muck.
> BÄUERIN KLEINSCHMIDT: You'll go to school for spite.[17]

And then, betraying her individualized personal motivation, she adds: "Study him to death, the dog."[18]

At this point, the predominant motivation of Bäuerin Kleinschmidt's action is still her personal individualized reaction to the man Großmann. By the third act, however, after her own economic situation is somewhat improved and some positive results of the transfer of power to the people have become evident, Großmann is no longer seen as a personal threat to her existence. Her conflict with him, deeply rooted in his previous exploitation of her labor, now takes on social

---

[16] Strittmatter, *Katzgraben*, pp. 98–99.
[17] *Ibid.*, p. 23.
[18] *Ibid.*

rather than individualized overtones. Although she still reacts against Großmann with personal distaste, Bäuerin Kleinschmidt reacts with the awareness of her role as an individual whose power rests in the growing power of the collective. Now society's Großmanns are no longer the redoubtable figures they traditionally were. They can be overcome through mobilization and organization of the collective effort. Thus, when Bäuerin Kleinschmidt hears of another effort by Großmann to hinder the construction of the crucial road to the city, she expresses the changing perspective:

> I wish Großmann's gut would bust with anger.
> Spund!
> The Women's Organization has to help. Even if I
> have to break down all the doors.
> I'll get out two brigades on Sunday
> to work the road, in spite of Großmann's ranting.[19]

There is, of course, still a healthy amount of personal motivation. Nevertheless, she has grasped the importance of her social role with the call for collective action toward a common goal. In this way, Strittmatter demonstrates that his characters are basically real people although they must necessarily be drawn schematically. The socialist perspective they attain does not appear magically out of a hat. There are no instant insights. There is a slow but clearly defined, plausible development from individualized points of view to collective points of view. The impetus for this development comes from real material changes in the economic environment, a process much more realistic than the sudden and unmotivated conversion to progressive socialist ideology which is the trademark of standard socialist realism in literature. Once they have laboriously reached their collective awareness, Strittmatter's characters remain realistic (although not in the socialist realist sense). They do not cast off their natural and personal emotions—Bäuerin Kleinschmidt's animosity is natural and personal—in favor of an idealized socialist perspective.

Georgi Malenkov's speech of October 1952 legitimizing satirical criticism of the negative aspects of Soviet society in socialist literature had an immediate effect on the Soviet stage. The year 1952 was a time when the works of socialist realism had plumbed the depths of dullness and sterility; they were little more than political propaganda. During 1951 and 1952 there had been widespread discussion by Soviet artists of the problem of conflict in the Soviet repertory.[20]

---

[19] *Ibid.*, p. 91.

[20] "Many dramatists felt that it was safer not to talk about contradictions and clashes, and they produced pointless but highly optimistic plays which resembled 'wine without alcohol,' according to a daring reviewer.

"The spectators reacted to this dull and contrived repertory by deserting the theaters when the contemporary Soviet plays were presented. At the same time all the other shows were crammed, and throughout the country theaters were attracting huge and appreciative audiences. In 1952 the current

Malenkov's expression of the new possibilities, coupled with Stalin's death a few months later, launched the first postwar "cultural thaw" in the Soviet Union. The initiation of the Malenkov era brought on radical changes. Artists who had been banished were recalled. Meyerhold and Mayakovsky, for example, were "reha-bilitated" and could be openly discussed for the first time in more than two decades. Plays were suddenly written about personal individualized problems, and the stodgy and stratified bureaucracy with its complacent ideology was bitingly satirized.[21]

It did not take long for this cultural heat wave to reach Berlin, arising as it did so soon after the general reforms of the New Course urged by the Soviet Politbüro. A few days after the debacle of 17 June 1953, a contemporary satire reached the stage of the Deutsches Theater. Heinar Kipphardt was the author of *Shakespeare, Where Are You? (Shakespeare dringend gesucht)*. A play about the local theater, it presented a devastatingly funny satirization of bureaucracy, official opportunism, and the gutless and brainless cultural functionaries of the SED.

Kipphardt was born in Heidersdorf, Silesia, in 1922. He studied medicine and, like Friedrich Wolf, was both physician and dramatist, although he did not practice medicine actively and intensively, as Wolf did. He came to East Berlin's Deutsches Theater with Wolfgang Langhoff in 1950 and was Langhoff's chief dramaturgical assistant until he moved to West Germany in 1959. In the Federal Republic he became one of the leading exponents of documentary theater with his world-famous plays *In the Matter of J. Robert Oppenheimer (In der Sache J. Robert Oppenheimer* [1964]) and *Joel Brand* (1965)—the latter a documentary treatment of the Nazi attempt to sell the lives of a million condemned Jews to the Allies in 1944 for ten thousand heavy trucks—an offer which the Allies rejected.

The plot of *Shakespeare, Where Are You?* concerns the attempt of the dramaturge of a provincial GDR theater to first find, and then stage, a com-petently written contemporary play. Like the main play, the play within the play is a satire. It was, no doubt, during his experience as dramaturge at the Deutsches Theater that Kipphardt developed his incisive insight into the cultural situation

joke in Moscow was: 'You will find good Soviet theater at the cemetery, and the cemetery at the Soviet theater.' In 1951, Soviet plays made up 55% of the whole repertory, and they dropped to 41% in 1952. But these figures did not reflect the number of performances. For instance, in the Moscow Art Theater only 86 out of 467 performances were of contemporary Soviet plays; in the Maly, 128 out of 523; and in Vakhtangov's classics numbered three times as many as the 'topical' Soviet plays. Some second-rate comedies had more success with the public than political or 'industrial' plays highly pub-licized in the Communist press. Already by 1952 *Pravda* stated in an article which deplored the situation in the theaters: 'The reason for dramatic poverty is that the playwrights do not base their works on deep conflicts. If one had to judge our life by those plays, one would come to the conclusion that everything is ideal, marvelous, that we have no conflicts. The playwrights think that it is prohibited to criticize the negative aspects of our reality" (Marc Slonim, *Russian Theater from the Empire to the Soviets* [New York: Collier, 1962], p. 366).

[21] Cf. Rühle, *Das gefesselte Theater*, pp. 425–30.

in the first years of the Five-Year Plan. This insight reveals itself in passages such as the following one in which the dramaturge, Färbel, is being examined for insanity:

> PROFESSOR (*to the interns*): Illusions and hallucinations following a brain concussion. (*To* FÄRBEL) You talk with birds?—Well?—Mr. Färbel? Are you giving them instructions? You talked to the birds about your play, isn't that so?—Don't be embarrassed, these gentlemen are all doctors.
> FÄRBEL (*screaming*): I'm normal. I know the date. I know the month. I know the multiplication tables. I know why a rainbow has colors. I'm a normal, fully competent human being who wants to stage a contemporary satire in the year 1953!!!
> PROFESSOR (*ad spectatores*): We have here the most beautiful hallucinatory illusion in the second half of the twentieth century.[22]

The critic Jürgen Rühle, who was present at the premiere, reports: "After the performance the audience arose to a man and applauded. Ill at ease, the party functionaries who were in the parquet eyed the government box, questioning whether they too should applaud. Then Otto Grotewohl, the prime minister, approached the very edge of the railing and applauded vigorously and for a long time."[23] The New Course was—for the time being—a reality and not an illusion.

Kipphardt's play had come at the right time. It was the greatest theatrical success in the German Democratic Republic, to be equalled only by the stage version of Hermann Kant's *The Auditorium* (*Die Aula*) and Plenzdorf's *The New Sorrows of Young W.* (*Die neuen Leiden des jungen W.*) more than a decade later. Heinar Kipphardt had examined the theater itself, and in his play he launched his satirical barbs in all directions. Wangenheim, Hauser, Grünberg, and even Brecht and Strittmatter had to take their share of the volleys along with the cultural ideologists of the SED.

Interestingly enough, they also had to turn the other cheek. Kipphardt's exercise had a consistent Marxist point of view. Since he called for a true revolutionary perspective in order to overcome the socialist doldrums of the bureaucracy in the Five-Year Plan, he could not be contradicted in terms of ideology. He had reduced the inanities of the planned society of that time to the world of the theater. The audiences responded gleefully, and found shoes that fit a number of actual political feet. For example, Kipphardt's satire on the plays dealing with industrial and agricultural production is a little unfair to Brecht and Strittmatter, but priceless nevertheless:

> ZAUN (*a young man of artistic looks: horn-rimmed glasses, crew cut, black marketeer's cap, in tailormade proletarian dress*): My name is Zaun. I am a partisan of the scientific

---

[22] Heinar Kipphardt, *Shakespeare dringend gesucht* (Berlin: Henschelverlag, 1954), pp. 91–92.
[23] Rühle, *Das gefesselte Theater*, p. 431.

theater. Following the method of historical-dialectical materialism, with rational poetical imagery, I have decided to liquidate all experience on the stage.

FÄRBEL: May I say "Hello" to you first?

ZAUN: Why? Let us cast aside these bourgeois formalities. I await the cutting edge of your critical intellect.

FÄRBEL: Well, about your play—

ZAUN: *Feed Contract*—a didactic play.

FÄRBEL: Look, your *Feed Contract* . . .

ZAUN: I agree entirely. Isn't topical with the development of agricultural collectives. In my head I've already changed it.

FÄRBEL: Oh, that's fast. Does it still start with a poem about the development of high-energy feed containing protein?

ZAUN: Naturally not. In an agricultural collective it has to be a chorus.

FÄRBEL: Please, you can't take a play and—

ZAUN: Precisely. I'll start with statistics.

FÄRBEL: I beg of you—you can't use statistics to start . . .

ZAUN: Quite right. Not original enough. I've already thrown out that idea . . .

FÄRBEL: Oh, that's fine . . .

ZAUN: And transferred it to weaving.

FÄRBEL: Wow, that's quick. And *Feed Contract?*

ZAUN: Is transposed into *Workday.* Documentary report on the socialist workday. Accordion, laughter, optimism, flags. Final chorus: We are building the world in the Three Man Method! How do you like that?

FÄRBEL: Bad.

ZAUN: Of course, not dramatic enough. I've got it: Blast furnace, explosion behind the curtain.

FÄRBEL: Also bad.[24]

Very familiar with Zaun's type of play, and not too fond of it, the public loved *Shakespeare, Where Are You?*, and socially critical plays prospered for a short time thereafter. The most crucial element of the play, however, was its consistent perspective on real socialist commitment as opposed to careerist opportunism, which is perhaps the reason it received a National Prize for Literature for 1953. The dialogue is expressive of the problems of functionaries in the new state as well, as the director of the theater, Schnell, tries to justify his blunders: "I? I—(*loudly*) I wanted the best. I worked and worked! I wanted to do right by everybody. Who can tell what it is you want! What do you really want?"[25] To this, Mellin, the enlightened party functionary from Berlin, replies: "Not careerists and not phraseologists! We want people—who know their work and are responsible for it. We want people who turn their faces to the masses, and not to their superiors!"[26]

[24] Kipphardt, *Shakespeare*, pp. 20–21.

[25] *Ibid.*, p. 112.

[26] *Ibid.*

Kipphardt's message was clear. It was a message directed to the party to revitalize itself. The character of the Comrade Mrs. Mellin represented the ideal and not the status quo. Kipphardt's view of the party is thus positive and idealized. He shows the party the way it should be, in a fine comic reversal of socialist realism, which had always shown the workers as they should be. Färbel, at the point of despair, talks with his office boy Fridolin, a classic parrot of Free German Youth ideology:

> FÄRBEL: I'm not a coward, Fridolin, I'm just tired. We're alone.
> FRIDOLIN: With a good cause one is never alone here.
> FÄRBEL: Who is with us?
> FRIDOLIN: The party.
> FÄRBEL: The party—that's good! The party is a concept, Fridolin. What we need are influential people who can help us.
> FRIDOLIN: The party, those aren't individual people.
> FÄRBEL: What is the party?
> FRIDOLIN (*stubborn, pathetic*): The party. It is the conscience of the world today. The party. It is the brain of the world of tomorrow.[27]

Fridolin's machine-like conception of the party as a general but also machine-like panacea is not what will help them put on the play. Färbel realizes that only individuals *qua* individuals can constitute the moral essence of the party:

> FÄRBEL: I've got another idea!
> FRIDOLIN: Now we've got to go to the party! Now we must fight!
> FÄRBEL: I'm going to the party—I'm fighting already—I have a colossally militant idea—you go to see a woman.
> FRIDOLIN: What?
> FÄRBEL: To a woman. Women, you know, are more diplomatic.
> FRIDOLIN: A comrade?
> FÄRBEL: Yes. Comarde Mellin in the Ministry of Education in Berlin. A great woman.[28]

What Färbel means, of course, is that Mrs. Mellin is above all an individual and that, as a party functionary, she has not lost her individuality or her responsiveness to the people. What Kipphardt asks for, then, with great socialist conviction, is a more humanized party.

But far from being a negatively critical response to the political system, Kipphardt's play, in its utterly comic essence, is a play of approval. It says a convincing "yes" to the larger order, while urging, in a most entertaining way, the advancement of the liveability quotient in the state. The satire actually shows that the larger battle has been won. It presupposes that people have a personal

27 *Ibid.*, pp. 88–89.
28 *Ibid.*, pp. 89–90.

stake in their state, support it, ask for a personal response, and therefore feel free to criticize some nonideological shortcomings. This is a true historical reflection. The early days of the regime were over. One could truly not be convinced anymore that an evil saboteur or *agent provocateur* was hiding behind every telephone pole on Friedrichstraße—or behind every funny line spoken at the Deutsches Theater. June 17 had shown that the real problems of advancing the new socialist order came from within. Hardening of the ideological arteries had caused that thrombosis. Kipphardt, a licensed physician, was ready with the diagnosis and a fitting prescription.

Traditionally a favorite literary tool of politically engaged authors, satire became, for a few short years, the favorite mode of expression in the German Democratic Republic. But, as in the case of Kipphardt, this satire was solidly based on the general approval of the system and the disapproval of particulars or incompetent individuals. And this movement was by no means restricted to the theater. Three 1953 poems by Bertolt Brecht also illustrate these tendencies. "Not Meant That Way" ("*Nicht so gemeint*") reports on the demand for more literary freedom by the German Academy of Arts (Deutsche Akademie der Künste) and the West Berlin press (which, in turn, used this request for its own propaganda). The poet, in a scathing dialectic lesson, tells propaganda-mongers from both sides that literary freedom is needed by authors to fight for peace—against the narrow-mindedness of one side and the "war-mongering" of the other. The poem "Indeterminate Errors of the Commission on Art" ("Nichtfeststellbare Fehler der Kunstkommission") recounts another episode from the Academy of Arts. The Cultural Commission is invited to discuss problems with a committee from the Academy. The functionaries of the commission bare their souls in obligatory self-criticism. However, when these functionaries are asked to be specific, Brecht records:

> Despite active reflection
> They could not recall making specific mistakes, but
> They urgently insisted
> That they had made mistakes—as is the custom.[29]

And the nice facade of Brecht's satire crumbles as its sharp cutting edge slices into the party press and propaganda machine:

> The Bureau for Literature
> It is known that the Bureau for Literature measures the distribution
> Of paper to the publishers in the Republic, so many tons
> Of the rare material for welcome works.
> Welcome
> Are those works with ideas

[29] Brecht, *Gesammelte Werke*, X (*Gedichte 3*), 1007.

Known to the Bureau for Literature from the newspapers.
This custom
Should, by the nature of our newspapers,
Result in great savings of paper, if
The Bureau for Literature would always allow only one
Book for each idea in our newspapers. Unfortunately
It lets mostly all books into print which rehash
One idea of the newspapers.
So that
The works of many a master
Are lacking paper.[30]

We must, however, not overestimate the effect of such a poem, since the Bureau for Literature was not very likely to appropriate too much paper for poems of this type. Brecht's roars remained those of a highly theoretical lion.

More effective than expressions of this type were the more subtle, more honest critical efforts in the framework of the drama, a vehicle that could get the message before a larger audience. Paul Herbert Freyer was another of the young dramatists who had a great stake in and an identification with the new republic. Freyer, born into a working class family in 1920, joined the merchant marine in 1936. His first theatrical activity commenced after the war in 1947, in his home town theater of Crimmitschau, where he became the chief dramaturgical assistant before moving on to the same position in Gera, and then to the Maxim Gorki Theater in Berlin in 1953. On the strength of the success of his contemporary plays, to be discussed below, Freyer became the general director of the City Theater of Plauen in 1955, and the head of the stages of Karl-Marx-Stadt (formerly Chemnitz) in 1956. Thus his playwriting was infused with considerable practical experience in the growing theater of the GDR's developmental years.

Freyer's industrial production play of 1953, *The Steamer* (*Der Dämpfer*), is an interesting synthesis of the prevalent socialist drama about industrial production with social satire. Freyer, who was 33 at that time, had established himself with a very successful play about the French Colonial War in Vietnam, *The Lost Outpost* (*Auf verlorenem Posten*). This play had seen more than 7000 performances in the GDR after its appearance in 1951.

The Steamer is named after the machine in which yarn must be steamed after it is spun, and deals with cultural, production, and morale difficulties in a people's textile factory. This, in itself, is a reflection of the liberalized atmosphere. Only months before, to acknowledge publicly that there were any "objective difficulties" (*objektive Schwierigkeiten*) in the GDR would have been considered "objectivism," "negativism," and a host of other dastardly pro-capitalist,

---

[30] *Ibid.*, pp. 1007–8.

defeatist deviations. The tone of the play is quickly established with a "Song at the Beginning":

> Today we want to name the names
> —That's why this play was made—
> To show you how you've made mistakes
> So we can cure them all by laughing.[31]

A suitably optimistic refrain follows with accordion accompaniment, and the play opens in the cafeteria of the factory. Here the many problems in the factory are identified: bad food, bad working conditions, small paychecks, loafing on the job, petty envy among workers, inefficient administrators, lack of understanding of national objectives and the Plan, and, worst of all, a party functionary who is a phraseologist. The latter, Ewald, is described as follows: ". . . He is the Production Committee Chairman. He is middle-aged, and the union functionary of the factory who is the most socially and politically active on all levels. Through overburdening he has earned, in jest, the title of Multifunctionary [a widespread pun on the German form of multimillionaire], and has lost the ground from under his feet. . . ."[32] An excellent instance of his removal from reality is his manner of speech toward the workers. He uses the newly invented, abominable Party Jargon German, and Freyer slices it to the bone. At a meeting of workers who suggest a progressive way to overcome the production problems and to increase efficiency, all the facts fly past Ewald's comprehension, but he responds nevertheless:

> Good! Fine! Colleagues, if we view the hegemony of the Economic Plan, the structure of the execution results, when we consider the constellation of previous fiscal quarters, in an acceleration of the positive factor similar to a logarithmic curve. In an analysis of the present economic condition, however, there appear certain symptoms which are conducive to the indication of discrepancies, often, of course, purely discontinual, which are usually in direct correspondence to nonmatured underdeveloped suggestions which some institutions, respective to the coordination and in the concrete application of acute acceleration. . . .[33]

The workers, however, have had it, and they won't let him get away with this gobbledygook. In the following episode of required self-criticism, Freyer, from a deep conviction that there is a better socialist path than the one deformed by bureaucracy, rocks the foundations of the "functionary system."

The play also contains one of the truer and more humorous satires on the cultural policies, and especially the theater policy, of the GDR. Ewald, also the

---

[31] Paul Herbert Freyer, "Der Dämpfer," MS (Berlin: Henschelverlag Abteilung Bühnenvertrieb, 1953), p. 4.

[32] *Ibid.*, pp. 5–6.

[33] *Ibid.*, pp. 25–26.

cultural functionary of the factory, is trying to pass out theater tickets for a contemporary topical play:

WILLI: What's up?
EWALD: The theater sent us these tickets again, for tomorrow night. You want two of them?
WILLI: Tomorrow night, for the theater?
EWALD: Yes.
WILLI: What's playing?
EWALD: Well . . . I don't know the title, you know, one of those plays . . .
WILLI: Does it have music?
EWALD: I don't know.
WILLI: No . . . If there's no music, my wife won't go anyway.[34]

Whereupon Ewald launches into one of his involved lectures on the workers' cultural responsibility and the national cultural heritage, with quotations from Karl Marx. But when someone asks him if he is going to the play, he has to admit that he isn't. Actually, he hasn't been in a theater for more than six months, and he further reveals that it wasn't even for a play, but for a party celebration instead. It seems that he is too busy distributing culture to partake of it himself.

The production problems are resolved by the institution of a new method that demands genuine self-criticism and a new, more progressive orientation on the part of all of the people involved. The success of the play, however, rests simply on its unpretentiousness and its disarming presentation of the work process in a people's factory. One simply could not, at that time, argue with a playwright who presented the facts, an optimistic view, and valid suggestions for improvement within the system. Even today socialist critics cannot complain about the play. It remains a piece of entertaining and engaged theater.

Freyer's next two plays, *Upward Bound* (*Die Straße hinauf* [1954]) and *Cornflowers* (*Kornblumen* [1954]), are also topical treatments of GDR society which again are based on objectives of the economic plan. *Upward Bound* presents actual conflicts between the complacently conservative and more progressive Communists in the construction projects of Berlin's Stalin Allee. *Cornflowers* deals very objectively, even negatively, with the problems of an ill-conceived agricultural collective. Neither play is on a level with *The Steamer*, although *Upward Bound* has perhaps the best dramatic conflict of any topical play of that period. Hermann Kähler again completely misses the point when he tries to slough off this play with these few words: "Here we find conflicts between workers which developed during the introduction of new production methods. But the fight of the new against the old was reduced to the fight of new against

[34] *Ibid.*, p. 6.

42

old methods of production. The characters remain undeveloped."[35] Nothing could be further from the truth. When Engineer Bark arrives in Berlin from Eisenach with his new method, the masons on the project work individually without any view to the collective effort. In the meantime, great ideological fisticuffs develop, even involving a State Secretary, who is shown in the worst, most reactionary light. Little by little, in skillfully arranged scenes, the merit of Bark's new method catches on, and its emphasis on interdependence and team-work actually transfers the essence of the method from the hands to the minds of the workers. Freyer shows this as the natural result of a battle between conflicting concepts in which the more progressive one wins and finally permeates the total perspective of those who have been converted to the new way. Freyer demonstrates this process in an extremely credible, logical, and historically accurate manner.

But perhaps Freyer, in his objective treatment, had already gone too far for an era of thaw that was rapidly refreezing. His portrayal of an old party member who rests on his laurels and has become a completely self-satisfied defender of the status quo, coupled with the dissection of the character of a very high party official, the State Secretary for Construction Planning, was perhaps too much too late. Even though the characters are both fictional, the narrow-minded opportunism they epitomize was actual and prevalent. And despite the fact that Freyer again includes the mandatory session of self-criticism at the end of the play, the damage to the party image was irrevocable. The master bricklayer Wieland asks to be allowed to start anew and to be given another chance to learn better ways, while the State Secretary admits that "the fact that Wieland wants to start all over again relieves me greatly. And the same . . . I'd like to tell you openly . . . now, before you leave Berlin . . . I'm going to have to find myself too. I've got to re-earn the trust put in me. I won't try to avoid the responsibility for my actions anymore, but will actively seek it from now on."[36] But again, we must consider historical influences. Perhaps from Hermann Kähler's perspective in 1964, when a State Secretary is again officially infallible, the development of such a character is indeed hard to recognize.

In 1955, the Deutsches Theater, which had presented one of the first critically realistic plays of the New Course, also produced the last significant play to appear before the glacier advanced once more from Moscow, as the "New Course" era ended with Khrushchev's dismissal of the more liberal Malenkov and, finally, the Hungarian revolt of 1956. The play in question was Alfred Matusche's *The Village Street* (*Die Dorfstraße*).

---

[35] Kähler, *Gegenwart auf der Bühne: Die sozialistische Wirklichkeit in den Bühnenstücken der DDR von 1956–1963/64*, (Berlin: Henschelverlag, 1966), p. 194.

[36] Paul Herbert Freyer, "Die Straße hinauf," MS (Berlin: Henschelverlag Abteilung Bühnenvertrieb, 1955), p. 128.

Matusche is another of the writers whose Marxist convictions developed during the fascist rule in Germany after 1933. He was born in Leipzig in 1909 where he attended the Technical University until 1927, when he "dropped out" in the modern sense. Searching for stability in the turbulence of the Weimar Republic, he became active in the socialist workers' movement, and worked for Leipzig Radio until the Nazi takeover in 1933. His first manuscripts were confiscated and burned at that time. After 1945, he resumed his radio work in Leipzig, and extended his writing to the stage and film. His work is characterized by a serious search for the human elements in any social system in a process that accepts no postulates. Although Matusche's work is highly esteemed by his fellow GDR authors, he has not enjoyed the acceptance and success which has fallen to lesser talents with less political conviction—perhaps because he consistently refuses to accept postulations of ideology and insists on examining them from a thoroughly critical perspective.

In *The Village Street*, Matusche presents a super-realistic and critical treatment of an incident in a small town on the Polish border immediately after the end of the war. A German army officer had received an "involuntary" cornea transplant from a Polish girl, who was blinded as a result. But the officer is not your standard Evil Nazi; he had, in fact, rescued a large number of Polish women from SS troops during the final weeks of fighting. The girl in question appears in the village, and, realizing that her condition was beyond the former officer's control, does not blame him for her loss of sight. There are more such uncomfortable dichotomies. The refugees in the village and the "new" farmers who receive the benefits of the Land Reform are full of Nazi sympathies. On the other hand, the Baron and his family, dispossessed by the postwar Land Reform, had been victims of Nazi persecution. In the situations of dramatic conflict provided by Matusche, nothing is easy, pretty, or optimistic.

But the play's extremely critical realism, which already provided a historical perspective, had overrun the rapidly narrowing official limits. The play simply asked too many embarrassing questions about the morality of the crass utilitarianism that governed the formation of the new social contingencies in the early period of GDR history. To the SED, it was undesirable. The critic and playwright Armin Stolper reported "conflict with critics. Matusche hits back: It's possible that the play has errors, but it is a true play."[37] But official tolerance of dramatic representations of the "truth" was again declining.

At this point it must be admitted, however, that the developments in the contemporary topical drama discussed in the preceding pages, though they were important, were perhaps not quite as widespread or significant as their treatment here would indicate. An important qualification is pointed out by Freyer himself

[37] Stolper, "Begegnung mit Alfred Matusche," in Matusche, *Dramen* (Berlin: Henschelverlag, 1971), p. 210.

in the ticket distribution scene of *The Steamer*. The people of the German Democratic Republic, in an era of emphasis on "people's culture,"[38] certainly preferred *Die Fledermaus* to plays of socialist realism, and their preferences were largely accommodated. While the contemporary topical drama was tentatively searching for a perspective, the traditional entertainment-oriented theater of German origin flourished in the repertory of the New Course era. This was partly a result of the new cultural direction, which placed emphasis on the national cultural heritage (*nationales Kulturerbe*), especially in the drama. This idea of the national cultural heritage encompasses all of the great works of German literature, since the revolutionary proletariat is now in a position to experience those cultural goods that had been withheld from it, but which are a part of its national cultural history.

One cultural result of the New Course had been the formation, in 1954, of the Ministry of Culture, under the direction of Johannes R. Becher, as a separate entity from the Ministry of People's Education (*Ministerium für Volksbildung*). Becher, born in Munich in 1891, was, and still is regarded as the "grand old man" of GDR letters. An early Communist like Friedrich Wolf, Becher had been a Communist member of the Weimar Republic's Parliament. He was an organizer of a proletarian writer's movement in the twenties. With Ulbricht, he was one of the German Communists who prepared for the postwar Communist takeover in Germany as a member of the Central Committee of the German Communist Party exiled in the Soviet Union from 1933 to 1945. Before 1933, Becher was one of the most famous of German expressionists and later became a visionary poet of the revolution. In the GDR, he liked to think of himself as the classic "poet and statesman," a role he played earnestly from a deep commitment to Marxist ideology until his death in 1958.

One of Becher's first plans or programs for achievement in the GDR's cultural affairs focused on the idea of the national cultural heritage. "Classical works are the basic elements of the repertories,"[39] was his formulation for GDR theater.

This renewed focus on the socialist treatment of the traditional heroes of German literature resulted in corresponding attention by critics to classical forms and traditional aesthetic principles. This critical direction was, in itself, not very conducive to the propagation of new treatments of the contemporary situation. A work seminar for dramatists sponsored by the German Writers' Union (Deutscher Schriftstellerverband) early in 1955 provides an example of this trend

[38] On 12 October 1954, Johannes R. Becher, the Minister of the newly formed Ministry of Culture, released a program declaration titled "Program of the Ministry of Culture on the Development of a People's Culture in the GDR." The title of the third section of this declaration is "Our Immediate Objectives and Goals in the Development of a Democratic and National People's Culture" (*Sonntag*, 17 October 1954).

[39] Supplement to *Neue Deutsche Literatur*, II/5 (1954), 15.

toward traditional concepts in theater arts. In a keynote speech, "A View on the New Drama," the critic Heinz Hofmann bemoans the fact that true tragedy and true tragic characters had not been presented in the new plays of the past season. This must have been very interesting for the writers of the new plays, who justly wondered how tragedy was to be accommodated within a revolutionary theory of socialist theater. Furthermore, Hofmann concentrates his discussion, to a large extent, on the historical and anti-fascist plays of Hedda Zinner and Friedrich Wolf. When he does talk about contemporary topical plays, he unfairly criticizes them because they lack the traditional dramatic elements he loves so much in the works of Goethe and Schiller. Thus, when he speaks of Freyer's *Upward Bound*, he crucifies the play with weak, rusty aesthetic nails left over from the eighteenth century:

> The strong dramatic talent of this author [Freyer] has, for the time being, yielded to bad influences. Too many "discussants" caused him to write plays about subjects which had not yet become his own. This resulted in plays in which the effort was not to bring *one* conflict to a climax, and to resolve it, but in which a multitude of characters appear (among them also a few purely chemical "positive heroes") and undergo no development at all. Some of them are only "peripherally" maneuvered into a change.[40]

The fact that Freyer had definitely made typological inroads in form, content, and perspective into the contemporary topical drama which became the staple of the GDR theater a decade later went unnoticed by GDR critics in 1955. It seems that the interest in and emphasis on this type of work in the theater had been overshadowed by the national cultural heritage, even in literary criticism. In contrast, Hofmann praises Kipphardt's *Shakespeare, Where Are You?* not for its daring, its perspective, or its contemporary reality, but because the author "had his subject under control."[41] This, however, only means to the critic that the play is in a traditional comic form which can be traced back through the comic drama of the cultural heritage; that is, from his perspective, admirable in itself.

Thus contemporary dramatists such as Friedrich Wolf and Hedda Zinner, who reinterpreted the national cultural heritage in historical dramas from a socialist perspective, had more success. The same is true for their continued work in plays of anti-fascism, including the newest version, anti-West German plays. Even Hermann Kähler points out that these plays were in the majority: "On the whole these plays [the contemporary topical works] were completely in the minority, and could not determine the profile of our drama. Plays like *The Devil's Circle* [anti-fascist] by Hedda Zinner (1953), *Thomas Müntzer* [history] by

---

[40] Heinz Hofmann, "Blick auf die neue Dramatik," *Neue Deutsche Literatur*, III/3 (1955), 134.
[41] *Ibid.*, 135.

Friedrich Wolf (1953), and *At the End of the Night* [contemporary] by Harald Hauser (1955) were dominant."[42]

Another popular historical treatment by Hedda Zinner, *Lützower* (1955), fits into the scheme outlined by Kähler. This overemphasis on traditionalism in literature brought on by the New Course is seen by Klaus Jarmatz, a leading literary theorist of the GDR, as being especially harmful to the development of the topical drama: "The inhibitions which caused a general reduction in the literary treatments of life in the German Democratic Republic after 1953 were especially noticeable in the drama."[43]

These "inhibitions," meaning outlooks which were later considered revisionism, or bourgeois interpretations of Communism, did not affect two contemporary plays written by the "unrevised" dogmatic Communists Harald Hauser and Karl Grünberg. Hauser, who was roasted on Kipphardt's satirical grill in *Shakespeare, Where Are You?* (he is the model for the party propagandist Monhaupt in that play), continued to write propaganda.

Hauser's personal history provides a fascinating study worthy of literary treatment itself. He was another of the anti-fascist political activists during the turbulent demise of the Weimar Republic. Born in 1912 in Lörrach in southwestern Germany, he studied law in Freiburg and Berlin. He distinguished himself as a man of action early in his life, directing agitation and propaganda for the Berlin Red Students' League after joining the Communists in 1932. He emigrated to France after Hitler's takeover and became a volunteer in the French army and later a heroic fighter in the French resistance. No doubt his fierce pro-Communist stance in the early years of the GDR developed concretely from his physical struggles against the Hitler regime.

Hauser's play *At the End of the Night* (*Am Ende der Nacht* [1955]) treats the trials, tribulations, and subsequent conversion to socialist idealism of Jensen, an engineer in a Soviet stock company. As he is about to defect to the West, Jensen discovers the humanity and historical importance of the sociopolitical mandate of the GDR. The man who makes this clear to him and inspires his reconversion is Strogow, a Russian engineer. Hauser, an author whose background is similar to that of Strittmatter, Kipphardt, and Freyer—all of whom have their artistic roots in the new state—has opted to propagate the party line rather than to examine it and improve it. What conflict there is in his play does not arise from the system, or the situation of the characters, but rests again on a surgically inserted outside influence—that too familiar standby, the *agent provocateur*.

This allies Hauser closely with Karl Grünberg, who in 1954 tried his hand at another topical play, *Electrodes* (*Elektroden*). This was similar to his 1950 effort,

[42] Kähler, *Gegenwart auf der Bühne*, p. 194.

[43] Jarmatz, "Die literarische Entwicklung in der Deutschen Demokratischen Republik," *Weimarer Beiträge*, 5 (1964), 795.

The Golden Steel, but was more primitive in dramatic conflict. Again no organic conflict is developed; again, those indefatigable foreign saboteurs and agents are called upon to advance the action. The play also reaches previously unequalled heights of anti-American and anti-West German sentiments. Generally, in Grünberg's plays, there are two colors—black and white—and two moral values—good and evil. His character descriptions illustrate this profoundly:

> EVYLYN: . . . *beautiful, around thirty, Western-mundane. Her significant interests are: hunger for life, coquettery, self-assertion and egotism. . . .*
> MR. WESTINGHOUSE: *Boss of the secret spy center in Dahlem. Late forties. His bearing is American, self-assertive, and constantly overbearing. He tries to minimize this through false joviality. Hidden behind this are brutality, cynicism, and cold calculation. He speaks an almost flawless chewing-gum-German.*[44]

Unable to portray the complex realities and conflicts of the new GDR society, Grünberg resorts to confronting well-behaved little children (the people of the GDR) with the bogeyman (the spectre of the evil capitalist). This seems to indicate that it was too late for Grünberg to learn anything new from the progressive developments taking place around him at that time.

The era of the New Course essentially came to an end with the fall of Malenkov in February of 1955 and Khrushchev's consolidation of power at the Twentieth Congress of the Communist Party of the Soviet Union on 8 February 1956. As a direct result of Malenkov's demise, Walter Ulbricht brought the New Course into perspective at the Twenty-Fourth Meeting of the Central Committee of his party on 1 June 1955: "We never had the intention to embark on such a false course, and we shall never do so."[45]

This brought to a close the first larger epoch of the contemporary theater of the German Democratic Republic. From divergent international influences in the immediate postwar years, it had arisen with topical dramas staunchly in support of the new state in 1949 and 1950. After a hiatus of three years, brought on mostly by cultural policies of the strict Five-Year Plan that discouraged new works, it reached heights of social activism and criticism during the subsequent New Course, although its products were relatively few. The lack of impact of the new topical plays during this time was partly due to the SED's relentless application of a basic tenet of Marxism-Leninism, one that reflects Lenin's awareness of the importance of the cultural heritage in a socialist society: that a balance between representations of the national cultural heritage and of the new proletarian culture is ideal. However, during the epoch of the New Course, the pendulum swung for a time in favor of the heritage, bringing with it a sizeable

---

[44] Quoted in Rühle, *Das gefesselte Theater*, p. 345.

[45] Ulbricht on 1 June 1955, quoted in "Neuer Kurs," *SBZ von A bis Z: Ein Taschen- und Nachschlagebuch über die Sowjetische Besatzungszone Deutschlands*, ed. Bundesministerium für gesamtdeutsche Fragen (Bonn: Bundesverlag, 1966), p. 355.

chunk of non-socialist aestheticism. A socialist system in difficulty—and this one was in deep trouble in 1953—always seems to fear left-radicalism, or new revolutionary ideas, more than reactionary thoughts, which can always be purged when things get better. As the economic policies of the 1953 New Economic System asserted themselves, alleviating the disastrous economic situation in the GDR, such new ideas in play-writing as satire and critical realism were forced into a temporary decline. This was aided on an aesthetic level by "revisionistic" views which had established themselves against contemporary dramatic treatments in general.

Up to this point, the contemporary topical drama of the GDR was to a large degree rooted in conversions or adaptations of Soviet socialist realism. But by 1956, the new state had weathered its worst economic crisis and was ready to leave the past behind. The time was ripe to develop a dramatic theater from its own history and experience: it was the dawn, finally, of the socialist national theater of the German Democratic Republic.

III.
Toward a Socialist National Theater

In 1956 international diplomacy again provided an impetus that altered the course of the literary history of the German Democratic Republic. New and important political contingencies appeared. West Germany was rearmed and became a member of NATO; the National People's Army had been formed in the East; and the big powers failed to come to an accord on the German question. Basic historical polarization was in progress. In West Germany, Adenauer's "economic miracle" was hitting its stride, saturating that part of Germany with smug self-satisfaction and restorative national pride. The complete integration of the Federal Republic into the social, economic and cultural systems of Western Europe and North America had taken place. The East was watched uneasily, with a defensive eye. But there, the Democratic Republic was just overcoming the aftereffects of political unrest and a major economic disaster, and was doggedly propagating a socialist way of life which, admittedly, still depended on personal material sacrifices by the people. One thing, however, had become clear to everyone: there were now basic structural differences between the two states— and ideological differences in the perspectives of their peoples—that could not be reconciled without drastic compromises. The increasing political distance between the two states necessitated, in the GDR, a corresponding reorientation of cultural policy toward a more nationalistic perspective to counteract the "fat cat" complacency of the West. The West's conspicuous economic prosperity was opposed by a moral stance that implied, in essence, that the West may be rich now, but would lose in the long run because of its corrupt system. It was this by then fully developed ideological rift which led Walter Ulbricht, in 1956, to proclaim the necessity and mandate of the literature of the German Democratic Republic as a new German national literature:

> In Germany we now find ourselves in a situation of conflict between two systems, between the ruling monopolistic-capitalistic system which has integrated West Germany into the warmaking base of NATO, and the German Democratic Repub-

lic, which has become the base of peace and progress. Under these conditions, the new German national literature has its roots predominantly in the German Democratic Republic, because a higher social order was created in the German Democratic Republic and socialism was developed by the working people. The ideas of the great German humanists are cultivated in this part of Germany. The future of Germany finds its expression in the politics of peace, democracy, and progress.[1]

Starting in 1953, the New Course in economic and cultural policy had somewhat slackened the forced progression toward the complete socialist state. Although the end of the New Course in foreign policy and economics arrived early in 1955 with the fall of Malenkov and finally, in 1956, with the Twentieth Congress of the Soviet Communist Party, this Congress further relaxed the cultural policy of the German Democratic Republic. The liberalization was mainly the result of the German Communists' misinterpretation of Khrushchev's secret anti-Stalin, anti-dogmatism speech which was the high point of the Twentieth Congress in Moscow. Khrushchev's denouncement of the "Stalin personality cult," which had long dominated Soviet life, was wrongly interpreted as a move against "Stalinist" cultural policy, toward a more liberal climate. The fact that Khrushchev only used this maneuver to solidify his own power did not become evident until later. The result in the GDR was fairly unidimensional, giving confidence to so-called "bourgeois revisionists" and bringing them and their ideas out into the open.

The policy toward the theater in 1956 and 1957, however, reflected a dichotomy in the basic cultural position. On one hand, new forms and experimentation, and all of what used to be condemned as "formalism," were very strong and enjoyed official party sanction in *Neues Deutschland* as late as May 1957.[2] From another quarter, induced by the return to a more distinctly socialist economic policy, there were calls for a corresponding return to contemporary economic and social topics in the drama. While cultural policy had usually been implemented through party channels from the top down, the strong request for topical contemporary treatments came, this time, from the bottom up. The "Nachterstedt Letter," from the workers of the People's Brown Coal Factory Nachterstedt to the Writers' Union Congress of 1955, is the first rejection of the more traditional non-socialist aesthetics which had been tolerated under the policy of the New Course. It reflects an advanced degree of socialist awareness and clear perspective, and is certainly a tribute to effective party activism and cultural-political agitation at the Nachterstedt factory. These culturally awakened

[1] Ulbricht, Address at the Fourth German Writers' Conference, 9–14 January 1956, *Neues Deutschland*, 17 January 1956.

[2] Cf.: "Until now questions of creativity were treated like a cat on a hot tin roof, in the fear that any individualistic perspective which one may have had would be considered 'ideologically vague' or 'formalistic,' two terms which represented a scarlet letter for any artist in the realm of the theater" ("Eine Aussprache mit Theaterintendanten," *Neues Deutschland*, 4 May 1956).

workers give some cogent advice in this open letter to all GDR writers: "There are still not enough books in which our authors treat, artistically, the new developments in our factories and our lives. Therefore we ask our authors to consider this question very seriously at their Fourth Writers' Union Congress."[3]

The authors are providing a service to the workers, and these workers would like it to be more useful, and more to their liking. Any pretentious theoreticians on the aesthetics of socialism should mark this point well. The workers of Nachterstedt, led by their factory librarian, offer even more specific advice:

> We would like more works about our new people who make all the material things with their hands; about the activists in production who work and fight with awareness for all the workers, for the power of the workers and farmers. You can find such people in almost all of our people's factories. Write works in which our people can recognize themselves. We will read these works with special pleasure, gain many new ideas about our own life, and see many things with new eyes. Characterize the working man exactly as he is; flesh and blood; how he works, loves and fights. Show the enthusiasm, the passion, and the great awareness of responsibility which permeates the soul of the worker in his fight for progress.[4]

This grass-roots call for a reorientation toward socialist realism in literature was contrary to the prevalent development in the theater. For example, in the 1956–57 season, only roughly 17% of the repertory consisted of plays by GDR authors.[5] But as has been indicated earlier, even most of these were historical in subject matter, and were not oriented to the contemporary reality of life in the GDR. As a further indication of the trend of the theater thaw, the percentage of Soviet plays, both historical and contemporary, reached an all-time low of 6% at that time. Criticism was equally permissive. One result of the Twentieth Soviet Party Congress was the open reception and discussion of Western "decadent" drama and other literature (compare the objections of Friedrich Wolf in 1946) by such French authors as Jean Anouilh, André Gide, and Jean Giraudoux, the Americans Thornton Wilder and William Faulkner, and their West German followers. This, however, was finally too much. At this point, the Hungarian precedent, coupled with the non-party line interpretation of Marxism which threatened to undermine the party's power, finally, by March 1957, provoked *Theater der Zeit*, the GDR's primary theater periodical, to offer official words of caution.[6]

But the traditional Western aesthetic influences (which were supported by Wolfgang Harich and a group of intellectuals in key cultural positions who were

---

[3] "Nachterstedter Brief," *Tribüne*, 27 January 1955.

[4] *Ibid.*

[5] Cf. Heinz Kersten, "Theater und Theaterpolitik in der DDR," in *Theater hinter dem "Eisernen Vorhang*," ed. Reinhold Grimm et al. (Hamburg: Basilius, 1964), p. 26.

[6] Cf. "So denken wir darüber," *Theater der Zeit*, March 1957.

soon to be purged as "third way" revisionists because they propagated a Marxist philosophy not approved by the party) brought on by the recent liberalizations were not the only forces which worked contrary to the ideal of socialist realism. The revolutionary dramas of the twenties and thirties also exerted their influence. The previously "formalist" and "decadent" works and theories of Mayakovsky and Tairov, Soviet experimentalists of the twenties, had been "rehabilitated" in the Soviet Union during the New Course. Concurrently, the radical experimentation of the German theater of the twenties also came to be seen in a more positive light as part of a socialist German tradition which might be used as a model for the GDR. Thus Erwin Piscator, Germany's leading theatrical experimentalist of the Weimar Republic, was made a corresponding member of the German Academy of Arts in the GDR. Furthermore, Brecht's Interrogation of Lucullus, rejected as "formalistic" by the party in the rigid Stalinist cultural climate of a few years earlier, appeared in 1955 under the title The Judgment of Lucullus (Die Verurteilung des Lukullus). It was at this time, too, that Brecht's stock, never too high in the GDR cultural-political market, skyrocketed due to his international successes in London and Paris. Brecht, who had always been suspected of being somewhat subversive—whether by the House Un-American Activities Committee or the Politbüro—was suddenly heaped with eulogies following his death in 1956.

It comes as no surprise, then, that in 1957 two distinct schools of thought were openly vying for control of the development of the GDR drama. On the one hand, standard socialist realism was being propagated by the party, and on the other, playwrights—with a degree of tolerance by the party—were looking to a more experimental theater based on a radical German tradition of the twenties and on Brecht's theories. On 25 March 1956, Alexander Abusch had praised these open debates and conflicts about literary forms and functions in the GDR which had characterized the Fourth Writers' Congress as a positive sign of fruitful, progressive discussion.[7] Subsequently, the April 1957 issue of Neue Deutsche Literatur, the official literary magazine of the Writers' Union, provided more of the same. In a discussion entitled "The Contemporary Theater" ("Das Theater der Gegenwart"), Peter Hacks, Hans Pfeiffer, Joachim Knauth, Harald Hauser and Hedda Zinner provided their evaluations of the current situation of GDR drama and its future possibilities.

Peter Hacks develops his views, on the basis Brecht's 1956 collection of notes, Dialectics in the Theater (Die Dialektik auf dem Theater), which he cites frequently. Hacks is an extremely scholarly and intellectual dramatist who consciously follows the tradition of Brecht. Born in Breslau, Silesia (now

[7] Abusch, who would radically change his view within the year as a result of the Hungarian incident, stated at this time: "Since the Writers' Union Conference no one can dispute that the open discussions, the real arguments within the realm of a unified socialist world view, can be interesting, varied, and really productive" ("Aktuelle Fragen unserer Kunstpolitik," Sonntag, 25 March 1956).

Wroclaw, Poland) in 1928, Hacks studied philosophy, sociology, literature and theater in Munich. In 1955 he moved from West to East Germany. In the GDR he was a dramaturgical assistant at Langhoff's Deutsches Theater until 1963, when both Hacks and Langhoff were sacked in a dispute over one of Hacks's plays. Hacks, who consistently got into cultural-political difficulties with his contemporary plays because he followed the theories described below, was most successful in his historical comedies, in which he reinterprets history in accordance with a Communist view.

In "The Contemporary Theater," he states that "the theory of socialist realism is better than the use to which the contemporary theater has put it from time to time."[8] He interprets socialist realism as "a dialectic realism,"[9] and calls for its application in the contemporary GDR theater, pointing out that Brecht's theory of theatrical dialectics "means as much to the aesthetics of the working class as Aristotle's theory did to the slaveholders, and its regeneration by the French classicists and Lessing does to the bourgeoisie."[10] Thus Hacks believes that Brecht's theory of a "scientific" theater is more useful for a working class society such as that of the GDR than the Soviet model of socialist realism would be.

According to Hacks, the real problem, even failure, of GDR theater lies in its cultivation of a false tradition, a point on which Bertolt Brecht would have agreed: "Techniques of writing and acting were tied to the idealistic tradition of of German classicism and its followers, and the mechanical tradition of naturalism."[11] He sees the greatest fault of the GDR's cultural effort in the fact that any orientation toward the truly realistic models of the cultural heritage has been contrary to policy. Hacks is blatantly critical of the combination of the cultural heritage with socialist realism, because this situation "only resulted in a proletarian version of courtly theater."[12] Hacks ascribes this confusion to the neglect of "the great realistic tradition of the German theater which, originating with Shakespeare, comes to Bertolt Brecht by way of J. M. R. Lenz and George Büchner."[13]

Another young new dramatist, Joachim Knauth, whose efforts, like those of Peter Hacks, had been restricted until this time to historical treatments,[14] supported Hacks's view in the same discussion: "The best works of our dramatists show the return to dialectics and therefore to the realistic way of writing."[15]

[8] Hacks, in "Das Theater der Gegenwart: Eine Rundfrage," *Neue Deutsche Literatur*, V/4 (1957), 128.

[9] *Ibid.*

[10] *Ibid.*

[11] *Ibid.*

[12] *Ibid.*

[13] *Ibid.*

[14] Up to this time Knauth had written *Heinrich VIII oder der Ketzerkönig* and *Der Tambour und sein Herr König*. His first contemporary topical play, *Die Kampagne*, came much later (1963).

[15] Hacks, in "Das Theater der Gegenwart," pp. 130–31.

Knauth is undoubtedly referring to the recent historical plays *The Advent of the Indian Age* (*Die Eröffnung des indischen Zeitalters* [1955]) and *The Battle of Lobositz* (*Die Schlacht bei Lobositz* [1956]) by Peter Hacks, as well as to Strittmatter's *Katzgraben*. This becomes more evident as he goes on to state that the new direction must be under the influence of Brecht's work.

This view seems to be prevalent among a new, younger generation of intellectual dramatists in the GDR who wish to orient themselves toward a model closer to home. Knauth, born in Halle in 1931, studied law in Leipzig during 1950-51, and then switched to literature from 1951 to 1955. Like Hacks's, his drama is conditioned by his early study of literature rather than by practical writing experience.

Hans Pfeiffer is even more adamant in his support of the "dialectic theater," although he too was conversant only with historical subjects, and did not apply the theory to contemporary topical drama. Pfeiffer also came to the theater with the scholarly background of a literary historian. He was born in Schweidnitz in 1925 and spent the last two years of World War II as a medic. In 1946 he became a teacher and developed that career with the growth of the GDR, eventually becoming a secondary school principal. He then studied German literature in Leipzig from 1952 to 1956, and turned to the drama as his primary activity. From his contribution to the 1957 discussion on the contemporary GDR theater comes a very Brechtian statement which would not have been tolerated four or five years earlier: "Since the socialist society continually collects new experiences, being therefore in a state of experimentation, its stage must continually find new ways, be experimental—less in its content, but most of all in its form."[16]

The other half of the dichotomy is represented by the views of the more conservative, definitely party-oriented writers. Their ideological roots reject any transplantation into a medium other than the doctrinaire socialist realism of the immediate past. Harald Hauser is one of these. He was by 1957 the heir apparent to the role of leading party dramatist which had belonged to Wangenheim and Grünberg before him. Hauser provides a clear political analysis of the situation. First, he supports the Hacks view that the present state of the theater is in limbo, and second, he blames it on the fact that (in his opinion) it reflects neither the classical tradition of the German stage of past centuries, nor the revolutionary, avant garde movement of the pre-Hitler era:

> Too many directors [*Intendanten*] have taken the easily understandable loosening and dedogmatization following the Twentieth Congress of the Soviet Communist Party and the Third Party Conference of the Socialist Unity Party, and substituted for them an opportunistic, compromising liberalization of the repertory. The result: nice operettas, farces, and comedies overrun the stages, even in Berlin.[17]

[16] Pfeiffer, in *ibid.*, p. 131.
[17] Hauser, in *ibid.*, p. 129.

And Hauser was right. At the time, the "culinary" aspect—as Brecht called the purely entertaining part of theater—of GDR theater was thriving indeed. As a remedy, Hauser proposes that the repertory should belong, instead, to the really revolutionary efforts "which create works of art for the stage in fulfillment of real social needs."[18] Since Hauser represents the "hard" party line in cultural politics, it is not surprising that this view was to become the new party policy during the Cultural Conference of 1957.

Supporting Hauser's view was Hedda Zinner, a prominent playwright of the "old guard" who was married to the dogmatic Stalinist and Central Committee member Fritz Erpenbeck. She called for a reorientation to the contemporary topical drama—although she herself had never written a contemporary topical play—and castigated the young dramatists—obviously those quoted above—for their "vulnerability (especially the young authors) to seemingly progressive 'modern' formal experiments dragged in mostly from the West."[19]

And it was this deprecating use of the term "West" by Zinner which was taken up during the subsequent Cultural Conference of the SED on 23 and 24 October 1957 to bring GDR culture back to socialist realism. Already in July of 1957, at its Thirty-Second Plenary Meeting, and in October of that year at its Thirty-Third, the Central Committee waged a full-scale attack on the Western influences brought about by the recent liberalization.[20] Everything on and from the West was termed essentially decadent, and thus officially evil.

This Cultural Conference was the first official move back to specifically party line-oriented art and literature. It signalled the re-emergence of a cultural policy similar to that of the initial years of the first Five-Year Plan (1950–52). Much of the Conference was an ideological and theoretical justification for the action taken against the revisionists Wolfgang Harich and his followers among the editors of the Aufbau Verlag. (The Aufbau Verlag was one of the largest GDR publishing houses and the publisher of the *Berliner Zeitung* and the cultural weekly *Sonntag*, both eminently influential publications in the GDR cultural arena.) Furthermore, the Conference resulted in the doctrinaire rejection of "revisionistic" literary criticism, specifically the rejection of Hans Mayer, Alfred Kantoro-

<hr>

18 *Ibid.*

19 Zinner, in *ibid.*, p. 133.

20 Paul Fröhlich, at the Thirty-Second Plenary Meeting: "I am making a note of this because it is an ideological form of the battle which tries to smuggle bourgeois decadence into our Republic under the guise of the term 'modern.' We must also fight against this" (*Neues Deutschland*, 21 July 1957). And the report of the Politbüro presented by Hermann Matern at the Thirty-Third Plenary Meeting: "Only in this way can the fact be explained that there remains confusion about the social role of art and literature, about the concept of freedom, about the necessity of fighting decadence, etc., and also the fact that the Western post-bourgeois culture is spreading freely in many areas of our cultural life. This is true for the performances in concerts, guest artists, and the repertoire of many operetta theaters. . . ." (*Neues Deutschland*, 19 October 1957).

wicz, and Georg Lukács, who until this time had been the most respected literary critics and theorists of the socialist camp. (In this discussion it is noteworthy that both Knauth and Pfeiffer had been students of Hans Mayer at Leipzig.)

But the Conference did more than just rid the GDR of various "uncomfortable" people and find scapegoats for the confused cultural leadership of the party between 1954 and 1957. A positive progressive cultural policy was proposed by the Conference. Most significant was the wide scope of the cultural effort that was proclaimed and subsequently put into effect. No major sector of GDR life was without an organized, party-supervised cultural enrichment program after the designs of the Conference were implemented. Under the headings of "Socialist National Culture" and "Mass Cultural Activity" (*Kulturelle Massenarbeit*), this program permeated all levels of education, self-improvement, sports, industry, hobbies, and the universities. There was a special emphasis on rural areas and agricultural collectives. It was the start of the now historical "Socialist Cultural Revolution" (*Sozialistische Kulturrevolution*), the final step in the separation process which permanently eradicated any identification between the parts of a divided Germany.

The Conference's effect on literature was equally significant. Western "decadent" influences on GDR literature were trimmed noticeably, and a call went out, once again, for works that would reflect the contemporary reality in the GDR. To Alexander Abusch, this meant that writers should get their experience in the field: "The central requisite for the success of such books remains that the authors and artists must really gain an in-depth knowledge of the life of our people in the people's factories, the machine-tractor stations, and the agricultural collectives. . . ."[21] This, of course, is the point of view presented by the Nachterstedt workers almost three years earlier, when Abusch and his comrades were heralding the "great thaw." One thing becomes clear: cultural policy in the "Workers' and Farmers' State" has nothing to do—in its inception— with the desires of the workers and farmers, but depends, as it does in most societies, on the decisions of an intellectual elite. In this case, it took this elite four years and a considerable political trauma to decide what their point of view is, was, and, of course, always had been. Once again, Abusch shines in his role as number one rhetorical chameleon of cultural policy.

There could be no more doubt about the new policy for the theater. For the first time in years, it was clearly proclaimed, and, as we will see, rigidly enforced. In the plan of the Cultural Conference, "For a Socialist Culture—The Development of the Socialist Culture in the Span of the Second Five-Year Plan," the section on drama is explicit:

[21] Abusch, Address at the Cultural Conference of the SED, 23 October 1957, in *Zur sozialistischen Kulturrevolution: Dokumente* (Berlin: Dietz, 1960), II (*1957 bis 1959*), 279–316.

C) In Theater Arts

Our theaters do not exert enough effort to develop the socialist contemporary topical drama. They have not only neglected to encourage and to support authors in writing socialist drama, but they have been overcome by old fashioned and petit-bourgeois conceptions both in the theaters themselves and in the realm of the audience.[22]

The reorientation toward contemporary subject matter was complete. The first result, however, before another great push back to socialist realism was added by the Fifth Party Congress of 1958, was a fusion of topical subject matter with the dialectic method by young and talented writers. This "dialectic digression," which from then on was defined as "contemporary socialist drama" (meaning drama of and about life in the German Democratic Republic), had only a brief though successful tenure in 1958 and 1959. It too was rejected as being intellectualized and formalistic (an indictment that is not unfair) in favor of standard, uninspired fare, in accordance with the developments of the Bitterfeld Conference of 1959. This dialectic swan song, which lasted only two summers, has now been officially removed from the development of contemporary GDR drama by GDR critics. In the West, on the other hand, there has been a tendency to lionize and idolize it as the true and only important GDR drama. For some Western critics of GDR literature such as Fritz J. Raddatz and his mentor Hans Mayer, nothing else seems worth mentioning.

But the prevalent development from 1957 to 1961—one which ultimately led to today's prevalent plays—was that of the socialist realistic morality play of topical subjects. The two phenomena, the dialectic digression and the renaissance of socialist realism, deserve and demand separate, dispassionate treatments to bring them into perspective. They must first be related to each other and, secondly, to the whole of GDR drama.

---

22 "Für eine sozialistische Kultur: Die Entwicklung der sozialistischen Kultur in der Zeit des zweiten Fünfjahresplanes," *Neues Deutschland*, 7 December 1957.

IV.
The Dialectic Digression

The dialectic digression of the contemporary socialist theater in the German Democratic Republic actually comes in two phases. The first sidestep encompasses plays from late 1957 to early 1960, the earliest of which was Helmut Baierl's didactic play (*Lehrstück*) *The Inquiry* (*Die Feststellung* [December 1957]). Heiner Müller followed with the *Lehrstück*-like plays *The Wage Reducer* (*Der Lohndrücker* [March 1958]), *The Correction* (*Die Korrektur* [September 1958]), and the purely agitation-propaganda piece *Klettwitz Report 1958* (*Klettwitzer Bericht 1958* [September 1958]). Peter Hacks's first contemporary topical treatment, *The Cares and the Power* (*Die Sorgen und die Macht*, first produced at Senftenberg in May 1960, but under discussion since 1958), and Hartmut Lange's *Senftenberg Tales* (*Senftenberger Erzählungen* [1960, not produced]) round out the first phase. The second phase of the digression from the newly reestablished realistic dramaturgy on GDR stages took place during the years from 1963 to 1966. The contemporary topical treatments in this phase were Hartmut Lange's *Marski* (1963), Volker Braun's *Dumper Paul Bauch* (*Kipper Paul Bauch* [1964]), Heiner Müller's *The Construction* (*Der Bau* [1964–66]), and Peter Hacks's second attempt at a GDR topic, *Moritz Tassow* (1965). Of these plays, only *Moritz Tassow* ever saw an audience.

It must remain clear that the relationship between the two phases is not linear, even though some of the same authors are represented in both phases. The contingencies for theatrical work were radically different in 1964 and 1958, respectively. The most important political act of the GDR, the "securing of the border" on 13 August 1961, separates the two phases. We will at this point consider only the first phase, since in the later period the ground rules—and perhaps the whole game—were changed. We must therefore consider this first phase in its own historical context, after delineating the cultural, political, and historical processes which etched its profile.

For the first time in this entire developmental study of the contemporary topical drama of the GDR we are not embarking on virgin territory. The critical treatments of GDR drama which are available today usually consider this period the actual start of the history of the GDR theater. Even the GDR scholars neglect to look back beyond 1956. In 1964, Hermann Kähler starts his history of the contemporary socialist drama in the GDR, *The Present on the Stage (Gegenwart auf der Bühne)*, with a chapter entitled "The Prelude of the Didactic Theater." He deals there exclusively with Peter Hacks and the early plays of Helmut Baierl and Heiner Müller, regarding them as a necessary evil on the road to Bitterfeld. At the same time he casts off the period between 1945 and 1957 in a cursory footnote.[1] An editorial collective of the *Weimarer Beiträge*, the GDR's foremost periodical of literary scholarship, in 1964 gives the plays turning-point significance in the development of the GDR drama by referring to them as the "didactic-agitatory new beginning of Heiner Müller and Helmut Baierl."[2] The only previous play considered worthy of mention is Strittmatter's *Katzgraben*, and then it is in connection with the work of Brecht.[3] A similar view is presented in the already mentioned *Theater Bilanz* (1971), a retrospective summation of GDR theater work.[4]

This type of critical evaluation by GDR scholars shows two things. It demonstrates, first of all, an aversion to the early GDR dramas, which is understandable, since the cultural-political restrictions at the time they were written did nothing to enhance their general quality. But besides this, and perhaps more important, it shows that the drama, the stepchild of GDR literature until the First Cultural Conference in 1957, has now "arrived." The consideration of contemporary drama in the literary histories reflects the increasingly important role of the theater in that society.

Western scholarship presents a perplexing problem in this context. Whereas the GDR treatments of the drama start with this dialectic digression, Western critics go one better. Not only do they start there, but they tend to stop there as well. These dramatists are generally seen as being representative of GDR drama— or at least as the only dramatists worth studying. There is some merit in this view if we are content to study only "masterpieces" and "great talents." There is no doubt that this dialectic digression represents a qualitative level of drama which,

---

[1] Kähler, *Gegenwart auf der Bühne: Die sozialistische Wirklichkeit in den Bühnenstücken der DDR von 1956–1963/64* (Berlin: Henschelverlag, 1966), pp. 193–94.

[2] Klaus Jarmatz, "Die literarische Entwicklung der Deutschen Demokratischen Republik," *Weimarer Beiträge*, 5 (1964), 794.

[3] "In the 'Notes on Katzgraben' (1952/53) Brecht developed important theoretical conclusions, especially for the drama, based on an analysis of Strittmatter's play" (*Ibid.*, p. 795).

[4] Manfred Nössig and Hans Gerald Otto, "Grundlagen einer Bilanz," in *Theater Bilanz: Bühnen der DDR: Eine Bilddokumentation 1945–1969*, ed. Christoph Funke et al. (Berlin: Henschelverlag, 1971), p. 24.

viewed from traditional aesthetic perspectives, remains singular in the whole of GDR literature.

But this general qualitative improvement can easily lead to an overestimation of the literary and historical significance of these plays. In any historical presentation of GDR dramatists and their works, we must remember that the mainstream of the drama remained within the framework of the prevalent cultural doctrine which we have just outlined. Thus the following explication of this qualitatively excellent "dialectic digression" in the GDR theater must be understood for what it represents: a study of *possibilities* which never reached fruition as a model for further development. The mainstream remained characterized by positive presentations of GDR life. As the young American critic Helen Fehervary puts it, "Besides this epic-dialectic tradition, the second form of 'escape' appears in a clear tendency toward the situational. . . ."[5] And it was this "situational" mainstream that determined the further development of the work of GDR dramatists.

Curiously, but also naturally, new developments in the drama of the GDR can be viewed in terms of age groups. The rapid development of the new GDR social structure is nowhere as evident as it is here. In a matter of ten years, from 1947 to 1957, three age groups of writers have determined the changing profile of the East German stage, and a fourth is not far behind. From Wangenheim, Wolf, Grünberg and Brecht (born around 1900), to Strittmatter, Freyer, Hauser and Zinner (born around 1915), we come to Hacks, Müller and Baierl (born around 1930) in 1957. This "generation gap" is a determining factor in the approach which the latter group takes in presenting the realities of their country on the stage. For this is the first of the three generations whose educational, social and political profile has not been determined by a pre-socialist, antagonistic class society. The traditional prerequisite of socialist drama, massive social conflict with its inherent dialectic situation, is not within the concept of reality which these young Marxists have attained. The basis of the dialectics in the plays of a Friedrich Wolf or a Bertolt Brecht, no matter how different their individual approaches are, is the economic and social class conflict inherent within their society. But by 1957 society has changed. The objective for this generation of new playwrights is the dramatization of the developmental processes in a society for which internal conflict has ostensibly been removed by the socialist/Communist order.

Of the traditions to which they could orient their own work, the dramatists of the dialectic digression chose Bertolt Brecht's efforts as the most promising touchstone. In their estimation, it was Brecht's "scientific process" of demonstrating the causality of social processes (mainly economic) that held the key to

[5] Fehervary, "Heiner Müllers Brigadenstücke," *Basis: Jahrbuch für deutsche Gegenwartsliteratur,* II (1971), 103–140.

the possibility of "dramatizing" the non-antagonistic contradictions of their socialist classless society. Werner Mittenzwei, perhaps the most astute drama scholar of the GDR, categorizes the main factors that attracted this group of authors to Brecht's work, and differentiates their approach from that of non-socialist dramatists:

> The alienation technique developed by Brecht had the greatest influence on the German socialist drama and authors like Helmut Baierl, Peter Hacks, Heiner Müller, and Hartmut Lange. The alienation technique is used in the most significant works of the socialist drama since the foundation of the German Democratic Republic. Their authors learned from Brecht without imitating him slavishly. They used his lessons individually in a manner corresponding to their specific talents. Even if these young writers have not yet learned to handle all facets of Brecht's method, they do consciously try to demonstrate, with the means of alienation, a process in its social causality.[6]

The dialectics within the social processes of the GDR are at the heart of the dialectic digression. Mittenzwei's point that these authors avoid slavish imitation of Brecht is essential to an evaluation of their works. But the fact that these new dramatists have not learned to "handle" all of Brecht's techniques does not necessarily detract from their contribution. For Brecht's work shows that he himself never came to grips with the removal of the massive conflict. Whether he could not or would not is not the question. The fact is that he did not succeed in demonstrating his "method," as Mittenzwei would have it, in a play about the social processes in the new state. The reference is, of course, to Brecht's unsuccessful attempts to dramatize the life of Hans Garbe, the famous Siemens-Plania activist whose tremendous efforts in rebuilding a kiln while it was still under fire became symbolic of the reconstruction in the early years.[7] (This feat is also the basis of Heiner Müller's play, *The Wage Reducer*.)

Büsching, as Brecht called the character, is his only hero who is not a hero of the antagonistic class system. The difficulties which the topic presented were not overcome by the master, although he considered the project at length in 1951 and again in 1954.[8] Thus it remains significant that the dialectic, scientific playwriting process was applied to the GDR reality not by Brecht, but by a new generation which perhaps had a stronger grasp of life in the GDR.

Dedicated to the advancement of their state and the propagation of the party's cultural policy, these works of the first digression are an indication that the goal-oriented cultural policy of socialist systems does not necessarily preclude the development of genuine theater. We must remember Alexander Abusch's

---

[6] Mittenzwei, *Gestaltung und Gestalten im modernen Drama* (Berlin: Aufbau, 1965), p. 270.

[7] The most successful treatment of the Hans Garbe subject, besides Heiner Müller's *Lohndrücker*, was a 1954 novel by Eduard Claudius, *Menschen an unserer Seite*.

[8] Bertolt Brecht Archiv, No. 925/01, quoted in Mittenzwei, *Gestaltung und Gestalten*, pp. 165–66.

belated call for young writers to go to the people for their subjects at the First Cultural Conference in 1957. The new plays answered this call. Helmut Baierl's *The Inquiry*, written immediately thereafter, is the first rational treatment of the contradictions between the worker and the farmer, who have a common goal, the success of the agricultural collective. Heiner Müller's *The Wage Reducer*, taking up the call of the Nachterstedt letter, presents the heroic treatment of the activist and his inherent contradictions in the development of the socialist perspective. This was the play Brecht did not write. Müller's *The Correction* is even closer to the new cultural policy; it reflects the prime goal of the economic plan by examining the difficulties of the Brown Coal Complex Schwarze Pumpe, the most important industrial complex of the day. The GDR's "Brown Coal literature,"[9] which we will consider and define later, includes Hacks's *The Cares and the Power*, a contemporary treatment, and Hartmut Lange's *Senftenberg Tales*, which is a historical treatment of the early years of the GDR.

In short, all of the plays of the dialectic digression are close cultural reflections of the economic plan. Baierl, Müller, Hacks, and Lange gathered their materials by working alongside the people at the very locales they treat in their plays.

Helmut Baierl was born in 1926 in Rumburg, now Czechoslovakia. His career parallels the historic growth of the GDR. From 1949 to 1951 he studied Slavic languages and literature in Halle. He started his literary career in 1952 by writing plays for amateur and children's theaters. These early works were distinguished by a didactic socialist moralism with much humorous satire. From 1955 to 1957 Baierl attended the Johannes R. Becher School of Literature, the GDR's prime training ground for talented young authors and critics. Here he augmented his considerable talent with a thorough study of the orthodox Marxist-Leninist literary theory, the influence of which is evident in his mature works.

Baierl's *The Inquiry*, first produced at Erfurt on 27 December 1957, is a direct and forceful exercise in didactic agitational theater. Without any circumlocution, Baierl seizes the prime problem of the agricultural collectivization process, the quest to overcome the traditional property-oriented mentality of the German farmer, and subjects it to dialectic scrutiny. The impetus that starts the dialectic didactic *Lehrstück* process, aimed at teaching both actors and audience a political lesson, is the return of Finze, a farmer who had fled to the West. The

---

[9] In the aesthetic system of the GDR, where art must be functional, instructional, and moral, with social, economic and technical implications which work toward the absolute goal of a socialist world, the discovery of a conversion process on 10 July 1952, whereby bituminous coal will yield enough heat to smelt iron ore, became a literary phenomenon. The measure of strength of an economic system in the modern industrial world is not gold; it is steel. The production of steel until this time had been limited to the availability of anthracite coke, which the GDR did not possess in any relevant quantity. Therefore, this discovery was perhaps the most far-reaching event, in economic terms, in the history of the GDR. Thus there developed a quantity of literature which can be called *Braunkohlenliteratur*.

chairman of the collective, whose background is that of an industrial worker, declares that Finze's goods and lands, which were appropriated by the collective according to law, must be given back to him, also according to law. This creates a dispute among the members, who naturally resent having to give up land which has increased in productive value through their work to one who had essentially sold them out. Finze declares, however, that the chairman had forced him to flee by trying to blackmail him into joining the collective.

In order to arrive at the truth, the chairman and Finze reenact their conversation of the night before Finze fled with his wife. Nothing is achieved, since the two men only reinforce their original points of view. Then the scene is "alienated" by a character reversal; Finze and the chairman exchange roles. This results in a premature declaration that the chairman was indeed at fault. Some members find this too simplistic; so a third scene is played in which the farmer Benno, of the same sensibilities and background as Finze, takes the job of the chairman, trying to convince Finze to join the collective at the crucial moment.

This is the successful experiment. Finze falls out of his role of portraying himself on that historic evening, and asks to join now. The members find this good, but again too easy, and ask him to wait. No one was at fault. In the quest for the success of socialism, the chairman had been too impatient because he did not understand the traditional historical point of view of the farmer. The farmer, in turn, had been alienated—not by the idea of socialism in agriculture, but by his refusal to accept rapid wholesale changes. It had only been necessary to find someone who could speak to him in his own language.

The lesson Baierl teaches as well as any playwright can teach anything is in line with the position of the SED agricultural policy in 1957. The conviction for the ideals of socialism cannot come through power. The power of socialism comes from the individual convictions of its base of power, the class-conscious people. In the quest for truth, for true conviction, Baierl rejects the standard superficial thought processes which tend to cover up rather than expose the inherent difficulties, the contradictions of the socialist society. He urges a thought process of thinking, rethinking, and thinking again from different perspectives to uncover the dialectic process of the socialist system, a process he demonstrates in *The Inquiry* with excellent results.

This is agitation in the theater. GDR theater critic Christoph Funke sees this as having the best effect on an audience, much in the way the originator of this dramatic technique, Bertolt Brecht, had thought of it. He sees success in this play in that "the dramatist Helmut Baierl throws the stick of dialectics between the legs of his audience."[10] This causes the viewer to fall rough and tumble into an experience "which can only be presented through the efforts of thought."[11]

[10] Funke, "Über Helmut Baierl," in Helmut Baierl, *Stücke*, (Berlin: Henschelverlag, 1969), p. 235.
[11] *Ibid.*

The formal aspects of the play reveal a distinct application of the technique of the "classic" Brecht teaching play. Short scenes are prefaced by provocative descriptive titles. Commentary and introductions and conclusions are given in the form of songs. Each scene ends with a gong. Throughout the dialogue, care is taken to demonstrate problems rationally by means of forcing players to exchange roles, perspectives, and even ideologies. The play is nevertheless realistic in scope. Although there is no doubt that Baierl developed his technique of realistic portrayal independently of Peter Hacks, it is Hacks who describes the technique best in "The Realistic Theater Play" ("*Das realistische Theaterstück*"), the essay which provides a theoretical base for the whole of the dialectic digression: "the specific in collusion with the general is named by Brecht as the characteristic detail (in characterization: the social gest; on a large scale: the typical plot). The characteristic detail is the central aesthetic category of realism."[12]

Although Baierl draws his characters swiftly and schematically, it is this attention to the characteristic detail, already defined by Hacks, which makes his people more real and their problems more credible than any tedious naturalistic characterization could. A piece of dialogue from the fourth scene, "The Accusation" ("Die Anklage"), will serve to illustrate this. The farmer Finze categorizes at once his individuality and his historical role as a German farmer, while the chairman demonstrates his capabilities, rationality, and functionary mentality as they talk not to, but past each other:

THE FARMER: Yes, you said that; and you pressured me to join. So I went to the West. Do you think it was easy for me to leave my farm? Over there in the camp I had dreams every night. I heard my cows bellowing and I saw weeds grow in my fields. It is the chairman's fault, but forget it. I just wanted to clear this up. That's all.

THE CHAIRMAN: No, the case isn't closed. This is a grave accusation. Farmers! I'm not aware that I forced him to go. Look, you decide for yourselves. I discussed the situation with him; one. He didn't want to join; two. Result: He would have remained an independent farmer. Three. No one could have done anything to him for not wanting to join. Running away is not a part of this addition. You put that entry in yourself, Finze.[13]

This is realistic characterization as described by Hacks:

Now, surprisingly enough, is the time to break a lance for attention to detail against such people who fight against realism under the poetic flag. They don't notice that realism is also a type of naturalism. But it is widened through the category of the dialectic. They don't see that the most thoughtful thing in the world, the characteris-

---

[12] Hacks, "Das realistische Theaterstück," *Neue Deutsche Literatur*, V/10 (1957), 92.
[13] Baierl, *Die Feststellung*, in *Stücke*, pp. 13–14.

tic detail, is differentiated from the emptiest thing, the naturalistic detail, only because it is selected from the perspective of the social essence. [14]

It is essentially Baierl's process to identify and describe his characters in terms of their social roles. For him, the worker or the farmer cannot exist as such without his role in his class, and such a class cannot exist without the awareness of that existence by individuals who are workers and farmers. This is also the central conflict in the play. How can industrial workers—the chairman had been one—assume a role in a productive collective of farmers who have a greatly different social background? The answer: by emphasizing the essential similarity of their basic objective, socialism, while still respecting their individuality.

The process reconciles their inherent differences by changing the conditions around them. This is not a traditional conflict situation but a contradictory one, according to Hacks's view in this "programmatic essay." [15] Conflict is seen here as the private manifestation of the social category of contradiction. Conflict is obsolete in this scientific age, according to Hacks, since it is based on the theory of the unified soul. Hacks further postulates that contradictions, on the other hand, exist, and that they are the basis of the situation expressed in the socialist drama because they show "reality as changeable, thus beautiful" [16] in a dialectic process. But Hacks is on shaky ideological ground here. By postulating contradictions as the force of change toward the "beauty" of a Communistic ideal, he himself contradicts the basic tenets of socialist realism as interpreted in the party line, where the positive solutions, and not the problems, should predominate.

A close look at the dialogue in the play reveals that the chairman and the farmer use essentially the same diction. Would it not be more realistic to differentiate the social roles through the use of dialect and other speech peculiarities? For Baierl, and again Hacks, that technique is obsolete because it is simply camouflage and not a relevant dramatic expression of social functions. The action of the farmers Benno and Finze in telling jokes to each other is a characteristic social gest. If they would use dialect in talking to each other, the social gest would lose its significance in favor of superficial non-characteristic detail, or naturalism.

Hacks identifies the special use of language demonstrated in *The Inquiry*, the plays of Heiner Müller and Hartmut Lange, and his own *The Cares and the Power:*

[14] Hacks, "Das realistische Theaterstück," p. 93.

[15] "Remarks about conflict: Contradiction is something other than conflict. Conflict is the private side of contradiction, it is its inner reflection since contradictions are not manifested except in contradictory actions. This private side is artistically irrelevant since its third rate meaning in the realm of social causality is evident: Its existence is, at the least, debatable. The theory of conflict rests on the theory of the unified soul, on the assumption that there is inherent in man a working, ordering, systematizing force which has as its goal to eliminate all contradictions" (*ibid.*, pp. 102–3).

[16] *Ibid.*, p. 93.

The working class does not speak its own language. Since it now rules, it speaks the old language of the rulers, except better. Dialect is not typical of its language. That is classbound and agrarian. The individualistic expression of the plebian original is not typical of it either. The working class has taken the highly developed medium of communication of the bourgeoisie, and uses it for its better ends.[17]

Baierl, whose experience before this play was restricted to amateur plays and children's theater, was understandably rewarded for this effort. He was named a dramaturge at the Berliner Ensemble, and served there from 1959 to 1967, where he also fulfilled his own "social role" as the Ensemble's party secretary.

From a similar bourgeois intellectual background, but with political sensibilities developed in the new state, comes Heiner Müller. Müller was born in Eppendorf, Saxony, in 1929. Immediately after the war, he worked as a librarian and a journalist before acting as a research fellow for the German Writers' Union in 1954–55. After this, he was the editor of the journal *Young Art* (*Junge Kunst*). Among his first works for the stage was *Ten Days That Shook the World* (*Zehn Tage, die die Welt erschütterten*), written jointly with Hagen Müller-Stahl and adapted from John Reed's book. This play about the Russian Revolution premiered at the Neue Volksbühne am Luxembourgplatz in Berlin in 1957. His *Klettwitz Report 1958* (*Klettwitzer Bericht 1958*) was produced by Armin Stolper and Horst Schönemann at the Landestheater Senftenberg. *The Wage Reducer* (*Der Lohndrücker*), perhaps his most successful contemporary play, premiered at the Städtische Theater Leipzig in 1958. *The Correction* (*Die Korrektur*) was produced at the Maxim Gorki Theater, where he was a dramaturgical assistant, in the same year.

Müller's treatment of the Hans Garbe topic was, along with Baierl's *The Inquiry*, a play that prophesied a new direction in GDR theater. "Retrospectively, *The Wage Reducer* in particular shows itself as a 'turning point' in our dramatic development, as something entirely new," writes Hermann Kähler.[18] This, one of Kähler's more lucid critical statements, is just praise for the wrong reasons. Kähler's reasons for rating the play highly are that "in this play, the German workers stepped out of their lives onto the stage as historical subjects; as characters to be taken seriously; as history-making personalities."[19]

But what Kähler describes here is not Müller's play; instead, it is closer to *Büsching/Garbe*, the play Brecht did not write. Neither characterizations nor personalities receive the major thrust of Müller's attention. Whereas Brecht was concerned with characterizing Garbe, the individual, as a semi-tragic hero of the socialist revolution, Müller's primary concern here is not with individuals, but

[17] *Ibid.*, p. 101.
[18] Kähler, *Gegenwart auf der Bühne*, p. 26.
[19] *Ibid.*

with social processes. Specifically, Müller explores how workers relate to work as a social process in building a Communist society.

Brecht's "great play" concept, coupled with the inherent difficulty of portraying the first of his heroes to support rather than oppose the prevailing political-economic system, necessitated an extensive barrage of alienation techniques, including a chorus and various theatrical devices.[20] In contrast, Müller's approach is disarmingly direct, simple, and designed to prevent the characters' domination of his dialectic exercise. This depersonalization technique is excellently indicated in the play's prescript: "The action takes place in the German Democratic Republic in 1948–49. The story of the circular kiln is known. The characters and their histories are fiction."[21] Where Brecht had planned a broad historical chronicle showing the development of an individual, Müller concentrates on a short period of time, a crisis situation. There is little, if any, psychological motivation, even less detailed characterization, and virtually no examination of the causality of the action. There is only action in a series of short scenes which start just before the dramatic climax which brings them to a close.

This actively inserts the audience into the process on the stage and forces it to take sides again and again. It means that reactionary points of view expressed by some characters appear equal in strength and conviction to the revolutionary views of others. The playgoer is caught in the squeeze. Müller does not develop the socialist perspective through the dialogue; instead, he postulates it and dialectically demonstrates its superiority. He shows no shining examples, only alternatives of action in crisis situations. The playgoer chooses.

The Wage Reducer's plot is relatively simple. The scene: the beginning of the German Democratic Republic. The situation: a need for increased production, a lack of labor, materials and food, and bad living conditions. Given: a disparate group of masons and mason's helpers, old Nazis, old Communists, fence sitters, and one *new* Communist. Balke has the new perspective: Increased production comes first, then better working and living conditions will follow. His perspective, however, is unimportant. The important thing is how all the others react to it and how it influences their work.

Balke works hard and thereby increases the production standard. The others call him names. He works harder; they threaten him. He tries the impossible, to rebuild a kiln while the fire chambers are still in operation. When a brick is thrown at him while he works on the kiln, one of his companions suggests that he keep it as evidence. But Balke just rubs his sore spot and asks if the brick is dry. When he learns that it is, Balke simply applies mortar and uses it to continue his work. Dry bricks are rare.

[20] Cf. Käthe Rülicke-Weiler, *Die Dramaturgie Brechts: Theater als Mittel der Veränderung* (Berlin: Henschelverlag, 1968), pp. 172 and 258.

[21] Heiner Müller, *Der Lohndrücker*, in *Sozialistische Dramatik: Autoren der Deutschen Demokratischen Republik* (Berlin: Henschelverlag, 1968), p. 174.

But all this is to no avail. The workers who oppose his ambitious efforts beat him up, and the management distrusts his motives because he had denounced a Communist saboteur during the Hitler regime. But again, his tenacity gathers support. Gradually, it becomes obvious that the economic sustenance of all depends on the success of the project. The collective effort is not a matter of choice, but of necessity.

But this even Balke must learn. Karras has been his foremost adversary, but more men are needed to repair the kiln in order to meet the demands of the plan. Karras is impressed only by the necessity. The director asks: "Karras, what about you? You're a kilnmason." Karras looks at Balke, who turns away, and replies: "That's Balke's soup; let him eat it."[22] At this point, Schorn, the party secretary who was imprisoned by the Nazis on the strength of Balke's testimony, interjects: "Balke didn't climb into the kiln for himself."[23] Karras answers simply, "When should I start?"[24]

But now Balke's own personal motivation and stubborn pride break into the open. Karras had been one of those who had beaten him up. Consequently, Balke tells Schorn: "I can't work with Karras."[25] This crystalline example of Müller's dialectic dialogue concludes with Schorn's reply: "Who asked me if I could work with you?"[26] In the final scene of the play, Müller again effectively demonstrates the dialectic process between the individual, the collective, and necessity:

15. (*Factory gate. Morning.* KARRAS *appears. Behind him,* BALKE.)
BALKE: I need you, Karras. I'm not asking out of friendship. You've got to help me.
KARRAS: (*Stops*) And thought you wanted to build socialism all by yourself. When do we start?
BALKE: Now. We don't have much time.[27]

With an economy of plot, action, and characters, a simplicity of structure, development, and diction, Müller's play is reduced to the essential. Hacks had called for a realism dependent on the characteristic detail. Müller presents nothing but characteristic detail. In this play, playwriting is reduced to an arrangement of essential dialectic structures which determine social behavior. There is an obvious artificiality in the terse dialogue and the concentrated scenes. In addition, the condensed diction at times turns the language into abstract poetic modules. Thus in Müller's play, alienation is internal rather than external; there are no songs, commentary, or reflective digressions. No one can escape noticing that it is a realistic *play*, and not a realistic representation of reality.

[22] *Ibid.*, p. 205.
[23] *Ibid.*
[24] *Ibid.*
[25] *Ibid.*
[26] *Ibid.*
[27] *Ibid.*

This technique is effectively agitatory and provocative on a highly intellectual level. The dialectic structure of the play does not rely on inherent massive conflict or a confrontation of old and new, but relies instead on the contradictions of the new situation, the conflict between what has already been realized and the reaction against further progressive development. Müller thus postulates a utopian view. His dialectic process actually moves between two poles, the socialist society of the GDR which he postulates, and a future socialist society of the GDR which could be better. Müller agitates his audience by presenting the victory of the new processes as completed before the final curtain. Thus the play "tries to carry it [the battle] into the new audience which decides it."[28]

With the success of these two works by Baierl and Müller, it could now be assumed that the didactic theater play was a strong base for the future development of GDR drama. This became an even safer assumption when dramatists responded artistically to a crisis situation in the GDR economy and a series of plays appeared using brown coal production as subject matter.

---

[28] Müller, *Der Lohndrücker, Neue Deutsche Literatur*, V/5 (1957), 116.

V.
Brown Coal Dialectics

The first play reflecting the importance of the brown coal industry in the overall economic plan was Heiner and Inge Müller's *The Correction*. The scenes, first published in *Neue Deutsche Literatur* in 1958, are subtitled "A Report on the Construction of the Industrial Combine Schwarze Pumpe, 1957" ("Ein Bericht vom Aufbau des Kombinats Schwarze Pumpe, 1957"). With this play, the Müllers anticipated the next cultural offensive to be launched by the SED, the "Bitterfeld Movement" ("Bitterfelder Weg"). This movement was the result of a conference held in Bitterfeld, a brown coal producing city, in April of 1959. It was a broad discussion by writers, workers, and party theoreticians about the role of literature in society. Here literature was declared a mass cultural activity. Writers were to write about work from the worker's perspective, workers were to learn about literature by reading and writing, and literature was to treat topics of national significance. Thus the Bitterfeld Movement attempted to break down the traditional dichotomy between the producers and the consumers of cultural objects.

Schwarze Pumpe, an industrial complex for brown coal production, is one of the proudest industrial achievements of the GDR. (Thus, in his choice of subject and setting, Müller already presupposed a major aspect of the Bitterfeld Movement.) It was started near Hoyerswerda (Lausitz) in the fall of 1955. The complex is an essential energy producer for the state, since its production ranges from brown coal coke for steel production to gas, tar, oil, and electricity. Brown coal is especially important to GDR industrial development since it is the country's only abundant natural resource.

In dealing with Schwarze Pumpe, the Müllers focus on its construction. All this pouring of cement and laying of brick upon brick serves as the continuous Müller metaphor for the total social and economic development of the GDR. This symbolic process combined with the required realism of the characteristic detail were to cause Müller great difficulty with the critics.

Just as there were in the formative stages of the GDR, there are serious organizational problems in the construction of Schwarze Pumpe. The play's workers are to a large extent selfish adventurers, slow-working, hard-drinking, hard-fighting frontiersmen of the socialist society who hop from one construction project to another in search of the big money. Their perspective is questionable, and certainly far from ideal. The reflection of the worker Franz K. is characteristic:

> I'm a construction worker, 'been red since 1918, but not so much since '46. I plowed up the Erzgebirge for the Wismut-Works; in unsafe mine shafts for eight hours a day. If you didn't drown down under, you drowned in booze. If the booze didn't get you, the broads took you to the dogs. It was hard to stay out of getting into the shafts, the broads, and the booze. It's gotten better now: The tunnels are safe, and the women are married. I don't break my back here. If the pace is too slow for the front office, why don't they ever show up on the site?[1]

The engineers and functionaries in the leadership roles are not exemplary individuals either. The bureaucratic jumbles and buck-passing result in slow-downs. The brigade system, the institution of the collective work process which the Müllers analyze here, does not progress. Into this situation comes Bremer, an old-guard party member who has had trouble adjusting to life during the building of socialism. He has not yet grasped the fact that the party of the working class is in power, and that the position of the once illegal party is now "We don't need barricades anymore, Comrade Bremer; we need industrial combines."[2] He is named the leader of a difficult brigade which has a habit of "correcting" production quotas with a pencil instead of with work.

As one might expect, Bremer's honesty creates conflicts with his men. He is responsible for their work, and thus is blamed when their almost willful negligence causes one of their freshly poured foundations to collapse. As a result, Bremer's whole outlook must undergo a correction, and he is ordered to apologize to an engineer. Bremer replies: "So that's how far we've come. Now I'm wrong. Did the engineer do time in a concentration camp for the party; did I build bombers for Hitler?"[3] Bremer must learn about the new reality, the new historical process, and role of the party. The Party Secretary asserts: "We can afford to build socialism with people who are not interested in socialism. That's how far we've come. Nobody is expendable. But when we've come so far that they are, it won't be necessary to make them expendable, because then we'll have them interested in socialism."[4] Bremer, however, is not yet ready to accept these new and necessary contingencies: "So the party says I've got to crawl in front of a

[1] Heiner and Inge Müller, *Die Korrektur, Neue Deutsche Literatur*, VI/5 (1958), 22.
[2] *Ibid.*, 31.
[3] *Ibid.*, 30.
[4] *Ibid.*, 31.

bourgeois engineer?" The Party Secretary replies: "To correct your mistake."[5]

But by the following scene, Bremer has become convinced of the necessity of the pragmatic party position. He tells a young colleague who wants to join the party: "It's not our objective to break noses. We are the ruling class. Our state is our weapon. So you want to join the party? Do you know what that means?"[6] He then brings his own role as a party member up to date: "Less beer, more work. Up to your gut in the muck if that's the way it has to be. Getting up when you fall down, and getting up again when you fall again."[7]

The play was published in *Neue Deutsche Literatur* with an introductory paragraph of criticism, which is understandable since the play concentrates on far from ideal situations in GDR industry. The Müllers present the grim side of the building process, the road toward socialism. The editors think that Müller and his wife Inge try too hard "to ferret out the contradictions of reality, but they treat the resolutions in a summary, schematic, and nonconcrete manner."[8] The editors call for changes. Even though Müller has included long reflective monologues by certain characters which move him as close to psychological motivation as he ever gets, the editors want more. They want all characters and actions motivated in detail, especially the transformation that Bremer undergoes.

In short, the editors of *Neue Deutsche Literatur* judged the Müllers' play with a yardstick made to measure the works of a Friedrich Wolf. They do not recognize the playwriting process in which the audience supplies the third step of the dialectic process, the synthesis. Instead, their view is traditional; in the place of problems, they want demonstrations of positive solutions. "To gloss over the deciding phases of the action is already a dramaturgical-aesthetic mistake, because it makes the end seem abrupt and inadequately motivated."[9] This view is reminiscent of the objections Friedrich Wolf raised to Brecht's *Mother Courage* in 1949. The editors also offer a word of advice to Müller about his style: ". . . we must warn against making a fetish of economy in language. It should not become barren. Too much 'poeticizing' can lead to inadequate content."[10]

In the discussion of the play held by workers of Schwarze Pumpe, which appeared in the same issue of *Neue Deutsche Literatur*, one of the aesthetic problems of any GDR playwright writing a contemporary topical play becomes clear: frequently, the play is not discussed as a play, but as reality. While the workers find the play a truthful representation of what has actually happened ("What [the authors] have shown is correct, it's the truth"[11]), while they find the play itself

---

[5] *Ibid.*
[6] *Ibid.*, 32.
[7] *Ibid.*
[8] *Ibid.*, 21.
[9] *Ibid.*
[10] *Ibid.*, 22.
[11] *Ibid.*, 32.

all right for themselves, they consider it too strong—or honest—for the rest of the GDR populace. In the opinion of the workers, the positive sides of the work at Schwarze Pumpe have not been accented enough.[12]

More optimism was required, and Müller, whose theory is that "the new literature can only be developed *with the new audience*,"[13] corrected *The Correction* to make it more palatable to this audience. The corrected *Correction* was directed later that year by Hans-Dieter Mäde at the Maxim Gorki Theater. The changes which were made reduced the reflective monologues and added more action scenes showing developmental steps, thus reducing the dialectic nature of the structure by adding more causally determined action. Also added was an optimistic final scene, of the type admired by the party; this addition was seen by Mäde as the result of "productive criticism."[14] But in effect, Müller's postulation of a dialectic conflict between the current reality and a future possibility was adjudged blatant negativism, and thus a literary transgression. For this reason, *The Correction* was the last of Müller's contemporary topical plays to be produced in the GDR until his *Women's Comedy* (*Weiberkomödie*), a play about the role of women in the GDR's industry, was produced in 1971.

Probably the most brilliant piece of agitational theater in GDR history, Müller's *Klettwitz Report 1958* is one of his least known works. Its reception was radically different from that of *The Correction*. Christoph Funke outlines its history: "Originally a radio play, it was only going to be read, but then the actors became so involved in the scenes that they decided on a detailed dramatization."[15]

The actors and their director at the Landestheater Senftenberg, located in the center of the brown coal region, tackled the project with great energy, for nothing could have been more topical. One of the great bulk conveyors had broken down, thereby devastating the production plan. Müller's *Report* explores the background, action, and ideological conflicts of the extraordinary voluntary work effort (*Braunkohleneinsatz*) by the workers, students, and the National People's Army, who, despite the breakdown, met the plan's goals through sheer physical effort. Never was an artistic treatment of an event in the GDR so close to the point of crisis in time and locality.

The scenes are short, potent, randomly in prose or verse, and directly propagandistic. Commentary and press clippings are used effectively. Central to the structure are the changes in perspective of various "types," which are demonstrated in short dialogues like the following:

---

[12] About *The Correction* the *Betriebsfunkredakteur* concluded: "But you have to show at least as much positive material as you've shown on the negative side. That's missing. The scenes which were presented are 100% correct. But also show the positive side" (*ibid.*).

[13] Müller, "War 'Die Korrektur' korrekturbedürftig?", *Neue Deutsche Literatur*, VII/1 (1959), 120.

[14] *Ibid.*, 122.

[15] Funke, *Der Regisseur Horst Schönemann. Bericht. Analyse. Dokumentation* (Berlin: Henschelverlag, 1971), p. 27.

d.

Conversation while working

WORKER: How does socialism taste?

STUDENT: It tastes like sweat.

WORKER: Better to sweat for a good thing, than to bleed for a bad thing.

e.

WORKER: You worked well, students.

STUDENT (*laughs*): With these bourgeois hands.

WORKER: Hands which work are worker's hands.[16]

Theaterdienst, the GDR's theater trade journal, described the performance of the play as an ideal result of cultural and political teamwork: "The performance of the colleagues from the Stadttheater Senftenberg at the Cultural Conference of Lauchhammer demonstrated the fruitful exchange between artists and workers, that on one hand helps the workers to attain culture through the political use of artistic means, and on the other hand helps the artist to consciously use art as a weapon."[17] This is, of course, the highest critical acclaim that can be granted in the GDR. It was Müller's highest point of official appreciation, a point he has not reached again, although in 1973 and 1974 his stock was once again definitely on the rise.

Müller's next play, *The Refugee* (*Die Umsiedlerin oder das Leben auf dem Lande*), written between 1956 and 1961, was a professional disaster for him. It succumbed after only one university performance in 1961. The play was "recalled" because it "contained an inadequate characterization of realism, and a formal use of dialectics,"[18] as the *Schauspielführer*, the GDR version of *Masterplots*, cogently puts it. Hermann Kähler, whose word in these matters is rather official, speaks of the play as a miscarriage, an "unsuccessful attempt."[19] But Klaus Völker, a West Berlin reviewer who saw the only performance, judges it in slightly different terms when he succinctly states: "*The Refugee* is one of the best pieces of new drama in the GDR."[20] He surmises that Müller's decision to postulate rather than demonstrate socialist development caused most of the flak. But the real reason is to be found in the new cultural-political emphasis. By 1961 the Bitterfeld Road was being travelled, and Müller's type of play was no longer a part of the plan.

---

[16] Heiner Müller, "Klettwitzer Bericht 1958," MS (Berlin: Henschelverlag Abteilung Bühnenvertrieb, 1970), pp. 14–15.

[17] *Theaterdienst*, 16 November 1958.

[18] *Schauspielführer*, ed. Karl Heinz Berger et al. (Berlin: Henschelverlag, 1968), II, 739.

[19] Kähler, *Gegenwart auf der Bühne* (Berlin: Henschelverlag, 1966), p. 26.

[20] Völker, "Drama und Dramaturgie in der DDR," in *Theater hinter dem "Eisernen Vorhang*," ed. Reinhold Grimm et al. (Hamburg: Basilius, 1964), p. 69.

Before we can discuss the official rejection of these dialectic plays, however, we must consider two more of these brown coal dramas, Peter Hacks's attempt to stage his theoretical "realistic theater," *The Cares and the Power*, and Hartmut Lange's *Senftenberg Tales*. Hacks's first contemporary topical drama premiered in the coal city Senftenberg in May of 1960, and was again produced, with fatal repercussions, at the Deutsches Theater in 1962. To gain an insight into the industrial process, Hacks went to work in the brown coal region of Senftenberg. In terms of realistic theater, he could have saved his time. For in the play, it becomes evident that Hacks went to Senftenberg to observe working people the way others go to look at animals in the zoo.

The dialectics of the play move between quantity and quality of production. In *The Cares and the Power*, Hacks has taken the bull by the horns and demonstrates some obvious weaknesses, some objective difficulties of the socialist economy such as: How does one guarantee quality when the market is ensured? How can one demand better work at lower pay, when the labor force is minimal? How can one postulate party orientation and perspective from the workers, when the functionaries lack the same? In the prologue, the top/bottom, subject/object, and state/individual conflicts are again set up as the basic dialectic impetus, as we have seen with Müller and Baierl.

> to improve
> the quality of the briquets; which means first to improve
> the quality of the party. And battles for quality
> rage from top to bottom
> in a good land[21]

And the director of the factory puts it this way:

> MELZ: Just as well I should chop off all my fingers. To improve quality is to slow down production which means less pay. That won't work with my workers. These people have caps. And when they tip them, Goodbye, dear Melz, we wish you well, dear Melz, then I sit here between these grimy walls which once were yellow. Socialism has more work than workers. When the workers rule, workers are rare.[22]

Hacks, however, cannot handle either the realistic proletarian language or the characteristic detail upon which his "realistic theater play" rests. His greatest difficulty is that he oversimplifies the contradictions and hides the results behind what Völker calls "increasingly handicrafted verse."[23] The prologue is a precise indication of this process:

[21] Peter Hacks, *Die Sorgen und die Macht*, in *Fünf Stücke* (Frankfurt am Main: Suhrkamp, 1965), p. 301.

[22] *Ibid.*, pp. 333–34.

[23] Völker, "Drama und Dramaturgie," p. 65.

Fidorra, Max is poor, Hede Stoll rich.
She buys, accumulates, pays. Whoever pays, rules.
The honor of this German proletarian
Is deeply hurt. He has no assets.
And along with money's power, slips away
His strength of spirit, muscles, and his loins.
A Terrible conjunction: This love fails
Because one gave up money for love.
What alone can rescue love? Money.[24]

The play is a skeleton. In characterizations, the details which are given fail to reflect the typical essence of the characters. The hand of the master playwright— and Hacks is certainly a master—is discernible here only through tricks of comic juxtaposition. But the true comic base is lacking. The structure of the play does not require these tricks, and they are obvious as adjuncts.

When Hacks, like Müller, attempts to develop a statement of contradiction between socialism today and Communism tomorrow, he cannot sustain the pressure. Unlike Müller, he is unable to display the basic contradictions which, according to his own prologue, form the essence of the play. In one instance, the dialogue approaches that point:

STOLL: It isn't right that we are poor and you are rich. We're all workers. You've got a part in the reconstruction just like us, and it's 1956 for all of us, and we don't have separate calendars. You don't work as well as you live.
ZIDEWANG: The age of equality isn't here yet.
GENERATORWART: The age of exploitation is over.
STOLL: It isn't right that we are poor and you are rich like this.
RAUSCHENBACH: Colleague, I could be your father.
STOLL: Only if I had a blind mother.[25]

But Hacks characteristically escapes the consequences of his own dialogue by dissolving the tension with humor. Perhaps here he takes neither himself nor his topic seriously. It is probably a little of both, because he continues the scene by playing formalistic games, juxtaposing aphorisms—a technique which Brecht uses to much greater advantage in his *Galileo*:

RAUSCHENBACH: I think you are so just, because you are so young.
STOLL: It's better to be too young to cheat than too old to do good.
RAUSCHENBACH: But the worker has learned to think of himself.
STOLL: He who thinks only of himself, thinks little.
RAUSCHENBACH: The quantity of thought is controlled by the quantity in the stomach.[26]

[24] Hacks, *Die Sorgen und die Macht*, p. 302.
[25] *Ibid.*, p. 336.
[26] *Ibid.*, p. 337.

In this manner, Hacks actually avoids the direct explication of the contra-dictory aspects of the socialist economy. Characterization is another means of weakening the dialectic situation: the play's token reactionaries are viewed either as fools (e.g., the intellectual Birkenbiehl), weak bourgeois sympathizers (e.g., Fromm), or neo-Nazis (e.g., Zidewang). Thus, the play is not contemporary, dealing with conflicts in the socialist reality, but is instead historical, since it bases the conflict on extra-societal bogeymen. The whole plot rests, in fact, on the lack of quality production in the briquet factory, and not on any dialectic tension inherent in the socialist economic process. When Fromm goes to the West to tell the Americans "something about how I was unjustly persecuted, and about the monthly production figures,"[27] and Zidewang's reactionary ideology is out-voted, the entire conflict is removed, since they are shown to be actually respon-sible for the money-hungry perspective of the workers.

Hacks, however, continues the pose, and Max Fridorra undergoes an instantaneous conversion into an excellent Communist. But how? Did he have a dialectic insight like that of Müller's character Bremer. Hardly, since Hacks never develops any true dialectic situations. Finally, with Fidorra's closing statement reflecting his conversion, the possibility of a parody on the tradition of socialist conversions arises: "But lightning should strike me if I can understand how I got to this point so quickly."[28] Since that is precisely what the audience is wondering, Hacks only succeeds in parodying the convention to which he has just resorted.

The last digressive play to be discussed here, the unproduced *Senftenberg Tales* (1961) by Hartmut Lange, is also a brown coal drama. Lange was born in Berlin in 1937. He studied at the GDR Film School in Babelsberg before working as a dramaturgical assistant at the Deutsches Theater, where he was greatly influenced by Peter Hacks. Following his difficulties in trying to stage the *Senftenberg Tales*, he left the GDR in 1965, and now lives in West Berlin.

Senftenberg Tales is openly historical and treats the specific changeover of the economic base in Senftenberg from capitalism to socialism. Lange, only 23 when the play was finished, is indebted to Bertolt Brecht, as is also evident in his later play *Marski*, a "Puntillade." Lange's socialist engagement with the literary plan is evident. Yet, although the play reflects the dictates of Bitterfeld, it is also the start of Lange's political difficulties in the GDR.

Though he incorporates the principles of didactic, which means realistic, theater, à la Hacks, Baierl, and Müller, Lange's aesthetic godfather remains Bertolt Brecht. Lange uses such favorite epic devices as direct addresses to the audience, commentary on the action, and the play within the play for purposes of alienation. He also incorporates a Brecht trademark, the strange, abortive marriage scenes right out of Brecht's *Puntila* and *The Good Woman of Sezuan*.

[27] *Ibid.*, p. 338.
[28] *Ibid.*, p. 382.

78

Most of all, however, he is unrelentingly exact in his historical view of the real problems of the early years of the GDR.

Lange operates from the point of view that since the battle for socialism has now been won, a good look at the immediate past; telling it as it was, can only be beneficial. But this assumption was the source of his problems with prescribed aesthetic doctrine. Already it was the Age of Bitterfeld. It was the time of new socialist realism by, of, and for the workers, with the emphasis on character development. Thus, Lange's intellectual approach was already suspect.

In *Senftenberg Tales*, no one changes. Here, historical conflict does not present an experience from which characters emerge, cleansed of their doubt, striving for a new order. In contrast, we see Lange's penchant for extreme objective realism. The great socialist changeover is not made to look like a people's revolution, an image which the party likes to propagate retrospectively, but rather looks like what it was, a change brought about by raw force imposed from the top down. Lange demonstrates the change as occurring essentially without insight or dynamic participation by the people. At one point, for example, the party organizer in the play is faced with the problem of what to do with an independent businessman, Brack. He decides: "When the cock gets too fat, he'll be slaughtered."[29] Although the play justifies the exercise of power as historically necessary, such dialogue does not sound nice—especially to sensitive party ears.

Instead of presenting optimistic details, Lange painfully focuses on the objective problems in the formative stages of the GDR. For example, one scene is built entirely around the national pastime of GDR citizens, standing in line for food. This "Sauerkraut Scene" is one of the most depressing scenes in any GDR drama to date. Despite the positive perspective the overall synthesis of the play generates, some individual components were bound to seem questionable to the SED. A "Worker with hat," for instance, says: "You can feel that the right hand is missing here. We were liberated from it because it exploited us, they say. Right. Now we can starve."[30] And Adam states: "They did it! The pumps work. Starting next week there will be money and a warm lunch—for those who believe it. September made a speech in which he used the word socialism a hundred times. That made me so thirsty that I ran to Brack [the *Klassenfeind*]."[31]

Scenes like the Sauerkraut Scene, and statements such as these were bound to offend the political power structure despite the affirmative final synthesis of the play. They are not only too explicit, but also too factual. Lange's Marxist perspective is not in doubt. The play—in the tradition of Brecht—simply asks too many objective questions about the nature of the power structure. These ques-

---

[29] Hartmut Lange, *Senftenberger Erzählungen oder Die Enteignung*, in *Deutsches Theater der Gegenwart*, ed. Karlheinz Braun (Frankfurt am Main: Suhrkamp, 1967), II, 226.

[30] *Ibid.*, pp. 213–14.

[31] *Ibid.*, p. 219.

tions, however, were not regarded as valid for or conducive to a system whose necessary objective was to remodel a whole people which had, a short time earlier, been participating or at least consenting National Socialists. The GDR, understandably enough, does not like to admit that its "revolution" was enforced by the presence of the Soviet army. Therefore, the play could not be produced.

Thus, by 1960, it was clear that the dialectic digression had synthesized itself into cultural-political oblivion. Its intellectual authors, all coming from middle-class rather than workers' stock, were regarded, along with their works, as being abstract, unemotional, and alienated from the working class. They became ideologically suspect (except for Baierl, himself a party secretary) simply because the emphasis had shifted to antiintellectualism in favor of writing workers.

The Bitterfeld Conference in 1959 marked a turning point in the direction of GDR literature. Yet three months before the Conference, the Socialist Unity Party (SED) launched a series of sharp ideological/aesthetic counteroffensives against the authors of the dialectic digression. At the Fourth Plenary Meeting of the Central Committee on 15 January 1959, Walter Ulbricht, basing his criticism on the resolutions of the Fifth Party Congress of 1958, expressed extreme displeasure with the so-called "didactic" theater: "At present, there are still some tendencies to derange the clear line [of the Fifth Congress] by narrowing the concept of socialist art down to agitation-propaganda art, especially by a group of young dramatists who announced the so-called "didactic" teaching theater as *the* socialist art form, at the expense of true artistic characterization."[32] Although Ulbricht admitted the importance of agitational literature and the exploration of various forms and possibilities of applying socialist realism in the theater, he demanded strict adherence to the party line: ". . . the deciding factor in all areas of literature and art is that the party line is to be made the *determinant* line for the development of a great and broad socialist national culture."[33] This was only a restatement of party thoughts on the theater which had been voiced as early as 1957, but which had not been rigidly enforced. This too would change.[34] But for now, Ulbricht saw the dialectic digression as an indication that the influence

[32] *Der Weg zur Sicherung des Friedens und zur Erhöhung der materiellen und kulturellen Lebensbedingungen des Volkes*, ed. Central Committee of the SED (Berlin: Dietz, 1959), p. 92.

[33] *Ibid.*

[34] In 1957, the Secretary for People's Education and Culture of the Executive Committee of the SED, Magdeburg, stated at the *Bezirkskulturkonferenz:* "Above all we have to remember that there is only one party line and only one discipline of the party. This is the law for all comrades—even the comrade artists. Without the strict adherence to party discipline, it will never be possible to realize the leadership function of the party in our theaters" (*Volksstimme*, 11 December 1957).

of bourgeois decadence was still alive, a situation which had to be fought "with all necessary resolve."[35]

While Walter Ulbricht set the general tone, it remained for Alfred Kurella, one of the party's leading cultural theoreticians, to specifically attack the theories of Hacks, and especially those of Heiner Müller, concerning the "new audience" and the "new theater":

> A theoretical "New Human Being" who demands a new dramaturgy haunts the audiences. He has no feeling anymore, and should have none, and should only be addressed in terms of thought processes. This new human being (who incidentally looks desperately like the human being of the "industrial society," the "second technical revolution," this progeny of petit-bourgeois sociologists) demands a "new theater" for which standard rules of the theater, which were good for other social systems, are no longer applicable.[36]

Kurella further ridicules this conception of the dialectic digression as a development of artistic dogma designed by "a few theoreticians who claim to have a patent on the knowledge of the cultural needs and cultural understanding of our workers and farmers."[37] In case anyone has missed the message, Kurella concludes by putting it into unmistakable political terms, terms which have put the fear of God—or the Politbüro—into socialist writers since they were first used in Moscow in the thirties:

> These are the places where revisionism barricades itself today. It does not show up as revisionism as such, but on the contrary presents itself as the "most progressive of all progressive ideas" which has to fight against the misunderstanding and the conservative rigidity of a few antiquated experts or "functionaries." In reality, however, when we get to the bottom of it, this "avant garde" represents revisionism.[38]

These statements by Ulbricht and Kurella appeared in rapid succession in *Neues Deutschland*, in a vigorous public campaign against this type of theater. A similar view was expressed, also in *Neues Deutschland*, on 17 February 1959, by the Party Organization of Berlin Authors (Betriebsparteiorganisation Autoren Berlin) in an open letter to Wolfgang Langhoff, director of the Deutsches Theater. The letter accuses Langhoff of a lack of socialist engagement. It bluntly asks why Langhoff determines the repertory according to "aesthetic principles," and "Why are Remarque, Sartre, Orff, closer to your heart than Wangenheim, Hauser, Tschesno-Hell, Gorrish and others?"[39] The letter concludes with an

[35] *Der Weg zur Sicherung des Friedens*, p. 92.

[36] Kurella, "Wege zur sozialistischen Volkskultur," *Neues Deutschland*, 11 February 1959.

[37] *Ibid.*

[38] *Ibid.*

[39] Betriebsparteiorganisation Autoren Berlin, "Offener Brief an das Deutsche Theater," *Neues Deutschland*, 17 February 1959.

ominous warning: "We think that it is about time for you and your co-responsible colleagues to consider your responsibility to the Farmers' and Workers' State."[40]

The actions concerning the Deutsches Theater are a vivid example of the executive procedures of the GDR cultural policy, which are reserved for use whenever the suggestions and demands of the literary plan are neglected. For the open letter had been no idle threat. On 16 March 1959, the Cultural Commission of the Politbüro of the Central Committee, under the direction of Alfred Kurella, called the entire directorship of the Deutsches Theater to account. Among the members of the Commission were Alexander Abusch, the Secretary of Culture; Anton Ackermann, the Deputy for Culture, People's Education and Health of the State Planning Commission; Hans Bentzien, the Secretary of Culture of the Executive Party Committee, District Halle; Günter Dahlke, from the Institute of Social Sciences of the Central Committee; and Heinz Kimmel, the Secretary for Agitation, Propaganda, and Culture of the Central Committee of the Free German Youth. There was no doubt about it: this was the first team. They confronted Wolfgang Langhoff, his chief dramaturgical assistant Heinar Kipphardt, and Hans-Dieter Mäde, director of the Maxim Gorki Theater, who had produced Müller's plays.

It was effective. Kipphardt was cast as scapegoat. In the words of Neues Deutschland, "He professed his acceptance of socialist realism in words, but diluted it by trying to augment it with the concept of a 'dialectic theater'; he upheld the leading role of the party in cultural questions, but negated it in his work."[41] Langhoff, happy to save his own skin, agreed with this determination. According to Neues Deutschland, he agreed to his mistakes of the past in obligatory self-criticism and had already changed his views. "His relationship to Comrade Kipphardt," reports Neues Deutschland, "had not been determined by the necessary critical and party-oriented estimation."[42] For Kipphardt, Shakespeare had finally been found. Langhoff's excellent rendition of Brutus to Kipphardt's own Julius Caesar convinced him that they had indeed come to bury him. Unsure of his friends and countrymen, Kipphardt chose not to depend on the lending of ears, and left, instead, for the West.

At the Bitterfeld Conference a month later, Erwin Strittmatter officially disassociated himself from the "dialectic theater" and categorized it as basically alien to the workers: ". . . there is such an unfeeling approach to the work of our workers; all poetic renditions of workers and their work is scoffed at; processes and human beings are described nakedly and coldly as if workers are parts of

40 Ibid.
41 "Kulturkommission beriet mit Berliner Theater-Intendanten," Neues Deutschland, 3 March 1959.
42 Ibid.

machines which could, incidentally, think."[43] For the time being, the *coup de grâce* was given to the dialectic digression by *Neues Deutschland* in a report about "The Development of the Socialist National Theater," a seminar called by the Central Committee. This report interprets the goals of the Bitterfeld Conference for the theater, and categorizes the dialectic digression as being diametrically opposed to the plan, or socialist realism:

About the "Dialectic" Theater

Siegfried Wagner and other speakers of the seminar spoke in this connection—using a term which its originators had thrown into the debate—about a theory of the "didactic" or "dialectic" theater, which wishes to differentiate itself from socialist realism (otherwise we don't see the necessity for its own theoretical system). Although the discussion showed that the various tendencies cannot in all cases be thrown into one pot, some essential common denominators can be extricated: an abstract concept of reality; an emphasis on contradictions combined with the refusal to progress toward their resolutions; a prejudice against deeply human characterization, for which the demonstration of so-called social relationships (most often the wrong ones!) is substituted; a dislike of the great dramatic form, instead impressionistic dissolution of the action into episodes; a penchant for speakers, commentators and other figures who enter into the action from the outside; often mechanical vulgar-materialistic thought processes, characterization of the people as exclusively determined by stomach, groin, and wallet; no consideration of the role of awareness as a factor of social change.[44]

Considering this ideological/aesthetic campaign against one specific type of theater in the short span of four months, we come to an unavoidable conclusion: To label these plays as a digression from the development of the GDR theater is entirely justified. There are two delineating literary historical factors which even demand such a label to forcefully indicate that we are not dealing with the mainstream of the GDR drama when we focus upon this phenomenon. First, the dialectic/didactic plays are the minority group of the socialist drama evolving from the impetus of the Cultural Conference of 1957; and second, the authors and plays do not form a unified school or movement and digress even from each other. Furthermore, it cannot be stressed enough that the compiled body of plays and the theories and ideas behind them were experimental in nature; that the experiments had only limited success; and that the prevalent cultural climate was such that a continuation of the experiments toward the formation of a tradition was questionable from the beginning. And the reason for this was simple. There was a concurrent readjustment to socialist realistic dramaturgy which was not only of good quality, but also of a "non-experimental"

---

[43] Strittmatter, "An die Basis—gegen die Selbstzufriedenheit," *Neues Deutschland*, 28 April 1959.

[44] Henryk Keisch, "The Development of the Socialist National Theater," *Neues Deutschland*, 4 June 1959.

nature which, of course, developed with the nurturing support of the SED.

Thus the first dialectic digression consists of a very limited number of plays which only have two things in common: their experimental nature; and the fact that the contingencies under which they were conceived were already culturally and politically suspect by the time they appeared, rendering some of them ideologically questionable to the party and thus, from the party's point of view, politically unsafe for public consumption as soon as they appeared. The indications now are that the heavy artillery of the anti-dialectic campaign was a classic case of cultural-political overkill. The dialectic digression had defeated itself long before the war was openly declared.

VI.
In Search of the Mainstream

Meanwhile, the resolutions of the Cultural Conference of 1957, the after-effects of the Nachterstedt letter, and the call for party line adherence in all matters theoretical were determining the major flow of dramatic production. Although the cultural policy actively urged the writing and production of contemporary topical plays, a radical change from the standard repertories, which were heavily laced with the classics of the national cultural heritage and of other cultures, could not be effected immediately. And while the dialectic digression took up some of the slack, it was never regarded kindly, and was, by 1960, effectively removed from the scene. The strong, positive, pro-socialist topical drama, in which heroes and heroines overcome insurmountable problems and undergo a tremendous change of perspective, was also obsolete; for the theatrical socialist realism of 1950 could not be served to the complex, fast-developing GDR society, whose successful battle with the objective difficulties inherent in socialist development had taught better lessons. Since the dialectic digression had been found incompetent to cultivate and affirm perspectives of present-day socialism in the GDR, a new point of orientation had to be found. As had been the case many times before when a touchstone was needed, the SED, and especially Walter Ulbricht, provided one.

The Fifth Party Congress of 1958 was effective in two major areas. It postulated that the foundation for socialism in the GDR had been solidified, and that efforts must be made to achieve a completely victorious socialism as a model for both German states. Thus the party leadership was not interested in propagating a contemporary topical literature which would examine the society's foundations for structural cracks or contradictions, as did the plays of the dialectic digression. Instead, the party demanded a literature which would accept and portray socialism as having arrived, and depict the people, already good socialists, in their efforts to become even better versions of what they already were.

In order to aid the populace of the GDR in achieving their fervent goal,

Walter Ulbricht realized that something other than the outdated moral code of the Christian Ten Commandments had to be found to satisfy and guide his people. Therefore, he promulgated the Ten Socialist Commandments at the Fifth Party Congress of 1958. Since these commandments determine the overall point of view in the plays we will discuss shortly, we must list them at this point:

1. Always support the international solidarity of the working class and all working people, and the unbreakable bond between all socialist nations.
2. Love your fatherland and always be prepared to use all of your strength and resources for the defense of the Workers' and Farmers' State.
3. Help to eradicate the exploitation of man by other men.
4. Do good deeds for socialism, because socialism leads to a better life for all working people.
5. To aid the development of socialism, always act in the spirit of mutual help and comradely cooperation, respect the collective, and welcome its criticism.
6. Defend and propagate the people's property.
7. Always strive to improve your achievements, be frugal and solidify the discipline of socialist work.
8. Raise your children in the spirit of peace and socialism so that they may become roundly educated human beings of strong character and bodies of steel.
9. Live cleanly and properly, respect your family.
10. Practice solidarity with those peoples fighting for national liberation and those defending their national independence.[1]

When GDR life of 1958 is taken as a basis for the illustration and propagation of these commandments, only the old standby, the fascist-bourgeois *agent provocateur* is needed in addition to set the stage for a contemporary socialist morality play. It was Gustav von Wangenheim who again responded to the ideological summons of his position as semi-official dramatist of the Free German Youth and provided the model for this type of play in 1958. The exceedingly close causal relationship between the cultural plan and its effective literature is nowhere more evident than in his play, *The Students' Comedy (Studentenkomödie)*.

The play demonstrates a close working relationship with the Free German Youth. It was first published by the Verlag Neues Leben, the official Free German Youth publisher. A letter to the reader from the Central Committee of the Free German Youth is included as a supplement to the play and indicates the extent of the play's programmatic purpose:

> If some of us were not aware that often an individual needs time to take the steps to awareness, Gustav von Wangenheim gives us a deep insight into the process which many a young person has undergone in the last few months. Even though this process has been combined by the author with joyful comedy, it remains deeply serious in our contemporary situation.

[1] *Kulturpolitisches Wörterbuch*, ed. Harald Bühl et al. (Berlin: Dietz, 1970), p. 381.

We find that this work demonstrates the deep commitment of our authors to the education and life, to the battles and joys, of the academic youth of our Republic.[2]

It was this official mandate which resulted in the production of the play. In the report about the Cultural Commission's inquisition of the Deutsches Theater on 16 March 1959, *Neues Deutschland* states: "In order to make up for the omissions in the repertory of the Deutsches Theater, *Newly Plowed Lands* [Sholokov], *The Students' Comedy* [Wangenheim], and *Professor Mamlock* [Wolf] will be played this season."[3] From this, it is easy to see where the party line of the theater is heading. Besides the socialist morality play *à la maison*, the new socialist morality play of Russia and the anti-bourgeois and anti-fascist plays were to carry the cultural policy into the next decade.

Wangenheim proceeds simply and directly in creating his *Students' Comedy*. The order in the life of one physics student, Peter Hechelberg, is upset. The comedy proceeds, and puts things back in their proper order. Hechelberg is a candidate for a doctoral thesis at the Physics Institute of the Humboldt University in Berlin. He also has a child—whose mother died at its birth—living with its grandparents in West Berlin, who are no longer able to take care of it. One level of the plot line resolves the conflict with respect to the child, for which Hechelberg has no room or time, but nevertheless a moral responsibility. A second level of the plot resolves the conflict created by the fact that there are two other students, Lotte Neumann and Atze Schumm, who are competing with him for the appointment to the thesis. A third level of the plot surrounds the efforts of the Free German Youth group to incite Hechelberg to be more socially active and do agitation propaganda and voluntary brown coal work. A last level involves reactionary provocation from sources in West Berlin, who manage to get Atze Schumm arrested at Bahnhof Zoo and charged with political kidnaping (*Menschenraub*).

Wangenheim skillfully weaves these actions together into a satisfying whole. On each level he demonstrates the superior moral position of the Free German Youth activists, who succeed in reestablishing order on all levels. Since all the characters become involved in all levels of the plot, and all are directly involved in the resolution process, a true sense of the collective dominates the play. Peripheral to the action, but important as socialist reincarnations of the good and bad angels of the medieval morality play, are two members of the older generation, Frau Hampel and Professor Proband. Frau Hampel is the ever-present figure of socialist realistic drama, the old grandmother who has undergone a lifelong struggle against reactionary ideas. Her humane convictions, combined with her natural common sense, demonstrate a historical tradition of progressive thought which is the natural "people's" base for socialism in the GDR. On the

---

[2] Supplement to Gustav von Wangenheim, *Mit der Zeit werden wir fertig: Eine Studentenkomödie* (Berlin: Neues Leben, 1958).

[3] *Neues Deutschland*, 20 March 1959.

other hand, Professor Proband is a divided intellectual, once a student activist himself in the thirties, but now out of touch with the people and the socialist mandate. Impressed with the actions of the students' collective, even he regains the revolutionary spirit of his youth:

> PROFESSOR: I think we will have a protest demonstration because of what happened to our fellow student Schumm. Rally in front of the university. How would it be if your agit-prop group would perform?
> PETER: Excellent, Professor. My foot has also improved—I think it's our duty to support Schumm.
> PROFESSOR: You must show the spirit of solidarity which the youth of the "Hohen Meissner" had—and later the socialist and Communist student groups. We were enthusiasts in those days.[4]

At all levels of this play Wangenheim stresses the need for more social awareness, more social action. It is not enough for a student to study. He must actively seek involvement in the collective process. His problems are not individual, but social. Only by social action, as Peter must learn, can individual problems be solved:

> PETER: Look, kid, I've got problems.
> LOTTE: I know.
> PETER: What do you know?
> LOTTE: I know why you just called me "kid," Papa . . . ! Help us with our problems and we may be able to help you with yours.
> PETER: A private affair . . .
> LOTTE: . . . usually has social characteristics.[5]

Peter had tried to separate his life from his work. The resolution of the plot is simply his willingness to see that this is impossible and reactionary. He realizes this, undergoes self-criticism, and asks for advice from the collective. After an agit-prop practice session which parodies the uninvolved student as a lamb with nothing constructive to do but say "Baah!" he sees the reflection on himself: "Agit-prop, you sang the truth. But the innocent lamb couldn't cope with its time—it had no time for you, no time for brown coal—only time for idle talk, baah!"[6] He further explains that "I will explain everything in writing. I'm no longer a candidate for the thesis."[7] And "I declare myself undeserving of the scholarship."[8] He decides to go back to work in the factory, since he had violated the trust of the workers and farmers by letting his socialist perspective slide as a student.

[4] Wangenheim, *Studentenkomödie*, pp. 59–60.
[5] *Ibid.*, p. 53.
[6] *Ibid.*, p. 64.
[7] *Ibid.*
[8] *Ibid.*

It is at this point, however, that the play deteriorates into something akin to the American soap opera. Lotte has taken Hechelberg's child, Peter works in a factory, and both become demoralized. A positive view is needed. Wangenheim very simply presents such a view in three steps. (1) Lotte, Schumm, and Hechelberg are admitted to the thesis as a collective. (2) Lotte and Hechelberg finally decide that they love each other and have done so for a long time. (3) Frau Hampel overcomes her disinclination toward screaming children and asks the new happy family to live with her.

What had started out as a demonstration of socialist morality in the form of a true comedy is reduced to a Neil Simon, Broadway type of situation comedy in which the resolution comes essentially from individual forces and not from the social phenomena with which the play deals on the surface. The comedy thus loses its social-historical perspective and its true relevance to cultural policy in the GDR. The title *The Students' Comedy* indicates a claim to be representative, characteristic, and typological. The claim, however, is nullified by Wangenheim's, the Free German Youth's, and the party's determination to produce "happy" resolutions at all costs. In this case, the cost was the ideological integrity of the play.

Another drama which tries to demonstrate and resolve the new moral predicaments of everyday socialist life is *The Lorenz Divorce Case* (*Ehesache Lorenz* [1958]) by the screenplay and radio play author Berta Waterstradt. Waterstradt has a revolutionary background as a member of the German Communist Party in the anti-fascist movement in the early thirties. She was born in Kattowitz (today Katowice) in 1907 and in 1925 moved to Berlin, where she became exposed to Communist ideology. During the Nazi period, she was incarcerated for a number of years. After the war she resumed her writing with Radio Berlin (Eastern Sector) and, later, for GDR film and television.

The Lorenz Divorce Case, which was made into a film a year after it opened, had a very successful run on many stages.[9] Waterstradt chose an interesting topic: marriage in the socialist society. The protagonists are ideal examples of socialist development in the GDR. Willi Lorenz is an industrial production expert whose specialty is rehabilitating sick factories, while his emancipated, socialist wife is judge in the family (divorce) court. Through a friend, Trude Lorenz learns that Willi is having an affair with his secretary, that their seemingly sound marriage has large faults. The play is half exposition of the problem and half resolution, with the analysis of the problem given perfunctorily in one short scene.

With this age-old topic, the author had the possibility of examining whether or not some basic human changes have occurred in the moral, i.e., family struc-

---

[9] The *Schauspielführer*, ed. Karl Heinz Berger et al. (Berlin: Henschelverlag, 1968), II, 745, reports that "this play ... was her first work for the stage; written in 1956, it gained access to many GDR theaters only after its successful production at the State Traveling Theater in Prague in 1958."

tures of society through the development of socialism. This the play does not achieve, although it is openly stated as the main objective. An important functionary works hard for the state for years; his wife, equally important, does the same. Does this ideal state thus cause a necessary alienation between the marriage partners? Do the demands of professional social dedication, the long hours and the lonely trips cause a communication failure between two dedicated persons who found each other and survived during the "time of illegality," the period of fascist rule from 1933 to 1945? Is it possible that the socialist system is at the root of the failure of this marriage and other marriages conceived under a traditional bourgeois morality but now exposed to entirely different conditions? Are the new system and the old family antithetical? Is there a need for a new definition of marital morality?

These questions are neither asked nor answered. The play shams historical importance by tantalizing the audience with the prospect of analyzing one of these blockbusters. But like the diver at the top of the tower who decides that the wind is too strong to dive safely, Waterstradt holds the spectators in suspense but fails to follow through. The problem is reduced from the social, the characteristic plane, to an individualized bit of male chauvinism on the part of Willi Lorenz. This is irrevocably demonstrated by the author in the major section of analytical dialogue:

> WILLI: But how many times do I have to tell you that I don't want to marry her at all?
> TRUDE: Please, let me talk. I hoped you'd say: I lost my head, and we've got to straighten this out. The girl is still young and has no parents. I behaved irresponsibly. We've got to take care of her somehow so that she doesn't get hurt further. You see, if you would have said that, then I might have believed your promises. But the girl was just a little delicacy for you which you (how do you say it nicely?) just "tasted" as a side dish. Her mother was "tasted" that way by her boss, too. He was a capitalist exploiter, and you're a member of the Socialist Unity Party. But there's no difference in the act itself. You just walked over a human being with whom you had a relationship without any concern. You have no honor anymore, and that's why I want to be away from you.[10]

Thus morality remains an individual problem. The conflict in the Lorenz marriage remains a private conflict. The play, while holding up visions of the analysis of the socialist family, only unpacks the bourgeois baggage that this particular family has brought along on the long road to socialism. The resolution of the problem is simply the act of packing it all up again in different bags. Willi, thrown out by both his wife and his mistress, is transferred to a different city. This will supposedly give everyone some time to think things out. Waterstradt,

---

10 Berta Waterstradt, "Ehesache Lorenz," MS (Berlin: Henschelverlag Abteilung Bühnenvertrieb, 1963), pp. 36–37.

however, implies that Willi and Trude will get back together again, all the wiser for this little incident.

This straightforward, sentimental, melodramatic contemporary play is good, solid, and entertaining theater. The roles are well-defined and lend themselves to powerful portrayals. The dialogue is clear and there is a good amount of humor and "folk wisdom" in the supporting roles. In short, it has everything it takes to make a success. But it would also be a success in the United States, or France, or even Timbuktu, since no specific characteristic element of GDR life or society is vital to its dramatic structure.

A similarly successful popular drama was *Ring Three Times* (*3 X klingeln* [1960]) by the theater practitioner Hans Dieter Schmidt. Schmidt's comedy "was played by almost all theaters in the German Democratic Republic, and reached high production counts everywhere."[11] His pragmatic formula for popular success comes from his active work in the theater since 1950 as an actor, producer, director and playwright. He was born in Wurzen, Saxony in 1926. His secondary schooling was interrupted by active duty in the German army during the war, followed by a period as a prisoner of war. With the end of the hostilities, he became an apprentice teacher and attended the Theater School in Halle, where his major interests were directing and acting. He also worked as an actor and director in Potsdam and Leipzig. Since 1950 his primary activity has been in the realm of children's theater in Erfurt, Leipzig, and Berlin. In 1958 he was named head director of the Theater der Jungen Welt in Leipzig, one of the leading young people's theaters in the GDR.

In *Ring Three Times*, Schmidt's objective is to dramatize the everyday problems of the GDR in a light, pleasing, and politically innocuous manner. To insure the support of the cultural planners, whose demand for progressive socialist perspectives was continually increasing, Schmidt simply made two of his characters in this three-character play members of the Free German Youth. But this socialist overlay has even less bearing upon the action than the same sort of technique in Waterstradt's play. The play's connection with GDR reality rests in its subject matter: life in a boarding house. The GDR is a state in which housing is at a premium, and the nature of relationships among people living in close quarters is something that deserves national attention. But it also deserves rational attention, which it does not get here.

Again a sentimentalized situation comedy structure masquerades as a play about contemporary topical problems. Schmidt, however, is less pretentious than Wangenheim or Waterstradt. He acknowledges the nonhistorical, nonpolitical nature of his treatment in this work and subtitles it *A Lighthearted Play About an Almost Serious Problem* (*Ein heiteres Stück um ein beinahe ernstes Problem*). Old Mrs. Engler has reactionary cobwebs in her thinking process—not from any political

[11] *Schauspielführer*, II, 766.

conviction, but from convenience. The thorn in her side is one of her boarders, Petra Simmich, a fervent *Jugendfreund* (the name with which members of the Free German Youth traditionally greet one another). Mrs. Engler hopes for an alliance with Hinze, a young actor and her new boarder, against the unsettling influences of Petra. But Hinze, contrary to her expectations, is also a *Jugendfreund*. Predictably, Hinze and Petra fall in love, etc., and the two boarders become allied against Mrs. Engler. But it is not an evil alliance, because with a bit of strategy and cajolery, they bring the old lady around to their point of view. They are so successful, in fact, that when the lovers quarrel and therefore neglect their socialist duties, Mrs. Engler reads them the riot act and sends them scurrying to their *Subbotnik*,[12] the voluntary day of work for the common good.

There is no social or ideological conflict in the play. It is a comedy dependent upon a series of trivial situational misunderstandings which give the audience a nice satisfied feeling when they laugh at the resolution. Mrs. Engler's backward thinking process is in the petit-bourgeois tradition of the widow parroting the inane thoughts of her dead husband. Actually she is from the start, like most older people in the socialist drama, sympathetic to all the progressive ideas Petra represents, and is only put off by the sound and the fury. Mrs. Engler herself analyzes the situation this way: "And to re-think, and change one's habits, that's not as easy as putting on a different jacket. You've got to have patience and a little bit of tact [with us old people]."[13]

Thus the three plays we have discussed here contrast sharply with the plays of the dialectic digression in all respects. These plays enjoyed the support of both the party and GDR audiences. They sacrificed perspective for "entertainment"; rationality for sentimentality; dialectics for love; and the characteristic detail for universal generalities. Their socialist contents are external adjuncts, and thus the plays carry a light ideological payload. The authors have opted for reaching a great number of people with a little message, rather than trying to peddle great truths to an empty house—as the dialectic digression tried to do.

One of the most glaring inconsistencies of East German literary policy is the fact that these sentimental romances of the urban intelligentsia resulted from a literary policy which by 1960 had as its creative goal the configuration of the human character in accordance with the demands of socialist society. This formulation was made at the Cultural Conference of 1960: "The configuration of the *human character of socialism*—that is the main objective of all the arts. It concerns the picture of the new human beings with their characteristic traits as they fight

---

12 *Subbotnik* is the Soviet terminology for a voluntary work effort on a normally free day. It stems from the Russian word *Subbota*, the term for *Saturday*.

13 Hans Dieter Schmidt, "3 X klingeln," MS (Berlin: Henschelverlag Abteilung Bühnenvertrieb, 1968), p. 64.

for the socialist morality on the journey from the I to the we, and their concurrent development into manifold personalities."[14]

Although these plays deal with the problems of everyday life, it is doubtful whether "in these new characters of our everyday life, characters which are setting new criteria for us, the entire beauty and dignity of the human being freed from exploitation is realized,"[15] as was further formulated by the 1960 Cultural Conference. A much closer working relationship between the theater and the cultural plan of the planned society of the GDR was obviously needed. This was realized by a series of plays which were much more responsive to the economic objectives of the Fifth Party Congress of 1958, the plays which reflected the new agricultural policy of the SED.

[14] *Kulturkonferenz 1960*, ed. Central Committee of the SED (Berlin: Dietz, 1960), p. 426.
[15] *Ibid.*

VII.
Collective Bucolics

From the very beginning, literature dealing with rural topics was an important ingredient in the literary plan of the German Democratic Republic. In the development of the drama, we must remember the historical significance of Friedrich Wolf's *Mayor Anna* (1949), Strittmatter's *Katzgraben* (1953), and Freyer's *Cornflowers* (1954). While Wolf's and Strittmatter's plays reflected the importance of the Land Reform in constructing a base for the development of socialism "in the country," Freyer's *Cornflowers* already presents the first dramatic treatment of an agricultural collective by a GDR author.

But these tentative steps toward a socialist bucolic in the drama remained embryonic due to the radical change of emphasis in the national economic plan toward a concentration of efforts in heavy industrial production. In this planned society, the turning away from the rural problems in the development of national socioeconomic priorities is reflected in the lack of significant rural topics on the stages of the GDR between 1954 and 1958.

In 1953 and 1954, only 25% of the usable GDR agricultural surfaces were administered by collectives. From then on, the rate of growth of collectivization is completely uncharacteristic in relation to the socialist development of the society and the rest of the economy. Collectivized agriculture's share of all usable space increased only 4% in 1955, 3% in 1956, and another 2% in 1957. By the end of 1958, only 37% of the land, and 352,938 farmers and agricultural workers had been organized into 9,637 of the three types of collectives.[1]

---

[1] There were three basic forms of agricultural collectives: Type I, the collective use of fields; Type II, the collective use of fields and implements (machinery, etc.); and Type III, the complete collectivization of all movable and immovable inventory. Each member retains a portion of the inventory for "private" use corresponding to what is not collectively used in each respective "Type." The figures for 1953–58 correspond to those given in *A bis Z: Ein Taschen- und Nachschlagebuch über den anderen Teil Deutschlands*, ed. Bundesministerium für gesamtdeutsche Fragen (Bonn: Deutscher Bundesverlag,

But the Fifth Party Congress of 1958 made up for the slackened pace of the past few years, and called for concentrated party agitation in the agricultural areas. This was the first move toward the climate which produced the complete crop of collectivized agriculture in the "Socialist Spring" of 1960. In April of that year, the People's Parliament pronounced the complete collectivization as a *fait accompli*, and as law.

The time between the Fifth Party Congress and the Socialist Spring saw one of the SED's most concentrated and forceful campaigns. The Seventh Meeting of the Central Committee in December of 1959 resolved to send thousands of party workers "to the farm" in order to convince the remaining recalcitrants to join up. Their success is history. In fact, more than 50% of all GDR agriculture was collectivized between January 1959 and April 1960.[2]

The concentrated socialist offensive in agriculture and rural life during these years was reflected in a new regard for the human situation of the farmer in the GDR. Already in December of 1957, the critic Hans Jürgen Geerdts addressed the Theoretical Conference of the GDR Writers' Congress on the topic "Our Literature and the New Developments in the Country" ("Unsere Literatur und das Neue auf dem Lande"). In his essay, Geerdts calls for a reorientation of literary production toward rural topics and especially agricultural collectives. He reviews the promising developments of literature immediately after the Second Party Conference of 1952 (the conference which announced the collectivization for the first time), but notes that they did not progress from there. He warns against the dangers of producing harmless pastoral literature without socialist content, and sets the tone for what should be written: "The class struggle in the village is not an idyll, but a dramatic confrontation, even a matter of life and death in specific instances. It is a confrontation in which the fronts are not schematically preconceived, but where the issue is always a very complicated conflict which cannot be characterized harmoniously."[3]

In simpler terms, this means that those farmers out there are now ready to join the socialist society, and that their problems cannot be justly dealt with on a localized level, but must be developed in relation to the economic, social, and political contingencies of the GDR. The treatments which were desired were not of the *Inquiry* type, however. Gerhard Ebert, a reviewer for *Sonntag*, the most widely read cultural weekly, condemned Baierl's play as "superficial agitation

---

1969), p. 383–84. Other statistics for 1958 are given in Kähler, *Gegenwart auf der Bühne* (Berlin: Henschelverlag, 1966), p. 62. *A bis Z* lists the count on 31 December 1958 as 9,637 collectives using 37% of the usable agricultural lands. Kähler lists 8,000 collectives and 37.8% land use. The 1953–54 figures include an additional 15% of the agricultural lands under the administration of state-owned farms, *Volkseigene Güter*.

[2] Cf. *A bis Z*, p. 383.

[3] Geerdts, "Unsere Literatur und das Neue auf dem Lande," *Neues Deutschland*, 15 December 1957.

determined by a city perspective."[4] The socialist bucolic in the theater between 1957 and 1961 was certainly not dialectic theater.

The plays can be functionally divided into two groups, one dealing with the contemporary rural situation, and the other containing historical treatments of the Land Reform, the immediate changeover from agricultural capitalism to the early stages of agricultural socialism. This is not to imply, however, that the plays of each group represent a closed, distinct group. They do not. Among the contemporary productions were *Stories About Marie Hedder* (*Geschichten um Marie Hedder*) by the young working class author Gerhard Fabian, a play which dates back to 1956 but which was first produced in Greifswald in 1958; Strittmatter's *Katzgraben 1958* (1958); Fred Reichwald's *Maria Diehl Takes a Chance* (*Das Wagnis der Maria Diehl* [1959]), which began as a television play; Hedda Zinner's first and only contemporary topical drama, *What Would Happen If...* (*Was wäre wenn ...* [1959]); and Helmut Sakowski's first successful attempts, *The Decision of Lene Mattke* (*Die Entscheidung der Lene Mattke* [1959]) and *Women's Quarrel and Love's Cunning* (*Weiberzwist und Liebeslist* [1961]). The important historical dramas on the early problems of the rural GDR were Strittmatter's *The Dutchman's Bride* (*Die Holländerbraut* [1959]); Helmut Baierl's *Frau Flinz* (1961); and Heiner Müller's 1961 effort, the politically suspect *The Refugee, or Life in the Country*, which was, however, not officially produced until 1975–76, although the subject matter is virtually identical to that of Baierl's play.

Stories About Marie Hedder and *Katzgraben 1958* center on the new relationships between the individual farmer and the agricultural collective. Although this topic should lead to an ideal dramatic exercise in the cultivation and breakthrough of the socialist perspective—especially among those of the rural population who are non-proletarians, such as the owners of medium-sized and large farms—neither Fabian nor Strittmatter can show the positive influence of the socialist agricultural method on the people involved.

Marie Hedder is the owner of a farm which is too much for her to handle. She would like to join the local collective, but the members exhibit a good deal of moralistic truculence and refuse to admit her to membership because she is a "whore" (she has two illegitimate children). Instead of taking things as they are, and using them to their best advantage—as a socialist perspective would demand —the members of the collective, basically proletarians, display enmity toward Marie not only on "moral" grounds, but also because she is the daughter of a rich farmer. This pettiness is presumably quite uncharacteristic of dedicated socialists. Further, although Marie Hedder has obviously been the victim of sexual exploitation in her youth, some male members of the collective tend to keep up the tradition. Instead of seeing that their historical mission is to change the social structure in such a way that Marie's situation will never be reproduced in their

[4] Ebert, rev. of *Alwin der Letzte* in *Sonntag*, quoted in Kähler, *Gegenwart auf der Bühne*, p. 90.

society, they display a misogyny that clearly demonstrates that the change of the production method over the last few years had done nothing to change the workers' perspective.

In the same way, Strittmatter's *Katzgraben 1958* is an indictment of the failure to develop the socialist perspective on the farm. Certainly proletarians like Kleinschmidt are aware of their social role, but in this adjunct to the 1953 *Katzgraben* it becomes obvious that the socialist reconstruction of the economic and social systems in Katzgraben has had no effect on types such as Mittelländer and Großmann. In 1958, Großmann wishes to enlist the aid of Mittelländer against the agricultural collective, just as he did in the highway dispute of 1953. Thus, Großmann demonstrates that the socialist development all around him during the interval rolled like water off his back. But even worse, Mittelländer, whose vacillating position was comical in 1953, when the audience would assume that he would sway toward the socialist perspective and become solid in the future, shows that the winds of time have only kept him swaying. Thus, for Strittmatter, nothing has changed between 1953 and 1958. The socialists are socialistic, and the non-socialists haven't learned a thing.

The point of view expressed by Fabian and Strittmatter is therefore sharply critical of the party's agricultural policy—or lack thereof. Indeed, the party could only acknowledge the justice of this criticism, for, as the statistics proved, the rural socialist perspective had not progressed significantly since 1953. These 1958 plays, then, form an initial part of the new agricultural policy by simply defining the problem and bringing it up for public discussion. Thus *Marie Hedder* and *Katzgraben 1958* are double-edged in their effectiveness. In their positive effect, they augment a repertory that was lacking orientation toward rural topics, and in their negative effect, they necessarily identify GDR society's most reactionary remnant: the farmers. This second edge, which would once have been denounced as objectivism, was now seen as a useful cultural-political weapon.

The most explicit manifestation of this double-edged effect is seen in a close look at Hedda Zinner's first contemporary topical drama, the 1959 comedy *What Would Happen If . . . .* The comic plot in this play rests on a fantastic contrivance by Zinner which throws the normal events of a small town, Willshagen, into turmoil. Willshagen is located in an area of land which is one of the thorns in the side of West Germany. It is one of the small pieces of the GDR which literally juts into the belly of the West. Around 1958, the Western "propaganda" radio *RIAS Berlin* (Radio in the American Sector) actually did broadcast rumors of a "straightening of the border" by which these projections from each side would be erased in a mutual exchange of respective thorns. Conveniently, Willshagen was one of the many towns in the GDR where, after the first wave of collectivization around 1953, the socialization process had been lulled into regression.

Thus Zinner's historical situation shows the population ripe for the growth of the reactionary perspectives fostered by such rumors. When three strangers arrive in town in a West German automobile asking questions about how things were "before," the fuse is lit. Primed by the RIAS rumors, the population of Willshagen undergoes immediate social polarization, which exposes the true thought processes of the people. When the local party organization makes moves to restore the castle of Count Prittwitz, it is assumed by some that the rumors are true, and that the Count will come back and Willshagen will become a part of West Germany. The rich farmer Dahlke openly exhibits capitalistic aggressiveness, a hunger for land, and an arrogant bearing toward all others. The farmer Schäfer, less successful than Dahlke, but having benefited financially in the new state, goes with the prevailing Western wind and denounces the socialist way of life. A few weak characters, the social and economic parasites of the town, become the strongest advocates of the change, and swiftly resume their pre-GDR roles as the lackeys of a capitalist power structure.

Such objective characterization of the populace is a far cry from the early fifties type of socialist realism, in which characters had to be "pure types" to start with, or had to undergo a miraculous onstage conversion. But Zinner demonstrates some basic philosophical tenets of Marxism-Leninism in other characterizations which leave no doubt as to her ideological integrity. One example is the reduction process by which human relationships are affected when capital—in this case, land and property—becomes a basic societal force once again. Zinner shows how Gepfert, a progressive farmer who was about to join the collective, sways in his decision and reduces his daughter to a chattel, legal tender in the quest for land. He wants to marry her off to Dahlke's dimwitted but amiable son in order to seal a land deal. When the girl refuses, the state of his consciousness is thrown back decades, even centuries, and only violence remains as a direct result of this new capitalist influence in his life:

GEPFERT: You'll marry Christian.
INGE: No. I won't! No! You can't force me. Those days are long gone!
GEPFERT: I'll show you what's long gone, you . . . you . . . (*Beside himself with rage, he approaches her with his fists clenched.* MRS. GEPFERT *enters, screams, and comes between them.*)[5]

This rage is Zinner's version of the capitalist alienation of man from himself. It is obvious that the old land-oriented mentality, the basis of capitalist agriculture, is under heavy attack here, with covering fire from the new party policy after the Fifth Party Congress. The root of the rural reaction is centered in this historical attitude, which she denounces in the following speech by Scholz: "To hell with them! Those farmers! They'll do anything for a piece of land! Make themselves

[5] Hedda Zinner, "Was wäre wenn—?" MS (Berlin: Henschelverlag Abteilung Bühnenvertrieb, 1959), pp. 74–75.

unhappy, and their children! Land, land, always land—even if they choke on it!"[6]

As the turmoil created by the rumors proceeds to its comic climax and realignment, the polarization process isolates various groups. In the final tableau, the class struggle in the rural areas is presented rather effectively. For while it is the standard socialist realism final tableau, it serves an almost emblematic purpose here as well, by arranging the contingencies visually onstage. In this scene, a group of wealthy reactionaries and their parasites gleefully await the return of the Count; a group of "new farmers" and those in the collective march up en masse, armed with the tools of their trade—hoes, axes, picks, clubs—to throw the Count back out. They realize their stake in the new society, and have come to defend it. The local party group, aware of the hoax, waits to see what will happen.

What happens is this: In Willshagen the reactionary forces among the people are brought out into the open. Even reactionary tendencies deeply rooted in the individual psyches of progressive persons, as in the Gepfert case, are exposed and thus purged by rational analysis. Finally, the historical necessity of socialist agriculture is demonstrated by clearly showing that the capitalist agricultural and social systems are now historical relics only represented by the *Nachtwächter* Ebermayer, the one-time lackey of the Count. Here, *Nachtwächter*, normally "nightwatchman," also has the colloquial meaning of a semi-idiotic dolt who never quite knows what is happening. Ebermayer appears in his livery at the portal of the castle like an apparition from the past. At that point, the audience becomes aware of the hoax for the first time: The three strangers are exposed as a production crew of DEFA, the GDR film corporation, who have chosen Willshagen as the site for their next feature, entitled *What Would Happen If* . . . .

Even considering the obvious and gimmicky theatricality of the play, we must rate Zinner's effort very highly. As an integrated, specialized, cultural-political weapon, it was an efficient method of introducing the party's new agricultural priorities. By showing very competently and persuasively how the farmer's historical land hunger, a basis of the capitalist system, leads to dehumanization and manipulation of people, even within the immediate family, she leaves two provocative questions for the audience to consider: Am I like that? And what would happen if . . . ? But notwithstanding its agitational qualities, the play's entertainment quotient ranks high among all GDR plays, making it an ideal example of effective contemporary topical drama in a planned society.

Where the concentration had been on individual farmers and their process of joining an agricultural collective in Fabian's, Strittmatter's and Zinner's plays, the late Fred Reichwald's 1959 opus, *Maria Diehl Takes a Chance*, accepts the complete collectivization of GDR agriculture as a foregone conclusion and treats the conflicts within an established collective. Reichwald, like many GDR dramatists, had a colorful, turbulent background. He was born of Jewish parents

[6] *Ibid.*, p. 33.

in Berlin in 1921. Early in his life he turned toward the land as a career and studied agriculture. His parents died as victims of the Nazi genocide, but he managed to escape to England, where he was a farm worker for two years. In 1939 he traveled to Australia and India. Returning to East Germany in 1947, he became a cultural-political agitator for the party among farm workers. His literary talents were developed at the Johannes R. Becher Institute of Literature. But basically his interest remained with the land and the farming people. His promising career was cut short by his untimely death in 1963.

The major characters in his play *Maria Diehl* are certainly autobiographical, drawn from Reichwald's experience as a cultural agitator. Maria Diehl, a former refugee, is now the chairman of a successful collective. Concentrating upon this character would permit Reichwald to focus on inherent contradictions in the workings of collectives and the development of a woman as an independent, active, and integral part of the political-economic system of the GDR. But ensured success by the simple choice of a blue chip topic—and in 1959 the agricultural collective was a gilt-edged cultural-political issue—Reichwald opts for the most simplistic—and traditional—plot imaginable.

From the German naturalistic drama of the turn of the century. Reichwald resurrects the "messenger from the outside" who must enter the scene as a catalyst before any action can begin. Thus, Walter Buschow, a party troubleshooter, a strong, silent, straightshooting socialist John Wayne, the Lone Ranger of the SED, ambles into the play as a new brigade leader sent by the district office. In an almost unbelievably sentimental bit of bittersweet, he also turns out to be Maria's long lost lover. The agronomist Keding, who is living with Maria and who actually runs the collective because she is subservient to him, sees his position threatened and tries to get rid of Buschow.

Keding is successful in blaming a dastardly act of sabotage on our hero. But old Walter had been active in overhauling the slipping socialist perspectives of some other members, and together Walter and his converts suspect Keding of being at the root of various bits of reactionary ideology which are floating around the collective. Maria confronts Keding with the knowledge of his sabotage, and he confesses to it as an act of personal jealousy toward Buschow. Being an essentially weak and frustrated female who is ruled by her emotions (how did she ever get to be chairman of the collective?), Maria believes him and protects him. Through a stroke of luck struck by a socialist *deus ex machina*, however, Buschow and Maria discover Keding's true nature. They find proof that Keding is not only a West German *agent provocateur*, but a Nazi war criminal as well. The final scene of this sentimental "East German Western" marks a profound change in the awareness of Maria Diehl:

> KEDING (*reaching with his hand*): Maria—give me the gun! (MARIA *bends down and picks up the gun.*) (*Commandingly*) Quick. Let's have it!
> (MARIA *goes toward* WALTER, *stands next to him and holds the gun in such a way that he*

can easily take it and aim it at KEDING. KEDING *slowly steps back from the table, raises his arms and stops.*
MARIA, *without looking at him,'takes two steps away, turns her back on* KEDING, *without looking at* WALTER.)
MARIA: I loved him—but I hate everyone who wants to destroy our world.[7]

The drama, ostensibly about the development of one woman's social and political role in the GDR system, actually has nothing to do with the clarification of such a contemporary question. It is instead a schematic but successful attempt to counteract Western influences. For this reason, its demonstration of the failure of the collectivization process to increase the collective awareness in Maria Diehl and other characters was forgiven by the SED. The plot is simply "whodunit"; the fact that the action is located in an agricultural collective is incidental; and even the solution is not the result of collective awareness, but is accidental.

It was only because of the play's conspicuously anti-Western black-and-white characterizations that *Maria Diehl* was tolerated. Not only was it tolerated, however; it was hailed as a play "in which the author, now artistically matured, again confronts the problems which arose from the socialist reconstruction of agriculture."[8] So interested were the cultural policy-makers in plays which concerned the agricultural scene, that Reichwald received the National Prize for this play in 1959, even though its socialist content is restricted to external bombast which leaves only a sentimental detective story as substance. For Reichwald, setting an audience-pleasing socialist soap opera in an agricultural collective was the formula for instant success.

But the converse can also be true. The new emphasis on socialist-oriented theater about rural topics also produced at least one interesting result from a completely unexpected quarter. Peter Pons's 1959 play *Fire in the Village* (*Feuer im Dorf*), subtitled *A Detective Play* (*Kriminalstück*), is an unpretentious play for amateur theater by an author who is completely unknown outside the realm of amateur theater. Thus, if anything indicates the status quo of the mainstream, the work of Pons does. The first consideration of his play is the necessary attention to a suspenseful plot and an interesting story. Pons, however, does his job so well that his "simple" play turns out to be much more complex and significant than it at first appears. Although there is not a single piece of politically oriented dialogue in the play, its overall perspective reflects the new political developments in the GDR villages. This results from characters and characterizations in the play which are not only interesting as parts of the detective plot, but which demonstrate, in their various relationships, the effect of the cultural-political offensive in the "typical" GDR village. The play, then, is no simple detective story.

[7] Fred Reichwald, "Das Wagnis der Maria Diehl," MS (Berlin: Henschelverlag Abteilung Bühnenvertrieb, 1959), p. 51.
[8] *Schauspielführer*, ed. Karl Heinz Berger et al. (Berlin: Henschelverlag, 1968), II, 755.

The plot works toward the solution of a crime committed among characters demonstrating typical rural social roles; the interaction triggered by this crime is dominated by a clearly "progressive" perspective. The crime, arson, is also of national consequence, since it involves a town shortly before it is completely collectivized. Thus it becomes a political crime. Pons's use of the Western *agent provocateur* is consistent with this national perspective and his genre. Whereas Reichwald's agent was crucial to the plot, the agent Pons comes up with is only incidental. His plot does not demand an agent, but the insertion of this interesting female character enhances the overall theatricality of the play and thus fulfills it as amateur theater. A substratum of humor further enables Pons to secure a progressive historical perspective in his play: the attacks on the GDR by this "incidental" provocateur are seen as historically unnecessary and essentially anachronistic. Thus, from any perspective relevant to the cultural-political plan of the GDR, this play is an unexpected gem.

Before proceeding with our survey of the mainstream, we must consider the significance of the Bitterfeld Conference in terms of the theater. On 24 April 1959 the authors of the Mitteldeutscher Verlag met at a conference held in the Cultural Hall of the Electrochemical Combine Bitterfeld. The theme and location of the conference were integral with its purpose. The motto was "Reach for your pen, colleague, the socialist German national culture needs you."[9] The conference thus launched a two-pronged cultural offensive. It encouraged workers to write about their lives, and authors to write about workers. In the drama, the role of the writing worker had no immediate effect, since the less demanding forms of reports, short sketches, short stories, and lyric poetry were preferred by the workers in their first literary efforts. Thus it is the second prong, the already cited efforts of professional authors to concern themselves with the lives of the workers, which is of immediate interest in 1959. Ulbricht summarized the "Bitterfeld Road" ("Bitterfelder Weg") and its prescription for professional authors as follows: "The Bitterfeld Movement is and will remain the program of fusion between art and life, between the artist and the people and the developing socialist society. It is the proof that socialist realism remains the artistic method proper to the development of our culture."[10] Thus we find that the 1959 Bitterfeld Conference presents nothing new for the drama, but is simply another reassertion of the people-oriented cultural offensive going back to the Nachterstedt Letter of 1956, the Cultural Conference of 1957, and the overall cultural program announced at the Fifth Party Congress of 1958. It should not be elevated out of this context.

The Bitterfeld Conference is nevertheless an important literary tributary of

---

[9] Formulation of novelist Werner Bräunig at the 1959 Bitterfeld Conference. This became the slogan by which workers were actively urged to participate in the production of socialist literature.

[10] Walter Ulbricht, quoted in *Kulturpolitisches Wörterbuch*, ed. Harald Bühl et al. (Berlin: Dietz, 1970), p. 80.

the dramatic mainstream whose course is the issue at the present stage of this study. Mainly, the Conference resulted in a "people's" emphasis on the part of the drama. It is partly responsible for consigning intellectualized portrayals to the still backwaters while drawing the *Volksstück*—the gutsy, vital, small-man-oriented, comical, even farcical theater of the German literary tradition—directly into the current. And this was important in the continuing cultural quest for a socialist national theater.

The *Volksstück* is hard to define in English. The manifold connotations of the term *Volk* in German have no correspondingly complex cognate in English. Perhaps the best way to categorize the genre is to concentrate on the national aspect of the term, combine it with its popular aspect, and thus distill not only a workable definition—a play of national and popular orientation—but the qualities that enable it to subserve the cultural policy of the German Democratic Republic.

The dramatic work of Helmut Sakowski most readily exemplifies this "popular national" direction. Sakowski was born in 1924 in Jüterbog. With Strittmatter, Baierl, and Reichwald, he was one of the first GDR authors to come to terms with socialist development in rural areas. He has always had a close connection to the land and studied forestry before becoming a soldier in World War II. From 1947 to 1949 he attended the GDR's new College for Forestry and subsequently worked for the Department of the Interior as a forester in Salzwedel between 1951 and 1958. Thus the characters and conflicts of his rural drama are drawn from firsthand knowledge and infused with an understanding, even a love for and identification with, the people who live from the land.

Sakowski's writing career developed in a thoroughly modern medium, however: his first dramatic works were written for television and radio. He prefers dramatic structures that utilize few characters and abundant action, and he prides himself on being utterly anti-intellectual. His commitment to the cultural policy of the Socialist Unity Party (SED) was rewarded in 1971, when he was named a member of its Central Committee.

In 1958, Sakowski wrote a television play, *The Decision of Lene Mattke*, which became his first work for the stage, premiering on 14 September 1959 at the Volkstheater Halberstadt. Its similarity to Reichwald's *Maria Diehl* goes beyond their identical origins as television plays and extends to characters and plot. But while Reichwald's play presents the new socialist reality of the GDR only as a superficial veneer, in Sakowski's first play it is all substance. Solid socialist ideology and party commitment reveal themselves in a very basic plot and simple characterizations.

The central issue is the rehabilitation of a family that had been reduced to poverty and disgrace by the father, Mattke, a deadbeat and a drunkard. After a cataclysmic dispute with the chairman of the collective, Mattke is removed from his post in charge of dairy production, and ends up in a hospital for an alcoholic cure. Lene Mattke expects to be thrown out of the collective with her husband, but this does not happen. Jagosch, an archetypal positive hero, recommends that she take charge of the dairy barn. Overwhelmed at first, Lene decides to give it a try with the help of her daughter. The two of them are highly successful, and the barn becomes the pride of the town.

This new responsibility breeds awareness and consciousness in Lene. For the first time in her life she belongs somewhere, makes a social contribution, and is a necessary cog in the social structure. The collective ideal is the basis for this new role. Then Mattke comes back. The collective decides that Lene Mattke will run the barn; Mattke will be given other work until he demonstrates a positive change. Mattke decides that he will take his family to an independent farmer, for whom they will work together as hired hands. Lene Mattke decides that she and her children will stay in the collective because they have grown with it in a reciprocal relationship of mutual and lasting benefit and have attained a level of self-respect, responsibility, success and human dignity that she had never thought possible. She confronts Mattke with these undeniable facts. But Mattke sees only the traditional, outdated husband and wife roles: "Don't you have any scrap of honor in your body? Making a pact with them when they want to kick your husband's ass?"[11] The socialist perspective on the independent decision-making power of women has made its impact on Lene: "You do what you want! Hit me if you want. Go away if you want. Drink yourself to death if you want. But without me and the children. I have to stay. They need me. I always followed you all those years, but I just can't do it anymore. Get out!"[12] This perspective has also filtered down to Mattke's sixteen-year-old daughter, Lotte, who sees the future that has just been opened to her threatened by her own father. She chimes in: "We don't need anyone to take care of us: We can take care of ourselves. We don't need you. Why don't you leave if you want to? Better to have no father than to have one like you."[13]

Up to this point the play does exactly what most of its predecessors have failed to do: It demonstrates the basic positive changes in social and family structure wrought by the sensitive application of the all-encompassing socialist principles of the SED, using the decision of Lene Mattke as a model. It is a small play that fulfills a grand mission in demonstrating those elusive elements of socialist realism, the "typical" and the "characteristic" evidences of the development of the socialist social structure. The convention of the joyful, harmonious final scene accounts for the necessary inconsistency of having Mattke come around at the end with the sudden desire to better himself and to abide by the

---

[11] Helmut Sakowski, *Die Entscheidung der Lene Mattke* (Berlin: Henschelverlag, 1967), p. 45.
[12] *Ibid.*
[13] *Ibid.*

decision of Lene Mattke and the collective. An agitational open end, one that would require the audience to take the problematic and certainly dialectic question home with them, would have served Sakowski's intentions even better.

Although Helmut Sakowski does not approach a realization of "national popular" drama for the GDR until his next play, *Women's Quarrel and Love's Cunning*, his technique in *Lene Mattke* already exhibits some inroads toward that goal. The characters that are peripheral in the demonstration of the play's social thesis are not as typical as Mattke, Lene Mattke, or Jagosch. They become schematic: Sakowski portrays them with naturalistic instead of characteristic detail on a level somewhere between typical characters and caricatures complete with dialect and folksy humor. *The Decision of Lene Mattke* exhibits a nosy female innkeeper, a corpulent, hearty farm wife, and an old man out of step with the times but with his heart in the right place, all well on their way to becoming stock characters for a GDR *Volksstück*.

Written in 1960 during the party's strongest offensive toward agricultural collectivization, and premiering on 23 February 1961, also at the Volkstheater Halberstadt, *Women's Quarrel and Love's Cunning* perhaps comes closest to being "the" comedy of national and popular perspective. It can be seen both as a result, and, at the same time, as a vehicle of, the recent pro-agriculture policy in the GDR. Sakowski calls the play a farce, thus consciously trying to ally this play with a German literary tradition dating back to Hans Sachs, the famous "Meistersinger of Nürnberg," who wrote "popular" plays in the late sixteenth century.

Women's Quarrel exemplifies what "socialist national theater" means around 1960. It is an eclectic combination of the new socialist perspective and a goodly amount of traditional nationalistic pride in one's own cultural heritage. The *Schwank*, or farce, was truly the first popular (that is, German rather than classical or adapted) theater in German literary history. The fact that the origins of the genre are closely connected with the rise of the trades and guildsmen, the bourgeoisie of pre-capitalist sixteenth-century society, does not matter. What matters is simply that it is a genre which is German in origin, and is also representative of a social group that was mobilized toward power by historical developments, by that historical necessity to which the SED would like to ascribe events in the GDR since 7 October 1949. The fact that in the traditional farce and *Volksstück* the farmer was the butt of the jokes and satire does not prevent the remodeling of the form to do exactly the opposite, to upgrade and idealize the farmer's intellect and awareness.

In Sakowski's farce we are given a collectivized village with an inherent contradiction. There are two collectives in the same village, although one would be more economical and efficient, more beneficial not only to the individual members but also the state. The dominant female members of the two respective collectives, Paula and Minne, harbor personal animosities, and thus keep the collectives split. The plot strives for the resolution of their differences and the merger of the collectives "Harmony" (Eintracht) and "Peace" (Frieden) into one morally integral collective.

As one might expect, the use of the farce as a dramatic form entails some inherent dramatic limitations, and thus Sakowski does not really succeed in significantly raising the socialist perspective of this play. The play's conflict is resolved by the love subplot rather than by any new socialist awareness on the part of the combatants. Here, the son and daughter of the respective disputants are in love and cannot get together because of their bullheaded mothers. This, of course, takes away the possibility for social and economic development of the inherent contradiction, and makes the play not unlike a simplistic, individualized *Romeo and Juliet* in the not-so-socialist village.

In order to make Paula and Minne see eye to eye, the lovers conceive a strategy of tricks and misrepresentation, stock techniques of the traditional farce. They make Paula and Minne agree to a temporary merger of Peace and Harmony to impress some imaginary Russian visitors. When the Russians fail to show up and the lovers declare their responsibility for the hoax, the two quarrelers see the obvious advantages of the socialistically sound merger. When asked for their objections to a permanent merger, they must admit that their individual prejudices are insignificant in terms of the progress they have obstructed for years:

BERNHARD: And what do the brigade leaders think about the conciliation?
PAULA: Minne Martens and I . . .
MINNE: . . . both of us had . . .
PAULA: God yes, besides little things . . . never any quarrel.
MINNE: We've been at one with each other for a long time already. (*Handshake. Applause.*)[14]

Of course the message is simplistic: it is designed that way. The objective is to define, isolate, and humorously denounce individual stupidity on the part of the farmer—much in the fashion of the traditional farce—and to positively demonstrate the individual's decision to get rid of his personal motivations in favor of the collective good. Thus this type of play becomes an ideological tool during the recruiting process leading to the Socialist Spring. Here, of course, the didactic objective is no longer to convince the independent farmers to collectivize, but rather to convince inefficiently operating or competing collectives to increase their value as assets of the GDR by increasing efficiency by all possible means.

. Hermann Kähler sees this strongest current of the mainstream not only as a means of "plumbing the depth of this upheaval [collectivization] for its meaning in terms of human relationships and the national history,"[15] but also as having

[14] Helmut Sakowski, "Weiberzwist und Liebeslist," MS (Berlin: Henschelverlag Abteilung Bühnenbertrieb, [n.d.]), pp. 67–68.
[15] Kähler, *Gegenwart auf der Bühne*, p. 61.

"*a direct effect upon the social development.*"[16] In this connection it will suffice to list a number of the bucolic comedies of this period, all of which were similar in scope and directed expressly toward the popularization of the collectivization process. They appeared between 1958 and 1961, and include *The Love Potion (Der Liebes-trank* [1958]) by Werner Salchow; *Brothers Exchanged (Die vertauschten Brüder* [1959]) by Gustav von Wangenheim; *The Instructor Should Marry (Der Instrukteur soll heiraten* [1959]) by Jan Hall; *Alvin the Last One (Alwin der Letzte* [1959]) by Erich Heller and Margret Gruschmann-Reuter; and *Too Big for a Cowhide (Das geht auf keine Kuhhaut* [1960]) by Margret Gruschmann-Reuter.

Of these, *Alvin the Last One* had the broadest and most direct effect. It became a colloquial convention in the villages of the GDR that one mustn't be "Alvin the last one" to join the collective. In a review of the play, *Sonntag* wrote about this phenomenon: "Nothing speaks better for the extraordinary effectiveness of the play than the feeling which is developing in some villages of the Suhl District that no farmer wants to be *Alvin the Last One.*"[17] In the same essay, the reviewer Gerhard Ebert praises *Alvin* at the expense of Helmut Baierl's *The Inquiry*, which the reviewer considers a failure as a play about life in the country because it is, in his view, simply a theatrical version of an intellectual question.

These collective bucolics are essentially much like Sakowski's early work, the difference being merely that Sakowski is a better writer than the others. This official critical evaluation of Sakowski and his work is to the point: "The content and diction of Sakowski's dramas reveal an exact knowledge of the rural situation. . . . And his case especially demonstrates how the writer's fusion with life, in the sense of the Bitterfeld Conference, bears artistic fruit."[18] Official accolades of this sort attested to the nature of the cultural-political influences on the writers who produced these plays. In any case, official and deserving testimonials were not lacking. In Hermann Kähler's view—and his metaphorical view remains ominously official—the authors of these bucolic comedies succeeded in fulfilling their mission: "With their work, they succeeded in grasping the wheel of history and propelling the socialist development of agriculture."[19]

The current critiques leave no doubt, then, that quantitatively, qualitatively, and officially, the collective bucolics comprised the mainstream between 1957 and 1961. The utilitarian scope of these plays, and their openly tendentious ideological commitment to the party, made them ideal theater for the GDR. Aesthetic questions are legitimate, but not central in this context, for in the GDR traditional aesthetic values have been supplanted by criteria of a work's didactic effectiveness, its usefulness as a tool of political education. From the GDR

16 *Ibid.*
17 Gerhard Ebert, quoted in Kähler, p. 90.
18 *Schauspielführer*, II, 792.
19 Kähler, *Gegenwart auf der Bühne*, pp. 61–62.

perspective, if a play entertains the audience, *and* meets these criteria, as do these collective bucolics, then the play is "good." We must accept this in order to come to an understanding of the reciprocal relationships between a contemporary topical theater built on a base of Communist ideology and the society in which it functions.

History, however, provides us at this point with an unexpected bonus for those who prefer "good" theater in the traditional sense. With the mainstream solidly carrying them along, Strittmatter's *Dutchman's Bride* (*Die Holländerbraut* [1960]) and Helmut Baierl's *Frau Flinz* (1961) rise to the top of the genre, and are without a doubt the best combinations of political usefulness and artistic quality that the contemporary topical theater of the GDR has to offer during this era. *The Dutchman's Bride* premiered at the Deutsches Theater in Berlin on 10 June 1960 during the party's Socialist Spring; while *Frau Flinz*, written by Baierl with the cooperation of the Berliner Ensemble, was first produced at the site of its origin on 8 June 1961. Both plays openly display the heritage of Bertolt Brecht, which is not surprising, since both authors gained their practical experience in the theater from that quarter—Strittmatter from Brecht himself, and Baierl from the Ensemble, and especially from the famous actress Helene Weigel, the widow of Brecht who at the time was the director of the Ensemble.

Besides the obvious influence of Brecht's dramaturgical views, which already differentiate the two plays from the bucolic mainstream in matters of form and dramatic technique, the main difference is that of perspective. Strittmatter and Baierl have chosen to distance themselves from their subject matter by viewing village life and the agricultural complex historically. Both plays therefore exhibit a broad episodic plot structure akin to that found in Brecht's plays. Both authors try to demonstrate the impact of the new socialist order upon the individual characters. Like Brecht at his best, they realize that a person's ideological development, the changeover from capitalist to socialist thought processes, sometimes spans a person's lifetime, and thus cannot be credibly shown in the two to three hours of playing time if plot must correspond slavishly to the actual time portrayed. In real life, such "conversion" takes considerably longer.

Baierl's dramatic technique differentiates itself from Strittmatter's only in his "epic" extension of space to include all the sectors of GDR life from farm to village to city. While Frau Flinz moves from one locality to another to demonstrate the universality of the slow, sometimes accidental and unintentional development of her personal socialist perspective, for Hanna Tainz, the Dutchman's Bride, the various difficult social and individual problems thrown her way by Strittmatter are all relative to one setting, her village. These differences correspond to differences in subject matter requirements. Baierl's heroine is a refugee looking for a home, and thus must continue travelling until her development is complete. Hanna Tainz, on the other hand, already has a home, and actively grasps the opportunity to work toward the new state and the new life as a historical mission from the start.

Both plays excellently follow the cultural policy of their time in centering not only on the socialist upheaval in agriculture, but also in choosing the development of the socialist woman as the major idea content of the works. Female heroines in plays with overtones of socialist ideology are nothing new, of course. Bertolt Brecht, the dramaturgical influence in these plays, especially favored female protagonists for that kind of play, as is evident in his *The Mother (Die Mutter)* and *The Rifles of Mrs. Carrar (Die Gewehre der Frau Carrar)*.

Both *The Dutchman's Bride* and *Frau Flinz* deal primarily with developmental heroines: the women undergo changes in their basic world views from the play's beginnings to the plays' ends. Since in both plays the action spans a crucial historical period in the national development of the GDR, the changes the heroines undergo presumably are characteristic and therefore important for the understanding of the socialist woman. It is interesting to observe how each playwright artistically resolves the difficulties of this type of developmental characterization.

Strittmatter first established the peasant background of Hanna Tainz and then demonstrated presocialist society's supposedly characteristic fusion of social and individual exploitation through Hanna's lover, who impregnates, disclaims, and finally denounces her. Strittmatter makes things somewhat easy for himself by making Hanna a girl of exceptional intelligence and the daughter of a worker with a fully developed "proletarian consciousness." After the war, as the mayor of the village, having gained quasi-mythic stature in the community as a martyr of Nazi oppression, she practices a humane socialism of kindness, care, and personal involvement long before "socialism" is even a term of any consequence in that part of Germany. This comes from her natural inclinations, and not from her rational perception and awareness. Her lover returns, and succeeds in bamboozling her once again. The flesh, alas, is still weak. There is a repeat performance of the pregnancy, and this time Erdmann, the culprit, tries to use his personal power over Hanna for purposes of reactionary provocation.

A small riot in the village, a riot incited by Erdmann, proves to be the point of crisis at which Hanna's rational awareness, which has grown over the past years through the actions and influences of some progressive thinkers around her, meets her natural inclinations head on. It is a point of decision, and Hanna acts against Erdmann—against her "natural, weak female" inclinations—in favor of the coming state. And here lies the weakness of Strittmatter's plot. The inherent contradiction between individual inclination and social responsibility is not resolved through a developmental process, but by a crisis choice much in the same way Fred Reichwald got out of the corner into which he had written himself at the end of *Maria Diehl Takes a Chance*. The only difference is that the overall quality of Strittmatter's play is such that this weakness hardly hurts the play.

Although it loses some of its lustre as a result of this flaw, it remains intact as a rare example of a didactic and yet entertaining play.

Everyone who has written about *Frau Flinz*—and it is one of the most written-about GDR plays—starts with a reference to Brecht's *Mother Courage*. Now that we have paid our homage to that tradition, there are other things to be discussed. The most interesting critical problem of the play is the development of the comic heroine. Martha Augusta Wilhelmina Flinz has, over the years, developed an anti-power structure ideology solidly rooted in the slave-wisdom mentality by which the underprivileged have outwitted the privileged throughout history. She has become so expert at "survival" that she has managed to save five of her sons from the Nazis' war after a sixth perished. And she intends to save them from the new system too: "And they can yell '*Siegheil*' or '*Rotfront*,' but whoever reaches for them gets his arm chopped off."[20] Now a refugee after the war, she refuses to distinguish between systems in moral terms, but relies on her well-developed survival techniques to outwit any system and live in temporary peace after each upheaval.

Every one of her strategies backfires, however. When she has her sons sham a study of the *Communist Manifesto*, the content convinces them. One by one she loses her sons to the future, to the emerging socialist system. Once she is reduced to having only herself to worry about, the pattern comes to completion as she loses even herself to the new order, and in fact uses her pragmatic wisdom for progressive positive action rather than passive defense maneuvers. Finally she reaches the stature of a national heroine as the founder of one of the first agricultural collectives. With this final turn of events, Baierl also succumbs to the maudlin sentimentality that can now be termed characteristic of the final acts of most of the plays of this period. It is reminiscent of the emotionalism of *The Dutchman's Bride;* in view of the play's reflection of the general qualitative improvements within the mainstream, it is tolerable. Werner Mittenzwei analyzes parts of Baierl's technique in this play in a very positive evaluation of the Brecht influence:

> Baierl's alienation technique distinguishes itself—and this makes him a true student of Brecht—in that it exposes the character of the socialist social order to the audience. He demonstrates the persuasive power of the new social order, even over those who resist its influence. Baierl alienates a character or a process by confronting the contingencies and resulting actions of the exploitative society with the new social processes. The resulting divergence is used by the author for historical differentiation, and to explicate the new order. Correspondingly, Baierl inserts the alienation in such a way that comedy arises strongly from the action, and flavors the plot and characters.[21]

---

[20] Helmut Baierl, *Frau Flinz*, in *Stücke* (Berlin: Henschelverlag, 1969), p. 60.

[21] Mittenzwei, *Gestaltung und Gestalten im modernen Drama* (Berlin: Weimar: Aufbau, 1965), pp. 274–75.

From the dramatic techniques used by Strittmatter and Baierl, we can distill the essence of two of the three basic character types of the socialist contemporary drama of the GDR. The two women respectively represent the developmental character (Frau Flinz) and the sudden-change character (Hanna Tainz). The developmental character is led through a series of disjointed experiences, each of which requires a decision. Each new decision alters the previous situation and presses the character forward. The suddenly changed character, on the other hand, reaches a new way of behavior and new human qualities "instantaneously." These swift conversions are still contingent upon experiences and thought processes leading to the crisis point. But they are culminations of a process more subjective than the growth in awareness that changes Martha Flinz step by step, even without her knowledge, the dramatic irony being the essence of the comic element in the play.

These last two works we have considered are the culmination of a specific development of GDR drama before the border action of 1961. This development, which has too long been neglected by critics and scholars, can be considered only in conjunction with the policies of the SED, from which it is inseparable. This study tended toward the identification of the mainstream not mainly to put the last two plays into true perspective as a part of a broad new tradition, but primarily to isolate the major dramatic production of the GDR before the border action of 1961 in terms of its function in that developing society.

VIII.
The Bourgeois Aesthetic: Up Against the Wall

The single most important event in the history of the German Democratic Republic is without a doubt the border action of 13 August 1961. Although mostly identified as the raising of the Berlin Wall by Western observers, this action goes far beyond the laying of brick upon brick in the streets of Berlin. The national significance of this move for the GDR is rivalled only by the formation of the Republic itself.

In political terms, 13 August 1961, despite all its measures, supplied only a symbolic division of Germany. In fact, the real division had been concretely achieved through diplomatic moves among Eastern European countries over the previous few years. The process of active disassociation from Western influences began at the Cultural Conference of 1957, and anti-Western views were officially propagated in the ensuing years. At the Fifth Party Congress of 1958, the SED postulated that the standard of living in the GDR would surpass that of Bonn's Republic by 1961. It further declared an active "status war" on the other Germany, and claimed that the GDR was the only legal German nation. By 1961, the party itself could see that such goals and claims were totally unrealistic. It was, however, an easy transition from the postulation of national pride of achievement to the narrow line of political separatism that resulted from the gross failure of the 1958 plan. With their nation's economic progress thwarted by recurring problems of planning, production, and execution, problems exacerbated by the continual loss of valuable manpower to the West, the GDR policymakers decided on positive offensive action rather than a quiet capitulation.

No one could have been more surprised than the political strategists of East Berlin and Moscow when their desperate move had an overall positive effect on the GDR's population. The border action was, in fact, well worth the bad publicity that had to be taken in stride. It demonstrated, once and for all, the permanence of the state and its sovereignty. Finally things were drawn in black and white. Although there was serious disagreement even among party members, unanimous approval was not of first importance. The sides were defined. The third-way seekers, the compromisers, the dreamers, and those with rubber spines saw the writing on the wall. The result among the population of the GDR was shock, accompanied gradually by a new officially unexpected respect for their government—a respect gained through an exercise of power, the most persuasive of political arguments.

The allies of the GDR quickly supported the action by proclaiming the sovereignty of this and not the other German state. Between 3 and 4 August 1961, a week before the border action, the Eastern European "people's republics" had drawn up plans for a separate peace with "Germany"—i.e., with the GDR. After the action, on 2 October 1961, Poland and Czechoslovakia did sign sovereign peace treaties with East Berlin. This new international recognition brought with it another national action, the draft. On 24 January 1962, the People's Parliament proclaimed a military service law for all able-bodied citizens. Six months later the Soviet Union provided this new "legal" Germany with another national prize, a capital city. Protests by England, France, and the United States notwithstanding, the Soviets withdrew their administrative arm from East Berlin, officially the Soviet Sector of the Four Power Agreements, and turned the seat of government over to the GDR, which flaunted "Berlin, the capital of the GDR" in the faces of the Western powers and the "provisional" Bonn regime. Thus 1961 saw not just the building of the Wall, but also a quick series of political moves among the Warsaw Pact nations which actually define the GDR's present standing among all the European nations.

The cultural and especially the literary policy immediately following the border action demonstrates no radical change from the prevalent policies set at the Cultural Conference of 1957, the Fifth Party Congress of 1958, and the ensuing Bitterfeld Conference of 1959. It was a matter of power politics reinforcing the existing cultural policy. Against a background of overt political actions directed toward national security, the Socialist Unity Party continued the active propagation of literature that demonstrated a unified national perspective. The theater offered nothing radically new. The new wave of industrial-topical literature officially triggered by the Bitterfeld Conference in 1959 brought forth the first nationwide production of a dramatic work by a "writing worker" with Horst Kleineidam's *Schmidt's Millions* (*Der Millionenschmidt*) in 1962. Following another pre-Wall tradition, the socialist bucolic drama reached its pinnacle of perspective and quality with Helmut Sakowski's *Rocks on the Road* (*Steine im Weg*), also in 1962. But while the more or less "party line" playwrights enjoyed official sanction to the point of lionization, the wrath of the party was felt by those who had continued to exhibit "revisionistic" and "bourgeois" tendencies during the time of national crisis.

One of the targets was the GDR Academy of Arts, whose publication, the revered intellectual journal *Sinn und Form*, had fallen into disfavor mainly through its editor, Peter Huchel, who was later chastised as a "traitor to the workers."[1] Huchel was, and still is, one of Germany's best and most respected poets. *Sinn und Form*'s aesthetic and philosophical integrity under his editorship was a far cry from the "people's culture" proclaimed by Alfred Kurella, Alexander Abusch, and Willi Stoph (later the president of the GDR), who carried the banner of the party at a conference of the Academy with the Council of Ministers on 30 March 1962. At this meeting the lyric poet Huchel was effectively dispatched to an isolation that lasted almost ten years. Stoph accused the Academy of not being firmly committed to the national goals of the GDR. He promised that henceforth "it will be impossible for any artist, as was the case with many before 13 August 1961, to live as a traveller between two worlds, and to think with a double perspective."[2] The venerable proletarian author Willi Bredel supported this view and even took up the official phraseology in taking exception to *Sinn und Form*'s rather cosmopolitan style: "This periodical, if I can speak frankly, was, despite its high artistic level, essentially a traveller between two worlds. Therefore it is necessary that we finally bring about a change."[3]

This change was nothing less than the suppression of "traditional bourgeois" aesthetics. The cultural awareness of the political leaders of the GDR had moved into the scientific age, and, from their point of view, justifiably so. Communist political cultures demand that an artist be in reciprocal contact with the "real world" around him. They further demand that his work reflect a societal mandate and incorporate a social purpose. In short, they require that he make things of socially utilitarian value to those around him, and thus, also to himself. This aesthetic perspective is diametrically opposed to the toleration of the continuation of a subjective, individualized tradition. The so-called "artist" of Western tradition had finally been "exposed" in the GDR in his "true" nature as a neurotic, frustrated social misfit who had been marketing critical evaluations of a society to which he could not "positively relate" in the form of the literature of the nineteenth century and its contemporary extensions. In the GDR, "individualistic" art, historically considered the province of "frustrated bourgeois intellectuals," becomes theoretically and practically more and more obsolete.

If there was any doubt about the new rigidity and energy behind this newest antibourgeois literary policy, it was dispelled forthwith at the Sixth Party Congress of the SED. This Congress, held in January of 1963, postulated the final victory of the socialist production methods and the arrival of the socialist society.

---

[1] Huchel reports on the occurrences after his censure, when he protested as parts of his library were being confiscated: "I stood there and complained, but the official had learned all the sayings by heart: He quoted Kurt Hager, who had called me 'the English lord of Wilhemshorst,' referred to the Sixth Party Congress at which I had been called a traitor to the workers' cause" (interview with Peter Huchel by Hansjakob Stehle, *Die Zeit*, 6 June 1972, p. 10).

[2] Stoph, *Neues Deutschland*, 13 April 1962.

[3] Bredel, *ibid.*

The cultural policy emanating from the Congress, however, showed a marked similarity to the anti-formalism/objectivism campaign waged ten years earlier which had dominated—and restricted—the development of GDR contemporary drama during the first Five-Year Plan.

The emergence at the Sixth Congress of Professor Kurt Hager as the head of the Ideological Commission of the Politbüro—a job not unlike that of grand inquisitor—marked the rededication to a rigid line. Freshly empowered by the party, Hager lost no time in setting the new tone. At a joint conference of the Politbüro, the Executive Committee of the Council of Ministers, and writers and artists on 25 and 26 March 1963, Hager explicated the resolutions of the Sixth Congress to those who might have doubted the gospel. In his address, he concluded that the resolutions of the Congress were not only for a few enthusiasts to follow voluntarily, but that the rededication to the Bitterfeld Road was mandatory for producers of cultural goods. Hager identifies Bitterfeld's impetus toward people's culture not as an aesthetic issue, but rather as a social-political one:

> A few writers and artists regard these resolutions with diffidence and rejection. . . .
> The question is by no means only one of accepting the Bitterfeld Road—whether or not the artist should change his way of living and whether he should turn to contemporary subjects. Aesthetics is not the primary issue. The central issue is political and concerns the cultural policy of the party and the government.[4]

But Hager quickly left such theoretical generalities behind and turned to a specific attack on individual authors and on works which were found lacking in identification with party ideology and commitment to the goals of all the working people. In his discourse about theater, it was the vulnerable Peter Hacks (literally a traveller between two worlds, having come from the Federal Republic of Germany) who was again singled out as a major transgressor.

The theatrical debacle of 1962 had been a revised Wolfgang Langhoff production of Hacks's *The Cares and the Power* at the Deutsches Theater, a production Kurt Hager indicted for "distortion of our socialist reality, and schematic characterization."[5] In the same speech to the writers, Hager made a detailed analysis of Hacks's mistakes and thus sets the ground rules for dramatic production for the years to come by negative example.[6] Hager's scathing polemic

---

[4] Hager, "Parteilichkeit und Volksverbundenheit unserer Literatur und Kunst," *Neues Deutschland*, 30 March 1963.

[5] *Ibid.*

[6] "We believe that Hacks has not yet grasped the real life in our Republic, the pathos of the socialist effort, the new character of our human relationships and the social relationships. He looks at human relationships primarily from a position of bourgeois psychology. How else could he seek the motivating forces in the characters of his play almost exclusively in the drive for material possessions, the fight for money, and in sexuality?

"The tendency toward political mistakes becomes evident in this play wherever Hacks speaks

represented the party's final reckoning with Hacks. Hacks was forthwith removed from his dramaturgical duties at the Deutsches Theater.

But this was not the first time that Hacks's cares had clashed with those of power. Even earlier, his colleagues at the German Writers' Union had also ostracized him. In the March 1963 issue of their publication, *Neue Deutsche Literatur*, the editors, speaking as a committee of the whole, washed their hands of any connection with the playwright. The "Final Position of the Secretariat of the German Writers' Union in Reference to *The Cares and the Power*" ("Abschließende Stellungnahme des Sekretariats des DSV zu *Die Sorgen und die Macht*") reads, in part: "In the play the reality and the people of the working class are distorted, their conflicts simplified. Our reality is seen from a petit-bourgeois, vulgarized-Marxist base and is covered with robes of abstract dialectics."[7]

Wolfgang Langhoff also entered the scene. In another effort to rescue his own career, he again exercised the Brutus Maneuver, this time upon Peter Hacks. On 7 April 1963, Langhoff engaged in the obligatory self-criticism in *Neues Deutschland*, but managed to place the greater share of the blame upon Hacks and his play: "*The Cares and the Power* . . . has distorted the most important question, the question of the confidence of the people, the working class, in their party, and thus it played into the hands of the party's enemies."[8] But this time the party's displeasure with the developments at the Deutsches Theater during Langhoff's leadership was not to be appeased. Kurt Hager's spring cleaning action at the Deutsches Theater was thorough, and Langhoff found himself on the doorstep, a location usually reserved for his dramaturgical assistants.

There could no longer be any doubt. The socialist national theater had indeed arrived. In the official volume *Theater Bilanz*, Manfred Nössig and Hans Gerald Otto define the goals of the theater after the Sixth Party Congress. As the most important objective they see the effort "to demonstrate artistically the departure from the effects of the classbound society which has been achieved in everyday reality."[9] Since the Congress had postulated socialism as a completed reality that necessarily ended the massive social conflict of classbound societies, emphasis was now upon "the characterization of the continuing success of essentially likeminded socialist personalities in their practical relationships, their

about the perspective and the future. Again and again he constructs a basic contradiction between today and the communist future. Hacks sees only the birthmarks of the capitalist past in today's society, and cannot see the new and the beautiful aspects in the change of the human situation. Besides the lack of a view of beauty, if we must judge by this play, he also lacks a view of the greatness of our present epoch in the transition from capitalism to socialism" (*ibid.*).

7 "Abschließende Stellungnahme," *Neue Deutsche Literatur*, XI/2 (1963), 117–18.

8 Langhoff, *Neues Deutschland*, 17 April 1963.

9 Nössig and Otto, "Grundlagen einer Bilanz," in *Theater Bilanz: Bühnen der DDR: Eine Bilddokumentation 1945–1968*, ed. Christoph Funke et al. (Berlin: Henschelverlag, 1971), p. 29.

mastering of the scientific-technical revolution, and the international class struggle."[10]

These objectives were nothing new for the mainstream of dramatic production, however. The newer breed of party-oriented playwrights, whose work was rooted in and nurtured by the continuous people-oriented cultural policies originating at the Cultural Conference of 1957, only found their latest works ideologically substantiated. Already in 1962 three new plays, Helmut Baierl's *The Thirteenth* (*Die Dreizehnte*), Helmut Sakowski's *Rocks on the Road* (*Steine im Weg*), and Horst Kleineidam's *Schmidt's Millions* were so exemplary of the socialist topical drama called for by the Sixth Congress that they may have served as models for the theoreticians.

The "Ten Agitational Scenes" of *The Thirteenth* teeter precariously between political engagement and blatant political opportunism. The scenes that Baierl wrote in collaboration with Erwin Burkert and Herbert Fischer were first produced by the Workers' Ensemble of the Elektro-Apparate Werke (electrical appliance works; EAW) in Berlin-Treptow at the 1962 Workers' Festival (*Arbeiterfestspiele*). The authors reduce the conflicts leading up to the border action of 13 August 1961 to the economic drain on the GDR caused by East Berliners who worked in West Berlin, known as Border Crossers (*Grenzgänger*). This simplifying process is carried over into the necessary schematic figures which represent conflicting ideologies. Reducing agitation propaganda to the dialectics of black and white, good and evil, the scenes concentrate on characterizing West Berliners and sympathizers as spineless cowards and opportunists, and NAV (National People's Army) men, party members, and their sympathizers as the heroic vanguard of the working class who energetically jump into the breach to defend the principles of international socialism against the ogres west of the Friedrichstraße. Baierl loses credibility mainly in his persistent attempts to romanticize the average GDR citizen's reaction to the border action. This results in a sticky sentimental overlay, under which the possibilities for proborder policy agitation propaganda collapse. Just two excerpts will suffice to illustrate Baierl's maudlin treatment of this ostensibly revolutionary event. In a scene titled "Stumm Police" (after West Berlin's Chief of Police), an East Berliner who has been visiting his brother-in-law in the Wedding section of West Berlin is advised by the West Berlin police that the border is being closed:

FIRST POLICEMAN: Stop! Hey, man, this is the way to the East. The West is over there.
THE MAN: Thanks. (*He keeps going.*)
SECOND POLICEMAN: Stop! Listen. Turn around! You wanted to stay. You just decided.

10 *Ibid.*

117

THE MAN (*comes back*): You're right! I'm going across. (*He goes and comes back.*) I just thought about something: One transition in life is enough for me. (*He leaves in the direction of the East. He shouts:*) Brothers, I'm coming![11]

In another scene, Schulze, an East Berlin railroad employee, visits his old school chum who is now a senator of West Berlin. When they hear noises along the border, they realize what is happening. The man asks Schulze to stay, but he politely declines. When he is asked why he doesn't want to come to the West's "good life," Schulze replies: "I don't know how to explain it to you. On our side...life is...more normal...maybe that's why."[12] Thus, Baierl demonstrates the national solidarity of the GDR by having his characters exercise their freedom of choice in favor of petit-bourgeois normalcy. This is hardly in the best interests of agitational theater, nor does it demonstrate a particularly socialist perspective. Instead, Baierl comes up with an abundance of the national perspective and an emotionally positive view of the border action. It is, in short, a public relations play, selling the Wall to the people.

While Baierl showed the physical separation of GDR society from the classbound West with questionable results, Helmut Sakowski's *Rocks on the Road* postulates the socialist society. Sakowski's main objective is to demonstrate how individuals saturated by their historical classbound thought processes undergo the change into the new human beings required by the new social contingencies which are already reality. Originating as one of the most successful television plays in GDR history during the 1960–61 season, *Rocks on the Road* was first presented onstage at the Maxim Gorki Theater in October 1962. Sakowski, a modest writer energetic in his party orientation, has no difficulty turning the contingencies of a non-antagonistic social structure into solid entertaining drama.

In an effort to write positively and optimistically while maintaining perspectives of social significance—without inherent social conflict—Sakowski employs the disparity of appearance and reality as his basic source of tension. The author confronts his characters with an advanced socio-economic system in which they must function. But the individual consciousness of the characters has not advanced beyond a merely formal acceptance of the new realities. In most cases, Sakowski's characters are only going through the motions of socialist life, while their basic attitudes and thought processes are still derived from their presocialist behavior patterns. This becomes evident mostly in personal, emotional relationships. Thus Sakowski's excellent dramatic tension results from the dialectic process of bringing a character's individual consciousness up to date with his social reality. Since the emphasis is solidly on the process of integration into the new system, which is blocked only by attitudes derived from obsolete social roles,

[11] Helmut Baierl, *Der Dreizehnte: Zehn Agitationsszenen*, in *Stücke* (Berlin: Henschelverlag, 1969), p. 129.

[12] *Ibid.*, p. 135.

Sakowski successfully avoids any individualized psychological excesses. Even though an independent farmer's integration into a collective depends upon the successful transformation of his individual consciousness, this individual process, when coupled with the social and political implication of the collective, becomes a social process first, and an individual act second. It is this quality that makes *Rocks on the Road* an ideal example of a new type of play, the contemporary socialist drama about the post-capitalist society in the GDR, the significant social drama without massive black and white conflicts.

This does not mean that Sakowski's play becomes a sociological case study; far from it. Besides their socioeconomic relationships—which form a theoretical base—the three major characters are connected by a massive emotional conflict which could, in itself, carry the dramatic action. From the traditional *Volksstück* Sakowski borrows earthy human beings (*Triebmenschen*), a vital egocentric farmer and a former servant girl of bewildering sexuality. (As in a *Volksstück*, the epithet "the dark one" is used in connection with her name.) Ten years earlier, when Lisa was a servant, Bergemann, the farmer, had impregnated her and cast her aside because she was poor. But Sakowski advances the clock on them by ten years, and their natural vitality is only an undercurrent in their personalities, and actually represents their outdated social roles as farmer and servant, which are already obsolete.

The farmer Bergemann offers to bring his herd of high-yield dairy cattle into the collective under the condition that he be in charge of dairy production. Lisa Martin, who now holds that position, is against this move. But Paul, the chairman of the collective, decides in favor of Bergemann and the members agree. As a result, Lisa is removed from the job which had made her a human being in her own estimation.

Paul's decision, which is for the good of the collective and GDR society, dehumanizes an individual through the obsolete thought processes that force the decision: (1) Bergemann comes to the collective with demands tied to the exercise of power through property, the herd. (2) In their quest to rationalize production and to increase profit, the members disregard the fact that the acceptance of Bergemann's conditions means the affirmation of a morally inferior individual at the expense of a morally superior one.

The strong undercurrent of the emotional relationships of the protagonists as they affect their social roles is the key to the popular success of the play. Even the resolution of the conflict—which one might expect to slide into the tacky side of sentimentalism—remains dialectically sound, and still optimistic. Bergemann finds himself rejected as an individual by both Lisa and his own wife. He realizes that his egocentric motivations are at the root of the conflict; but he also realizes that his individuality must be at one with his social role in order for him to be the producer he must be to satisfy his natural inclinations. He knows that he cannot function in the new social structure with his obsolete consciousness. Therefore,

119

in a courageous/cowardly act (he could stay and face the music), he strikes out on his own to work as a laborer: "I'm curious. I want to look around on the construction sites, among the people."[13] He is faced with taking the huge step from his historical past into the socialist present. But though he is ready to take it, he needs time:

> ALFRED: It took me half my life to get this far. You can't expect me to turn myself inside out overnight and end up being one of you . . . which is what you demand . . . no. That's too much. I know I've got to start over. So I'm starting by leaving.
> PAUL: Where do you plan to go?
> ALFRED: It's a big country. New things are everywhere.[14]

On the surface, the plot may seem simplistic. It is. But the topic and the dialogue reveal a degree of substance that makes the play one of the milestones of GDR drama.

In November 1962, the Städtische Bühnen Leipzig presented Horst Kleineidam's *Schmidt's Millions*, the first professional production of a dramatic work by a writing worker. Kleineidam, the son of a shoemaker, was born in Gebhardsdorf in 1932. With a severely limited formal education, he started working as a laborer in a textile mill and later became a carpenter's apprentice. Endowed with a love of adventure and a basic restlessness, he crossed the GDR border for West Germany in 1952. There, in the classic style of the twentieth-century drifter, he worked as a farm laborer, coal miner and construction worker while experimenting as a writer in his free time. He returned to the GDR in 1958 and settled into the role of a construction carpenter, writing for amateur theater as a hobby. His real talent developed with the Bitterfeld Movement of writing workers. Kleineidam's major "literary" purpose is to develop strategies for mastering the practical day-to-day conflicts facing people who work with their hands in an increasingly bureaucratic society.

Kleineidam's first drama, *Schmidt's Millions*, was the direct result of the Bitterfeld slogan, "Worker, reach for your pen" (*Greif zur Feder, Kumpel*). The play came at an opportune time. Produced two months before the Sixth Party Congress, it served to punctuate the success of the movement of writing workers while serving as an incentive for further travel along the Bitterfeld Road. Kleineidam's play draws heavily on the author's experience on construction sites and develops a conflict similar to the one Sakowski resolved in *Rocks on the Road*. Kleineidam's characters have also accepted life in the new socialist system and are successful in their outward adaptation. But there are strong remnants of petit-bourgeois thinking which undermine the essence of the socialist way of life. In a

---

[13] Helmut Sakowski, *Steine im Weg*, in *Sozialistische Dramatik: Autoren der Deutschen Demokratischen Republik* (Berlin: Henschelverlag, 1968), p. 295.

[14] *Ibid.*, p. 294.

wise maneuver, Kleineidam does not overextend himself, but restricts his situations to what he knows best, socialist production methods and workers' thought processes.

Gerhard Schmidt is the brigade leader of a group of masons. Although the brigade leader is an essential cog of the socialist production method, Schmidt's actions are actually those of a foreman in the old capitalist system. The brigade is the socialist production unit which functions as a collective and not only determines the organization of labor on the job, but also enters into the social, cultural and personal activities of its members. Gerhard Schmidt nullifies this concept by ruling his brigade with an iron fist. He brings material benefits to the brigade because his commitment to socialism is simply that "the ruble must roll."[15] He analyzes life as being, and as having been for a few thousand years, "a matter of money, women and food."[16]

The large earnings accompanying this obsolete ideology also bring with them substandard quality. To overcome this, Schmidt imports his brother, a party member and an excellent mason. He wants to kill two birds with one stone, for Schmidt reasons that the progressive appearance of having a party member in his brigade will overshadow the defects. Walter Schmidt, however, will not allow himself to be used in this manner. Instead, he turns the brigade into a true collective by appealing to the individuals' pride in their trade; by raising their consciousness concerning the national importance of the work they are doing; and by exposing the reactionary base of his brother's leadership.

This social conflict in the play is largely superseded by the archetypal emotional conflict, the rivalry of two brothers. Kleineidam increases the dramatic tension further by insisting on a love triangle between Gerhard, Walter, and Gerhard's wife, Helga. This makes for solid theater, but also weakens the overall perspective of the play by individualizing the real conflict. One wonders for an instant whether the socialist content of the play is not merely opportunistic sugar-coating on an otherwise hackneyed dramatic conflict lifted from the dusty pages of German "bourgeois" theater history. For in fact, under the shadow of the genuine emotional conflict of the love triangle, the dialectics of upgrading the characters' social consciousness become almost invisible.

But Kleineidam met the plan for literary production. He characterized a situation from everyday productive life, and dramatized some basic difficulties in the socialist production method. Unlike Hacks, who wonders if these difficulties could be inherent in the system—which is heresy—Kleineidam, a master carpenter himself, ascribes all of the difficulties to the backward thought processes of individuals, thus giving the system a clean bill of health. As a final note of opti-

---

[15] Horst Kleineidam, "Der Millionenschmidt," MS (Berlin: Henschelverlag Abteilung Bühnen-vertrieb, 1963), p. 3.

[16] *Ibid.*, p. 20.

mism, even Gerhard Schmidt, who had been characterized as a reactionary tyrant, becomes convinced by the criticism of his colleagues, and accepts three months of demotion in order to prove himself a worthy socialist. He does realize, however, that it will be a hard transition: "Nothing is like it used to be. It's all changed. I don't know if I can handle it."[17] But armed with a new collective perspective, one of his colleagues counters with the final line of the play: "We will help you."[18]

These three plays of 1962 define the essential objectives of the contemporary topical GDR drama to the present day. Looking to these plays as models, the Sixth Party Congress continued a theater policy which was rooted in the Cultural Conference of 1957, and which was instrumental in bringing forth the new type of socialist theater play that dominates the GDR stage from the sixties into the seventies. It is a drama which finally does without the extra-societal bogeyman as antagonist. It affirms the system and concentrates mainly on demonstrating the integration of initially reluctant individuals into the socialist order that has become the determining factor for all human activities.

Already in 1964, Hermann Kähler, trying to isolate the "emergence of a new type of theater play" ("das Hervortreten eines neuen Stücktypus"),[19] developed socialist party line commitment as an aesthetic category—a criterion for this type of play—echoing Hager's earlier call for a political aesthetic.[20] Since these dramatic works are a basic cultural political tool of the society upon which they reflect, it is, for that society's committed functionaries, a valid category. Helmut Baierl, Helmut Sakowski, and Horst Kleineidam succeeded in developing dramatic works that satisfied the new criteria and confirmed their practical ascendancy.

---

[17] *Ibid.*, p. 103.

[18] *Ibid.*

[19] Kähler, *Gegenwart auf der Bühne* (Berlin: Henschelverlag, 1966), p. 12.

[20] Kähler formulates: "The principle of socialist orientation and commitment as an aesthetic category enriches our plays by one essential artistic characteristic: our drama took the dynamism, the effect as a socially developmental force, from the revolutionary socialist drama forged by the working class in the [previous] capitalist society. That's the source of its desire to change not only the individual, but also to force the change and progressive development of the whole society" (*ibid.*).

IX.
Heavy Traffic on the Party Line: The Plays of 1963–1964

In 1963 and 1964 a veritable wave of major dramatic works reached the stages of the German Democratic Republic. This wave demonstrated Hermann Kähler's—and Kurt Hager's—major criteria for "the new type of theater play." First, the plays have as their central subject matter the development of socialist living patterns in the GDR. Secondly, the authors of these plays demonstrate their unwavering commitment to the party's principles. This is evident in their perspectives on social, economic, and political issues, which necessarily determine the ideological content of their plays.

Joachim Knauth's *The Campaign* (*Die Kampagne*) was presented by the Worker's Theater Muskau on 1 May 1963; the Maxim Gorki Theater staged Rainer Kerndl's *His Children* (*Seine Kinder*) on 7 October 1963; *Barbara*, by Harald Hauser, first played in Rostock on 1 February 1964; Horst Salomon's *Fool's Gold* (*Katzengold*) appeared in Gera on 11 June of the same year; Rostock saw another premiere on 5 July with Kuba's (Kurt Barthel's) dramatic poem *terra incognita;* and, finally this flurry of theatrical activity concluded with the premiere of Claus Hammel's *Nine O'Clock at the Roller Coaster* (*Um neun an der Achterbahn*) at the Maxim Gorki Theater on 4 October 1964.

Joachim Knauth prefaces his first contemporary drama by citing these words of the Russian dramatist Nikolai Gogol: "And he who hasn't the courage to laugh about his own mistakes had better not laugh at all."[1] With this epigraph, Knauth makes a brilliant foray into the semi-virgin territory of comic satire, a genre which had been unexplored since Heinar Kipphardt's *Shakespeare, Where Are You?* ten years earlier. And like Kipphardt's play, *The Campaign* was a resounding popular success. The similarities between the two plays continue. Knauth, having also been a dramaturgical assistant at the Deutsches Theater, takes

---

[1] Joachim Knauth, "Die Kampagne," MS (Berlin: Henschelverlag Abteilung Bühnenvertrieb, 1963), p. 4.

Gogol's formulation to heart and subjects the complacent wing of GDR theater to some well-placed satiric jabs. But the most impressive element of Knauth's work is his expertise in making genuine theatrical fun while never sacrificing his overall commitment to the socialist perspective for the sake of a joke. In an afterword, Knauth himself characterizes his particular form of comic satire:

> Satire has many forms, in this case that of the comedy of types with a cabaret-like element. Some will find cabaret-like elements in the theater offensive, especially if one has elevated concepts of plot and character psychology. But this element is advantageous for the message because it permits considerably more attacks on the object of satire than could possibly be permitted in a plot conforming to the standard dramaturgical cookbook.[2]

This approach turns the comedy into a shooting gallery where the foibles of the new socialist society are set up and subsequently shot down. Using the random example of a People's Shoe Factory, Knauth unmasks the peculiar kind of opportunism which he sees rampant in the institutions of the GDR. This opportunism is the vice of insecure individuals in leading positions who follow the letter of every party resolution—thereby negating the revolutionary spirit the party's resolutions are designed to promote. These basically "bourgeois" individuals are the greatest roadblocks on the way to an improved form of socialism. Two such roadblocks, the marketing manager of the People's Shoe Store and the plant manager of the People's Shoe Factory, accuse each other of this fault:

> SPECK (*critically*): I see the evil stems from you yourself.
> ZEISIG: What evil?
> SPECK: The so-called new form.
> ZEISIG: True, and with that I am following the party's call for daring.
> SPECK: That's not daring, that's avant-gardism! Socialist daring is daring with moderation.
> ZEISIG: You're a nit-picker! The last Plenary Meeting demanded that we be daring!
> SPECK (*superior tone*): Wait until the next Plenary Meeting.
> ZEISIG (*excited*): People like you think only from one Plenary Meeting to the next, while completely missing the point of the resolutions![3]

Speck's confident manner, however, makes Zeisig, the factory manager, insecure, and he becomes guilty of the things he criticizes Speck for. Zeisig is afraid to stand his ground because he might be criticized in *Neues Deutschland*, which he regards as a fate worse than death. "Once they start criticizing, it's all over. Then the only salvation is self-criticism."[4] Therefore, Zeisig institutes a campaign to increase the socialist awareness of the employees, hoping thus to

[2] *Ibid.*, p. 59.
[3] *Ibid.*, p. 11.
[4] *Ibid.*, p. 13.

prove himself in the eyes of the ministry. Campaigns, however, are Knauth's real targets here. To him, these peculiar social-ideological offensives with great fanfares, publicity, and optimistic slogans only serve to mask the incompetence of those, like Speck and Zeisig, who introduce them.

True to its comic form, the play, after causing the members of the audience to laugh at themselves for one and a half hours, comes to an affirmative conclusion. Knauth's criticisms were not directed at the basic structures of the society, but rather at the socialist variations of typical human weaknesses. Thus they are consistent with the party's desire to agitate individuals to become better representatives of a valid system.

Knauth has walked the tightrope well. Satire of any kind is still a questionable genre in a society of Marxist-Leninist principles. Speaking of satire in socialist literature in March of 1963, Nikita Khrushchev warned that the weapon of satire must be wielded carefully in the manner of a surgeon whose scalpel removes a malignancy without damage to the organism. He reflects ominously: "Mothers are quite right in not permitting their children to handle knives and similar tools until they have learned to use them."[5] But Knauth has learned to handle his scalpel. Well aware of the dangers of surgery on any deeply-rooted malignancy, he carefully concentrates on cosmetic surgery, which rarely leaves a scar.

Rainer Kerndl, drama critic of *Neues Deutschland*, attempts to demonstrate how contradictions within socialist development can be resolved in his play *His Children*. In October of 1961 at the Gorki Theater he had presented another work, *The Shadow of a Girl* (*Der Schatten eines Mädchens*), which characterized one family's successful fight to overcome the spectre of a Nazi past by committing themselves to the socialist future. In that play, however, Kerndl still relied on extra-societal intervention in the form of the already obsolete *agent provocateur* to carry the dramatic action.

Kerndl was born in 1928 in Bad Frankenhausen. As a young teen-ager he was drafted into the German army during the final years of World War II. After returning from a POW camp, he resumed and finished his secondary education. He immediately became involved in organizational activity for the SED and functioned as editor of a regional SED newspaper and as a Free German Youth administrator. His journalistic career led him to drama criticism, and subsequently to his own dramatic writing. His first literary efforts were in the realm of children's literature and radio plays. His mature drama, under discussion here, developed partly from his practical dramaturgical activity at Berlin's Maxim Gorki Theater.

Kerndl's *His Children* is essentially the story of a socialist generation gap.

---

[5] Khrushchev, Address at a meeting of leading functionaries of the Soviet party and government with artists and writers on 8 March 1963, trans. from *Pravda*, 10 March 1963, in *Neues Deutschland*, 14 March 1963.

Karl Sorge is a man of Ulbricht's mold, a longtime Communist functionary whose life has been dedicated to developing a humane socialist German state. His children are Judith and Rolf, both adopted, who are now leading party functionaries. Karl's real son, Alfred, has become a West German journalist. Rolf and Judith love one another out of convenience: they have always been together, and can't imagine anything else. Karl and Alfred Sorge both come to visit Judith and Rolf at the same time, unbeknown to each other. Rolf and Judith are having difficulties, because Rolf's role as the area construction engineer is causing him problems. Rolf, it seems, is also a socialist of convenience—he has never known anything else—and he follows the letter of the Central Planning Commission's orders but not the spirit. This contradiction causes unrest among the people of the area, whose needs are not being satisfied. It remains for Karl Sorge, with his ultimate wisdom of experience, to put things into their proper perspective.

A most interesting development of this play is that Kerndl, the GDR's most official drama critic at the time, uses such formalistic techniques as flashbacks and time lapses in order to establish a complete pattern of psychological motivation for all the major characters. Since these flashbacks trace the play's contradictions to psychological traumas experienced by the characters in the Nazi era or its aftermath, we search in vain for socialist realism as the basis for Kerndl's dramatic approach. On the contrary, his characterizations reveal the naturalistic dramatic techniques for which he has crucified many a play in the pages of *Neues Deutschland*. But his dialogue, often reminiscent of a party resolution in the unmistakeable socialist jargon that characterizes the style of *Neues Deutschland*, was enough to ensure at least official success. In 1970 *His Children* was still listed among plays officially commended for having developed "important approaches in contemporary topical drama in which the emergence of a GDR national consciousness, a patriotic commitment to the first German Workers' and Farmers' State, is expressed."[6] As a dramatist, Kerndl is an excellent patriot.

Harald Hauser, always having written with a similar patriotic mandate, returns to the development of socialist dedication after a nine-year hiatus. After his 1955 opus, *At the End of the Night*, he had concentrated on imperialism and the "neo-fascist" restoration of West Germany in his plays *White Blood* (*Weißes Blut* [1959]) and *Night-Step* (1960). In *Barbara* he returns to life in the GDR as his prime subject matter. With it, he tackles his most ambitious dramatic conflict. The touchiest subject of GDR domestic politics is the problem of "flight from the Republic" (*Republikflucht*). By 1964 it had become conspicuous by its absence from the work of GDR writers.

Hauser sets his three-person play on the night of 12–13 August 1961. Uwe Jobst is an engineer in an electrical power plant in Berlin. He has decided to leave the GDR for professional, political and personal reasons. He is disappointed in

    [6] "Dramatik," in *Kulturpolitisches Wörterbuch*, ed. Harald Bühl et al. (Berlin: Dietz, 1970), p. 115.

the technical developments at his plant, which is being administered by a technical collective whose members have studied a lot of Marx but too little Edison. Consequently, their drive for progress has overtaxed the technical capabilities of the staff and the equipment, and Jobst is left with the impossible job of rectifying the resulting mistakes. To add to his troubles, Jobst's daughter Karin is the socialist society's version of a juvenile delinquent. Her problems arise from lack of a stable home—there is no mother—and a subsequent cynical attitude toward the state.

Instead of facing these difficulties squarely, Jobst decides on a westward change of residence. Just when he is ready to pick up his daughter and cross the border, his colleague Barbara, who loves him, becomes aware of his plans. There is a confrontation of all three characters. Barbara unsuccessfully tries to persuade them to reconsider their move, when the border action begins. At this critical point Jobst realizes his responsibility to the socialist order. Because all of the country's available electric power will be needed for the border action, he risks his life to disconnect an automatic transformer which was installed by the collective over his objections. He knew that it would fail at peak demand and that the security of the GDR would be threatened by the ensuing power failure. In his heroic action he loses an arm, but saves the Republic. Together, Barbara, Jobst and Karin resolve to face their personal problems within the socialist society of the GDR.

Technically the drama provides a vast array of modern theater practices, including flashbacks, time distortion, interruptions, and audience participation. The play opens with a director looking for something to play. He finds three interesting people in the audience, Jobst, Barbara, and Karin, and cajoles them into presenting their story on the stage. The result of this epic technique is surprisingly helpful in airing the "flight from the Republic" problem. Hauser shows that those who have fled need not be considered criminals, and that a greater degree of personal involvement is needed on the part of the party and other socialist institutions to convince those who leave reluctantly that they are needed and wanted. Hauser's combination of a naturally dramatic situation with sensitive manipulation of modern theatrical effects results in his best work to date. *Barbara* is a play in which the national perspective arises directly from the dramatic action, thus obviating the necessity for a rhetorical overlay.

Another new young playwright enters the scene here. Horst Salomon is a relative latecomer to literature, and another success story from the movement of writing workers. His background is properly proletarian. The son of an East Prussian farm laborer, he was born in 1929. In 1945 he settled in Thuringia as a refugee, and worked mainly in the reconstruction effort, clearing the rubble left from the war. From 1950 to 1958 he was a miner at the Wismut Mine, rising to the rank of safety inspector and leader of the emergency rescue team. During this time he began writing as a hobby. His obvious talent earned him a visit to the Johannes R. Becher School of Literature in Leipzig from 1958 to 1961. After the completion of his studies he moved to Gera, where he lives today, and became closely involved with the Gera Theater, one of the best experimental "provincial" theaters in the GDR.

Salomon's first play, *Fool's Gold*, brings us squarely back to the Bitterfeld Movement, to which he owes his literary career. The play traces production difficulties in an iron mine to the presence of opportunistic would-be socialists in the administrative positions. Thus, the point of view expressed in Heiner Müller's *The Correction*—that socialism can develop even with the help of those who are not interested in it—has changed radically. Now the phraseologists and opportunists are scrutinized carefully. Salomon indicates that the time has come when the state can afford to demand a true socialist dedication from its constituents. But the most interesting facet of this National Prize-winning play is that it is the result of a collective effort involving the author, the producer, the director, and the SED.[7] The dissolution of the bourgeois aesthetic has indeed removed the dramatist from his role as solitary genius and made him an equal member of a production collective. The National Prize for Drama in 1964 was undoubtedly conferred on this play for its progressive production background, since as a socialist drama it is only an adequate melodrama in which the political opportunist has simply replaced the *agent provocateur* in the play's structure.

1964 also brings one of the GDR's most colorful authors to the contemporary theater. Kurt Barthel, known simply as Kuba, is of the Strittmatter generation, born near Chemnitz (today Karl-Marx-Stadt) in 1914. Ironically, the lifelong Communist activist died while visiting West Germany, after a violent shouting discussion with leftist radicals of the Sozialistischer Deutscher Studentenbund (SDS) in Frankfurt/Main which led to a subsequent fatal heart attack. Kuba was a physical giant of a man. His artistic career began in the late twenties, when he worked as a painter and decorator. Active in the socialist workers' movement, he was forced into exile in 1933. In Prague in 1933 he led the theater groups "Red Star" and "New Life," both centers of German exile culture. With the Nazis' eastward advance, he was forced to flee to England by way of Poland. In England he worked as a farmhand and construction laborer. After his return to East Germany in 1946 he engaged in cultural-political agitation for the SED. He was the Executive Secretary of the German Writers' Union from 1951 to 1953.

---

[7] Ilse Galfert reports on the collective process which finalized the play: "Horst Salomon's co-workers at the Wismut Mine helped a lot, not least by letting him go on a lengthy working vacation. But more importantly they participated in real, artistically important thought processes which helped revise the plot of *Fool's Gold*. They can rightly regard themselves as co-authors of the play.

"The other co-authors are the comrades of the District Council of the party in Gera. They didn't just participate by submitting ideas of editorial glibness related to contemporary reality . . . but instead, they helped by thinking along creatively in terms of the basic substance of the manuscript and its inherent possibilities" ("Zur Entstehungsgeschichte von 'Katzengold,' " in "Katzengold," by Horst Salomon, MS [Berlin: Henschelverlag Abteilung Bühnenvertrieb, 1964], pp. 2–3).

Later he was a member of the party's Central Committee. His major works are in the realm of poetry, which is evident in the concentrated lyrical style of his drama.

In 1964 Kuba's second drama, *terra incognita*, also received a National Prize. In 1959 the prolific socialist lyricist had received the Prize for his first drama, a portrayal of the German pirate Klaus Störtebecker as an amphibious Robin Hood with Marxist overtones. This time, Kuba kept marching along the Bitterfeld Road by dramatizing the socialist production methods of the GDR's oil fields. He elevates the actions of an oil-drilling brigade to a truly heroic level. Here, roustabouts, drillhands, and technicians infuse a symbolic microcosm of the GDR with a free-spirited, unbridled vitality. Since natural energy sources are rare and thus extremely important to the industry of the GDR, the topic alone makes the play important. Kuba isolates the content of his play: "The victory over the natural resources and their development for the benefit of society characterizes the victory of society over individual solitary human beings. It is the victory of many individuals over the petit-bourgeois remnants in themselves."[8] He identifies his play as a "dramatic poem," a description which needs some clarification. As a drama, it is indeed poetic. As a poem, it is very long. Despite the play's pretentious overbearance, Kuba must be credited with a serious attempt to elevate the form of the contemporary topical drama. Actually his attempt does not differ substantially from Heiner Müller's work, with two exceptions: Müller shows considerably less party phraseology and pompousness, and considerably more talent.

The procession of new young dramatists continued in 1964 with the emergence of Claus Hammel, who was to become one of the GDR's finest playwrights. Hammel is a classic representative of the new breed of GDR career intellectuals who are now starting to filter into the leading governmental, cultural, and administrative positions. He was born in Parchim (Mecklenburg) in 1932, into a middle-class family. After completing his secondary education, he— like Rainer Kerndl—became a theater critic. In 1957 he assumed the editorship of *Neue Deutsche Literatur*, the GDR's leading literary magazine. In 1958 he joined the staff of the influential cultural weekly *Sonntag*. According to Hammel, he wants to use the stage as a 'testing ground' for new ideas on how to create a better world. His drama, however, never loses sight of his primary objective, that of entertaining the audience—and he is successful in doing this.

The conscience of a young girl is the subject matter for Hammel's first major work, the contemporary drama *Nine O'Clock at the Roller Coaster*. Having gained experience as a drama critic for *Neues Deutschland* between 1955 and 1957 and by doing successful adaptations from other sources, the most successful of which was his *Frau Jenny Treibel* after Theodore Fontane, the realist novelist of the late

[8] *Schauspielführer*, ed. Karl Heinz Berger et al. (Berlin: Henschelverlag, 1972), II, 771.

nineteenth century, Hammel wades into the mainstream with his portrayal of Sabine, the girl caught between East and West. The action takes place in the early sixties. After growing up in the GDR, Sabine is told that the people she considers her parents are not her real parents. Her real mother, who had abandoned her as a small child, reappears as a rich capitalist from West Germany. She demands that Sabine come to live with her. Sabine, who is somewhat immature, wants to stay in the GDR, but she also wants Moritz, the party secretary whom she loves, to make a public statement in favor of her decision. Although Moritz would like to do this, the legality of the real mother's demand is proven, thus prohibiting further party action on the case. Moritz is torn between his love and his party when an older colleague sets him straight:

> SCHMIDT: We don't give in, Moritz. We've never given in—not in '53, and not on the 13th of August.
> MORITZ: So we'd rather sacrifice a human being to keep our name clean. We risk everything just to gain recognition from the enemy.
> SCHMIDT: The party is not a whore. We want to convince people, not please them! No, we don't want to please your Sabine! If you haven't succeeded in convincing her of our cause and she wants to leave, don't blame the party. Miss Krause has freedom of choice. If she is silly enough to make the great decision between here and there dependent on a silly trial of strength between the party and herself, we're going to refuse to be the fool in her game.[9]

Moritz is convinced of his duty to the party at the expense of his inclination toward Sabine. Hammel's contemporary version of the Schillerian conflict of *Pflicht und Neigung* (duty and desire), which dominates classical German drama in the late eighteenth century, is the most successful attempt to humanize and dramatize that traditionally cardboard figure, the party secretary, that the GDR drama can offer to date.

Sabine chooses to go Westward, simply to spite Moritz. It was a bad choice. She returns disillusioned, lonely, and pregnant. Her Western fiancé-impregnator comes to take her back, but this time she exercises her options in favor of Moritz and the socialist system. Hammel's play, an epic exhibition of short fragmented scenes, utilizes a combination of impressionistic scenes and hard argumentation to deliver a persuasive message. Its run at the Maxim Gorki Theater was enthusiastically received.

Some general reflections about this wave of socialist drama come to mind. First, there is no doubt as to the ideological commitment of the authors. They are solidly behind their party, and their works demonstrate that position. A second facet is the emergence of a collective playwriting/producing process, which not only surfaces in the efforts of the worker/writers like Kleineidam and Salomon,

[9] Claus Hammel, *Um neun an der Achterbahn*, in *Sozialistische Dramatik: Autoren der Deutschen Demokratischen Republik* (Berlin: Henschelverlag, 1968), pp. 517–18.

but also characterizes the works of the all-out professionals Baierl, Sakowski, Kerndl and Kuba. Third, it is obvious that the removal of extra-societal conflict elements creates some difficulty for the dramatists, who thereby find themselves bereft of dramatic antagonisms. In order to make nonantagonistic contradictions dramatically palatable, they must invent or superimpose natural or even archetypal dramatic structures on their works, thus adding a needed dimension to the essentially sterile, nonantagonistic constellations. Kleineidam resorts to feuding brothers, Sakowski to a love triangle, Hauser to a historical crisis, and Hammel to the great internal conflict of the individual character as developed during German Classicism.

Finally, the most important phenomenon in terms of German literary development is the emergence of a national, politically oriented drama. The GDR theater regards itself as the legitimate heir of a "German national theater," the dream of the eighteenth-century "classicists." At the same time, however, the German Democratic Republic claims the progressive tradition of German drama—from Lenz, Büchner, and Hauptmann to Wolf and Brecht—as the historical source of its own socialist drama. But whereas the sociopolitical views expressed in the works of that tradition were directed mainly against the systems from which they arose and upon which they reflect, the GDR's socially and politically oriented drama strives to gather support for the system from which it emerges. Thus GDR drama has become, in a unique dialectic structure, at once socialist and conservative: It is socialist in content, and yet is in support of the current GDR status quo.

The contemporary topical drama of the GDR, as represented by these plays produced after the border action of 1961, has the historical mission to invert the standard socially oriented drama, to make it a positive commentary upon the human situation in its society. While we may be justly critical of the individual structural weaknesses that some of the works exhibit, we must acknowledge the overall success of this planned theater in terms of the rigid criteria of the planned society.

X.
Ruminations and Rejections:
The Eleventh Plenary Inquisition

Not all of the GDR literary production progressed as comfortably—and according to plan—as the contemporary topical drama in 1964 and 1965. While the Second Bitterfeld Conference, held on 24–25 April 1964, was heralded as a complete success in affirming the continued dedication of all literary artists to socialist realism ("The basic questions of socialist realism have been cleared up."—Ulbricht[1]), discussion of the crucial aesthetic questions which concerned authors and critics was scrupulously avoided. This second conference, much more organized and official than the one in 1959, deteriorated into a display of general self-congratulation on how well the country's cultural policies were progressing toward the final goal of the humanistic socialist national people's culture. The Germanist Hans Koch outlined the conclusions of the Second Bitterfeld Conference even before it was history in the April 1964 issue of *Neue Deutsche Literatur*:

> The step which must be taken now is not primarily the change of the thematic principles of our literature, as was the case after the First Bitterfeld Conference of 1959. Rather, our primary objective is to deepen and enrich the human characterizations in our art, which will develop primarily from the stronger efforts toward quality in literary works.[2]

Keynote speeches at the conference categorically rejected the suggestion advanced by the Prague Kafka Conference of 27 May 1963[3] that Franz Kafka's works be adopted as part of a redefined socialist realism. Walter Ulbricht attacked

---

[1] Walter Ulbricht, "Über die Entwicklung einer volksverbundenen sozialistischen National-kultur," *Neues Deutschland*, 28 April 1964.

[2] Hans Koch, "Fünf Jahre nach Bitterfeld," *Neue Deutsche Literatur*, XII/4 (1964), 11.

[3] The so-called "Kafka Conference" took place on 27 May 1963 in Prague. Prominent left-oriented Germanists from West Germany, Czechoslovakia, Poland, Hungary, Yugoslavia, France, Austria, and the GDR discussed the importance of Kafka's work for socialist societies. Cf. Konrad Franke, *Die Literatur der Deutschen Demokratischen Republik* (München: Kindler, 1971), pp. 121–23.

the crux of the discussion, man's alienation from his own nature, by declaring it a logical impossibility in the socialist society:

There are some intellectuals who have lately specialized in "alienation." Disregarding the historical contingencies, they talk about the alienation of the human being from his own nature. They talk about the self-alienation of the worker in production without understanding that there is a difference between the worker in the people's industries and the worker in the factories of the exploitational capitalist society.[4]

In this lengthy dissertation, Ulbricht further rejected "abstract realism," doubt, and skepticism as vehicles for attaining deeper socialist insight (*Zweifel als Motor des Fortschritts*), and clinched the conference with his formulation that socialist art must "elevate man and give him wings."[5]

Those who pleaded for a more relaxed literary policy—mostly novelists whose new, 1964 novels would run into heavy party artillery, such as Christa Wolf (*The Divided Sky* [*Der geteilte Himmel*]), Erik Neutsch (*The Trail of Stones* [*Die Spur der Steine*]), and Strittmatter (*Ole Bienkopp*)—were warned by Kuba:

There is protest against force which was never applied. There are calls for a "free world" of art in our Workers' and Farmers' State, a world into which the party cannot enter, and thus a world in which socialism has not achieved victory.

This demand is without substance, just as the art which is propagated in this connection is also without substance. Such a private world does not exist, did not exist, and cannot exist within or without the boundaries of the German Workers' and Farmers' State.[6]

The categorical rejection of the widespread discussion of realism and alienation at the Second Bitterfeld Conference was not without its consequences. It is now clear that authors were looking for some more definite, aesthetically productive guidelines within which they, as convinced Marxists, could operate. The result of the abundant but nonspecific cultural-political rhetoric they were served in their place was the development of some experimental tendencies in the literature of 1964 and 1965 that the Central Committee had not anticipated. In the novels mentioned just above, the authors try to develop new subject/object relationships between the society and the individual, engaging in explorations of the individual frustrations within obstructive bureaucracies committed to the preservation of calcified party-line attitudes. Further, there appeared excursions into crass realism, or "telling it like it is," especially in an excerpt of Werner

[4] Ulbricht, "Über die Entwicklung. . . ."

[5] *Ibid.*

[6] Kuba, *Zweite Bitterfelder Konferenz 1964: Protokoll der von der Ideologischen Kommission beim Politbüro des ZK der SED und dem Ministerium für Kultur am 24. und 25. April im Kulturpalast des Elektrochemischen Kombinats Bitterfeld abgehaltenen Konferenz*, ed. Central Committee of the SED (Berlin: Dietz, 1964), p. 260.

Bräunig's yet unpublished novel *The Iron Curtain (Der eiserne Vorhang)*, which was carried by *Neue Deutsche Literatur* in October of 1965.

But the Eleventh Plenary Meeting of the Central Committee of 15–18 December 1965 resulted in a retrenching action by the party against such subjective, "decadent," "bourgeois" tendencies. Among the casualties of this ideological offensive were the "skeptics," the radical singer/poet Wolf Biermann, the novelist Stefan Heym, the physicist/philosopher Robert Havemann, and the novelist Werner Bräunig. Erich Honecker made one thing perfectly clear: There was no possibility of coexistence between Marxism-Leninism and such "bourgeois" manifestations in the ideological sphere. He isolates Heym in the following manner: "He [Heym] uses his appearances in West Germany to publicize his novel *The Day X [Der Tag X]*, which, because of its completely false rendition of the events of 17 June 1953, could not be approved. . . . He writes articles for periodicals and newspapers in the West in which he falsifies life in the Soviet Union and the GDR."[7] Wolf Biermann fares no better: "Biermann's so-called poems signify his petit-bourgeois anarchistic attitude, his arrogance, his skepticism and cynicism. Today Biermann in his songs and poems is a traitor to basic socialist positions. . . . It is time to act against foreign and harmful works which, at the same time, demonstrate pornographic tendencies."[8]

The Eleventh Plenary Meeting effected a reform reaching into the top positions. Wolfgang Joho was removed from the editorship of *Neue Deutsche Literatur* because of the publication of texts by Bräunig and Heym. The same fate befell Hans Bentzien, the liberal cultural minister on whom the general trend of the ideological deviations was blamed. He was replaced by the more doctrinaire Klaus Gysi.

In the contemporary drama, 1965 is not noted for what was produced, but rather for what was aborted. The Eleventh Plenary Meeting effectively nipped a potential second dialectic digression in the bud. The GDR theater had long awaited the return of Heiner Müller with a topical subject. In 1965 his play *Construction (Der Bau)*, a liberal adaptation/transformation of Erik Neutsch's *The Trail of Stones*, was scheduled to premiere at the Deutsches Theater. But a pre-premiere publication of the text in *Sinn und Form* caused a furor among party regulars. Thus, Müller became one of Erich Honecker's primary targets at the Plenary Meeting. Müller was accused of lacking the proper perspective on the party's efforts in the development of socialism. Again, the functionaries refused to follow his dialectic structures, and took negative statements—which Müller synthesizes into a critical but positive whole—verbatim.

---

[7] The report of the Politbüro to the Eleventh Plenary Meeting of the Central Committee of the Socialist Unity Party (SED), as reported by Erich Honecker in *Neues Deutschland*, 16 December 1965.
[8] *Ibid.*

Especially offensive to the party was the characterization and dialogue of the brigade leader Barka:

KLAMANN: Leave me out, brigadier.
BARKA: When your party
    Straightens out the mess here, we'll raise a red flag, Klamann.
    Pluck out your third eye if it offends you.
    (*Rips off* KLAMANN's *SED pin*)
    The party comes and goes; we work.[9]

When questioned about diverting cement from other projects for his own, he states:

    The world is a boxing ring and the fist is always right.
    Let down your guard and you go down.
    One punch too many and you're counted out.
    Communism is for the newspapers.[10]

His evaluation of the plan is simple: "The plan is sabotaged by planners who get paid for it/ We've had to help ourselves since 1880."[11]

Construction is Müller's highly poetic vehicle in which the dialectic process flows between the heroic individuals (Barka, Donat, and Schlee) and the petty bureaucrats: between the present reality of the GDR and the possibilities for the future: between progressive imagination and restrictive planning. Barka's vision of himself at the end of the play is problematic for the socialist ideology of the party in 1965:

    Since I've become acquainted with the And between myself and me
    I want to be none other than I and I.
    My life is building bridges. I am
    The ferry from the Ice Age to the commune.[12]

But there are indications that this expression of a contradiction between the socialist here-and-now and a Communist utopia, an essential deviation from the SED's position, which rejects such dialectic formulations as left radicalism, was not even the main cause of the prohibitive action against the play. Instead, it would seem that the potentially most interesting, and certainly most aesthetically and ideologically ambitious of contemporary plays of the GDR, was squelched because of its deviation from Walter Ulbricht's reactionary, petit-bourgeois code of ethics, the socialist morality code. Müller's *Construction* contains erotic-poetic

---

[9] Heiner Müller, *Der Bau, Sinn und Form*, 17 (January 1965), 177.
[10] *Ibid.*
[11] *Ibid.*
[12] *Ibid.*, p. 224.

reflections on the extra-marital affair of a party secretary who does not remorse-fully crawl back into the conjugal bed, and who does not undergo the socialist moral rearmament which is required in the GDR if such a subject is to be treated at all.

Before he launched his direct attack on Müller's *Construction*, Erich Honeck-er, in his keynote address at the Eleventh Plenary Meeting, based his entire attack on moral premises:

> Our GDR is a clean state. In it there are immovable standards of ethics and morality, of behavior and good etiquette. . . . We join with those who have noted that the causes for these appearances of immorality and a life style alien to socialism are also evident in some films [*I Am the Bunny* (*Das Kaninchen bin Ich*) by Wolfgang Bieler], television plays [*Monologue of a Cab Driver* (*Monolog eines Taxifahrers*) by Günter Kunert], theater plays, literary works and periodicals. . . . Brutalities are described; human reactions are reduced to sexual libido.[13]

After categorizing these works as "representations of American immorality and decadence,"[14] Honecker turns directly to Heiner Müller:

> . . . the manuscript of *Construction*, published in *Sinn und Form*, . . . demonstrate[s] tendencies and concepts alien to socialism. . . . The individual is opposed by collec-tives and leaders of the party, and the state is often characterized as a cold and alien power structure. Our present reality is seen only as a hard, sacrificial, temporary state on the way to a beautiful, illusory future—as "the ferry from the Ice Age to Communism [sic]."[15]

Honecker demonstrates that as a literary critic, he is a good politician—a power politician.

This prohibitive wave lasted into 1966, when three plays exhibiting ten-dencies similar to those of *Construction* were also censored. On 5 October 1965 Peter Hacks presented his *Moritz Tassow* at the Berliner Volksbühne. The play, which had been collecting dust for four years, displeased the functionaries, and was removed from the GDR repertoire shortly after its premiere.[16] The dramatist Helmut Sakowski, a candidate for membership on the Central Committee, wielded the sharpest hatchet against Hacks at the Eleventh Plenary Meeting. Comparing Werner Bräunig's rejected novel and Hacks's *Moritz Tassow*, he spouted righteous indignation: ". . . Bräunig's pornography is harmless when compared to the vulgar obscenities which are paraded across the stage at the Volksbühne to thrill the petit-bourgeois."[17]

---

[13] Honecker, *Neues Deutschland*, 16 December 1965.

[14] *Ibid.*

[15] *Ibid.* It is interesting to note that Honecker has edited Müller's concept "commune" into "Communism."

[16] Cf. Franke, *Literatur der DDR*, p. 140.

[17] Sakowski, "Klare Konturen für die Kunst," *Neues Deutschland*, 19 December 1965.

Moritz Tassow, like Müller's Barka, is a great individual, a vital anarchist, a utopian Communist, and a much more interesting character than his counter-player, the party secretary Mattukat. Although Hacks's comedy sharply criticizes left radicalism and subjective interpretations of Marxism, this criticism was not enough to save the play. For the censure levelled against Hacks's dramatic procedure here rests against the figure of Blasche. This character is a spineless career functionary who represents an alternative to Tassow's utopian position, and in whom the median group of party functionaries saw itself characterized. Hacks's comic-historical reflection on the events in East Germany immediately after the war necessarily bares the pragmatism of the party in those hard times. It is a pragmatism of which the pragmatists do not like to be reminded.

The other plays with utopian figures that did not fit into the planned theater —or the planned society—were Volker Braun's *Dumper Paul Bauch* (*Kipper Paul Bauch*), published in 1966 but never produced in its original form, and Hans Pfeiffer's socialist production play, *A Meeting With Hercules* (*Begegnung mit Herkules*). This play was removed from the Städtische Bühnen Leipzig shortly after its premiere. Its fate was similar to that which befell Pfeiffer's first contemporary topical play dealing with industrial production, *The Third Shift* (*Die dritte Schicht* [1960]), which was removed after its second night onstage.[18]

At this point we must consider the work of the poet/dramatist Volker Braun, one of the youngest of the GDR's dramatists and without a doubt the greatest "raw" literary talent to develop in the German language since Heiner Müller in the GDR and Günter Grass, Peter Weiss and Rolf Hochhuth in the Federal Republic. He was born in Dresden in 1939. After completing his secondary education he worked in a print shop. In 1958 he turned to underground construction in the project Schwarze Pumpe, the scene of Müller's play *The Correction*. Later he worked as a machinist and oiler. From 1960 to 1965 he studied philosophy at the University of Leipzig. Then in 1965 he turned to the theater as an assistant at the Berliner Ensemble. His career, like Müller's, has had more downs than ups because of his outspoken manner and his critical attitude toward standard party politics. Today, however, after several first-rate volumes of poetry and the much-delayed production of his first drama, he is the young lion of GDR letters, finally enjoying recognition of his talents by critics of both East and West.

In Braun's *Dumper Paul Bauch*, Bauch is another character of archetypal vitality who singlehandedly tries to bring an advanced Communist perspective to the dumping area of a people's strip mining complex. His superhuman efforts, while upsetting the production plan, wrecking the inadequate equipment, and causing accidental industrial casualties, finally catapult his brigade into an ideal socialist awareness. Bauch is a character of great creative and destructive powers, and as a dramatic figure he bears a close resemblance to Brecht's Baal. The real

[18] Cf. Franke, *Literatur der DDR*, p. 462.

dialectic contradiction upon which Braun bases his play is outlined in the preface. For it is the nature of the dump, which inherently reduces the worker to a *pars pro toto* and alienates him from his human totality by reducing him to an arm:

> The area which you see here, called dump, is one hundred meters long, three wide. Sand. Those standing in the sand have a sad job. To do it, they need an arm. It lifts the lever on the dump wagon. But now they find another arm, long, thin, and what is it? A leg—and there: another leg. And all that hangs on them, and more, coldly attached, useless like warts.[19]

It is in this sphere of inhuman work that "socialism is not quite possible. It is a remnant of barbarianism. We don't talk about it."[20] After the Eleventh Plenary Meeting, where it was ruled that the alienation concept was not acceptable in characterizations of GDR life, the production of a play on such a dialectic base was impossible. Volker Braun has been rewriting his *Dumper Paul Bauch* ever since. The latest version, called *The Dumpers* (*Die Kipper*), appeared in *Sinn und Form* in 1972.[21] The play's dramatic impetus still remains the inherent contradiction of inhumane work in a humane society. It was finally produced in 1973.

Helmut Sakowski correctly analyzed the reason behind the rise of this new skepticism toward the state. Referring to an Ulbricht statement from the last Bitterfeld Conference, "definite contours in art demand definite contours in leadership,"[22] he cited the failure of the cultural leadership to hammer out a clear line of policy in the previous two years. Sakowski noted that the Cultural Department of the Central Committee had not done its job in discussing pertinent aesthetic questions with candidates for membership on the Central Committee who were writers and artists. Thus he transferred some of the blame for the rise in "revisionism" from the writers to the functionaries. He reasoned that artists always tend to experiment, and that it was the responsibility of the SED to channel that energy into positive and optimistic production. Finally, he asked: "Where are the contours in leadership? Why do we have an Academy of Arts, a Cultural Ministry, and a Cultural Department of the Central Committee?"[23]

The result was a long-range cultural plan announced by Walter Ulbricht. The literary goals were outlined by Ulbricht in his major contribution to the Eleventh Plenary Meeting, entitled "Problems of the Planned Perspective Until 1970" ("Probleme des Perspektivplans bis 1970"). Avoiding the hatchet quality

---

[19] Volker Braun, *Kipper Paul Bauch*, in *Deutsches Theater der Gegenwart*, ed. Karlheinz Braun (Frankfurt am Main: Suhrkamp, 1967), II, 9.

[20] *Ibid.*, p. 25.

[21] Braun, *Die Kipper*, *Sinn und Form*, 24 (January 1972), 90–145.

[22] Sakowski, "Klare Konturen für die Kunst."

[23] *Ibid.*

of the other contributors (except in his reference to the influence of the Beatles[24]), Ulbricht announced a positive line following the desire expressed by Sakowski. At the root of his formulation was his view of the GDR as the developer of a "Socialist Brotherhood" ("Sozialistische Menschengemeinschaft"). In his view, any artistic endeavor should be aimed at creating an awareness of and serving this "Socialist Brotherhood."

The first criterion Ulbricht established was the effectiveness of the work of art as a perceptive tool: "Works of art and literature have the potential to enable man to recognize his social position and human relationships."[25] Secondly, he established the subject matter that leads to this potential: "We are concerned with artistic quality in the characterization of the most contemporary problems. We are expecially interested in the problems that mark the period of the all-around development of socialism in the German Democratic Republic, and all problems of national significance."[26] As the third and perhaps central criterion, he cited the need for a never-ending process in which authors repeatedly submit proof of their own socialist awareness and perspective: "No one can say at any certain point that he has attained such an attitude once and for all time. It must be fought for continuously and subjected to proof with each new contingency. Otherwise comfortable, negligent and superficial answers will arise to the question of how a work of art can most effectively serve the Socialist Brotherhood."[27]

Thus, the essential function of contemporary topical literature in the socialist society is defined by its cognitive quality, which enables the society to recognize not only the positive manifestations of its overall ideological design, but also the everyday implementation of the literary message as established by each party congress. The Eleventh Plenary Meeting established that the writer's ideological commitment to Marxism is not sufficient in itself. Since in the GDR there is ostensibly no contradiction between ideological base and societal superstructure, the indication of an alternative superstructure in a literary work is sufficient proof of ideological heresy.

There is only one recognized contradiction in the German Democratic Republic: "GDR: *It is a great historical achievement*, a gigantic success of the German peace effort, . . . and at the same time it is something normal, everyday, a workshop in the process of constant development and characterization."[28] Walter Ulbricht further established that the writer must approach this reality

[24] Ulbricht was not sympathetic to rock music: "The eternal monotony of this 'Yeah, yeah, yeah' is intellectually mortifying and ridiculous" ("Probleme des Perspektivplans bis 1970," *Neues Deutschland*, 18 December 1965).

[25] *Ibid.*

[26] *Ibid.*

[27] *Ibid.*

[28] *Ibid.*

"with a constructive, cooperative attitude."[29] Thus, the successful treatment of GDR life depends on how cooperatively the author holds his mirror. If it does not reflect the view that this state is indeed the fairest Germany of them all, he may find his mirror confiscated.

[29] *Ibid.*

XI.
The Contemporary Topical Drama

1. CULMINATION AND CRISIS

Since 1949, when the beginning of a socialist realistic theater tradition in the German Democratic Republic was defined by the works of the veteran prewar Communist writers Friedrich Wolf, Karl Grünberg and Gustav von Wangenheim, the straightforward development of that tradition had always been threatened with interruption by exacerbations of an experimental drama essentially based on a development of Bertolt Brecht's theories of a dialectic theater. These upheavals were rejected by the literary policymakers first as formalism/objectivism (1951–52), then as revisionistic abstract dialectics alien to the interests of the workers (1958–59), and finally as petit-bourgeois skepticism and pornography (1965–66).

These dialectic digressions, as exercised for the last time in 1965 by Heiner Müller's *Construction*, Peter Hacks's *Moritz Tassow*, and even Volker Braun's *Dumper Paul Bauch*, are essentially revolutionary because they demonstrate basic dialectic contradictions of their society; they are revolutionary theater in a society which has itself ceased to be revolutionary. If that society acknowledges no contradiction other than the fact that it is great yet humble—which is the case in point—a demonstration of true contradictions implies a basic need for change in the social structure. But a dramatic approach based upon the utopian Marxist goal of continuing revolutionary development toward the ideal Communist state is not viable in a society in which socialism has been declared final and permanent. In crystallizing the ideological results of the Seventh Party Congress (17–22 April 1967), Walter Ulbricht maintained that "socialism is not a short-term transitional phase in the development of society, but a relatively independent socioeconomic system in the historical epoch of transition from capitalism to Communism on a worldwide scale."[1]

---

[1] Ulbricht, *Die Bedeutung des Werkes Das Kapital von Karl Marx für die Schaffung des entwickelten gesellschaftlichen Systems des Sozialismus in der DDR und den Kampf gegen das staatsmonopolistische Herrschaftssystem in Westdeutschland* (Berlin: Dietz, 1967), p. 38.

Between 1966 and 1971, with the last digressions removed, GDR contemporary drama truly became the theater of the planned society. Its development in those years, having been narrowly defined by the Planned Perspective Until 1970, followed the party dictates regarding subject matter, perspective, and attitude and eschewed "deviation" in its characterization of the so-called Socialist Brotherhood. For there is no room for deviation in a planned society. The digressors among the GDR dramatists found their socially and politically critical mirrors cracked by the Eleventh Plenary Meeting of the SED in the fall of 1965. This meant that the only valid subject matter of socialist realism, contemporary life in the socialist society, had been removed from the province of the dramatic work of a Heiner Müller, a Peter Hacks, and others who would follow the dialectic tradition and place the value of a critical treatment of GDR society above that of an uncritical acceptance of the status quo.

By 1967 the postwar era had passed. The economic necessities had been secured by the relatively successful implementation of the New Economic System[2] dating back to 1963. The implementation of incentives for individuals and collectives, combined with the technological advances in all production sectors, had brought radical economic gains for both individuals and the society as a whole. Political sovereignty and national security were guaranteed through an aggressive foreign policy built on a base of ideological identification with the Soviet Union. The cultural policy of the SED countenanced only two valid objectives for the contemporary topical drama in the fully developed and finalized socialist state proclaimed by the Seventh Party Congress of 1967: First, that drama was to demonstrate the validity of the system; and second, that it was to act as a cognitive tool to help the individual citizen of the GDR attain further integration into the Socialist Brotherhood by clarifying his role in the continuing scientific/technological revolution that had been established as the socioeconomic base of the modern socialist system.

Out of this situation, which could be viewed as the socialist version of the affluent society, arose new and crucial topics for drama which were immediately treated in a rapid succession of new plays between 1967 and 1969. The most interesting of these are Horst Salomon's second play, untranslatably entitled *Ein Lorbaß* (2 March 1967); Claus Hammel's second topical play, *The Chimney Sweep Comes Tomorrow* (*Morgen kommt der Schornsteinfeger* [25 November 1967]; Horst Kleineidam's second offering, *Of Giants and Men* (*Von Riesen und Menschen* [10 October 1967]); and Siegfried Pfaff's *A Day in the Life of Regina B.* (*Regina B.: Ein Tag in ihrem Leben* [10 October 1968]). All four plays develop a dramatic

[2] Neues Ökonomisches System (NÖS): the name of the economic reforms finalized during the Sixth Party Congress of the SED (15–21 January 1963). This refers to a contingency plan to modernize and economize the economic system at all levels. Cf. "Neues Ökonomisches System (NÖS)," *A bis Z, Ein Taschen- und Nachschlagebuch über den anderen Teil Deutschlands*, ed. Bundesministerium für gesamtdeutsche Fragen (Bonn: Deutscher Bundesverlag, 1969), pp. 447–50.

conflict based upon a tendency toward complacency, toward the deterioration of the revolutionary élan, toward "taking it easy," which the authors see as a negative manifestation of the secured existence provided by the fully developed socialist system. These dramatists see the ideological danger of a fat and lazy socialist society, and demonstrate the necessity for continued progressive action on the part of individuals, especially in their personal and group relationships, in order to avoid backsliding into socialist Babbitry.

Salomon's protagonist Harald Schmieder, called the Lorbaß, is an energetic young man whose talents are not being used to the best advantage. His personal characteristics are impatience, wit, and idealism. But he is employed below the level of his talents as a grease monkey on a strip mining shovel. From this position he observes a mining complex in the process of sinking into the socialist doldrums.

One day, out of sheer frustration with the inefficiency of the complex, he gets onto the shovel, which he is not qualified to run, and accidentally wrecks it, causing over 40,000 marks worth of damage. This action serves as the impetus that enables Salomon to demonstrate his thesis. The chairman of the investigating commission of the mine tries to avoid the responsibility and succeeds in transferring the case to the State's Attorney. But the Attorney rules that the case is an internal problem of the mine and does not belong to the court. The ensuing investigation confirms that the entire productive system of the mine has become inefficient. Key individuals in production, leadership, and organization are resting on the laurels of their past achievements as socialist activists. The mine's much publicized activist is a drunk, the managing executives avoid responsibility, the financial experts pinch pennies without vision, and the mine's political groups, the union and the Free German Youth, operate at cross purposes.

The State's Attorney, Kowalski, opened a Pandora's Box with his decision. As a result of the destructive impetuosity of the Lorbaß, there is a general shakeup of calcified perspectives. The commission rises to its responsibility and regains its role as a progressive socialist collective, essentially the conscience of the mine. The Lorbaß is officially censured. He must make restitution by doing 400 hours of extra volunteer work. Finally, he must attend technical courses and become a "qualified" skilled worker. But the mine itself must also change so that accidents like these, caused by the misappropriation of manpower, will be avoided: "And further, we recommend that the management clean up its personnel development program, especially in reference to young people."[3]

Horst Kleineidam's *Of Giants and Men* is also built around this problem of the utilization of "youth power." A people's electric motor factory serves as a microcosm of the society as Kleineidam branches out into some philosophical generalizations. Richard Barhaupt has risen from the ranks of the workers to

[3] Horst Salomon, *Ein Lorbaß*, in *Neue Stücke: Autoren der Deutschen Demokratischen Republik*, ed. Manfred Hocke (Berlin: Henschelverlag, 1971), p. 441.

become the plant manager. In Peter Principle fashion, he is now limited by his lack of theoretical knowledge. For in the modern world, computers, automation, and industrial cybernetics determine productive quality. Ulrich Barhaupt, his son, is the representative of this new movement as the technical advisor of the factory. Richard has settled down into a routine of practical administration and rejects the experimental theories of his son. Reinhard Barhaupt, the grandfather, acts as resident philosopher, a Walter Ulbricht incarnate, and forces the confrontation between father and son. This clash results in the dialectic dynamism which had been lacking in the plant. It becomes clear that the objective difficulties in production can only be overcome by the implementation of dynamic theories.

Kleineidam assails the middle-aged functionaries who control the system for their tendency to lose vision and daring, to become narrowly pragmatic. The GDR's most powerful men, once the vanguard of socialist development, are characterized as being well on their way to becoming socialist conservatives. But Ulrich's massive creative energy must be applied in a rational manner. Through the philosophical overview of the grandfather, the dialectics of this generation gap are synthesized into a positive goal for the GDR: to constantly augment the achievements of practical experience with infusions of youthful energy in order to continuously propel the society forward. The resulting character synthesis is one of gigantic scope. Kleineidam's play is an exercise that applies Friedrich Engels's formulation—that when the Renaissance needed giants, it made giants of its men—to the German Democratic Republic.

Kleineidam, in order to avoid the schematic, sterile, and artificial conflicts that necessarily result when characters become mere vehicles for ideas, again superimposes archetypal dialectic conflicts—this time that of father and son— much as he did in *Schmidt's Millions*. Again, this technique is successful.

Whereas Horst Salomon's and Kleineidam's main concern is the reconstruction of the Bitterfeld Road into a modern expressway for continued faster travel into the future, Claus Hammel and Siegfried Pfaff turn directly to the new attitudes and human relationships that must be developed by the various travellers so that the new highway can be utilized to its fullest capacity. Hammel calls his *The Chimney Sweep Comes Tomorrow* "an attempt at happiness" ("Versuch über das Glück"). A young, "modern," and intellectual couple, beneficiaries of the accelerated economic development of socialism, find their dreams fulfilled. They have moved into a new apartment building and anticipate a happy and comfortable life henceforth. Yet, not untypically, they find that their happiness is without depth and that they are uneasy.

The housewarming party, attended by their friends, who represent various degrees of socialist awareness—from that of the old-line revolutionary chimney sweep to that of the new "bourgeois" socialist career functionaries (socialism's "Beautiful People")—turns into a free-swinging ideological debate. Jette and Jule, the young couple, are forced to reevaluate their positions vis-à-vis their society, and, and, most of all, each other. In analyzing their life, they uncover the basic question, which makes them uncomfortable because they cannot answer it:

> But is that all? Is work everything? Okay, I enjoyed it: Because I knew we could use the money to buy a real carpet, a car, and a weekend cottage. Leather chairs, Meissen china, independence, freedom. But what happens when we have all that? What are we going to do for the rest of our lives? What a joy! We can assemble all of it on a couple of square yards: Oh what happiness, look at us, see what we've achieved! Then we can dust our life's work, wash it, polish it, paint it, vacuum it, and state proudly: It was worth it. That can't, *can't* be everything![4]

With this formulation, Hammel has crystallized the question central to the further development of socialism in the German Democratic Republic: How, when the requisites of material and ideological existence have been secured, can one retain a revolutionary attitude without challenging the system? Hammel's answer is predictable. The revolutionary bearing in such a socialist society manifests itself in a continually renewed dedication to the collective ideal within the framework of the party. The individual's primary task is the realization of the collective ideal, the Socialist Brotherhood, which can be achieved only by overcoming "individualistic," "bourgeois" tendencies. Socialism is not the means merely to a private independence: "The dream of our forefathers. My hearth and home are worth gold. Small, but all mine. Not bad."[5] Hammel demonstrates that this dream is invalid. This private island within socialism does not exist. Socialism is progress, development and growth permeating all facets of life. The final realization that socialism is *life* is the permanent revolutionary attitude. Quite credibly, Hammel forces his characters, and perhaps his audience, into that realization.

With the aid of a collective of the Gera stage, Siegfried Pfaff developed his 1969 radio play, *A Day in the Life of Regina B.*, for the theater. Pfaff is another young intellectual much like Kerndl and Hammel. He was born in Kreuzberg in 1931, but was raised and educated in Karl-Marx-Stadt. He was a teacher until 1953, when he began to study philosophy and German literature in Leipzig and Berlin. He worked as an assistant director and dramaturgical assistant at the Berliner Volksbühne until 1960 when he switched over to the electronic media and joined the Drama Department of Radio GDR.

For his central dramatic conflict in *Regina B.*, Pfaff goes back to Gerhard Fabian's *Stories About Marie Hedder* (1955), extracts the intelligent young woman with two illegitimate children from the rural situation of the fifties, and places her in a modern industrial environment in the developed socialist society. Regina Bayer has had to overcome a questionable reputation by becoming a productive member of the industrial society. She has made a decent home for her children,

---

[4] Claus Hammel, *Morgen kommt der Schornsteinfeger*, in *Neue Stücke*, p. 312.
[5] *Ibid.*, p. 280.

improved her professional status through hard work and evening courses, and thus gained the full respect of her neighbors and co-workers. She is ready to settle back into a well-deserved family routine, when Krüger, her fiancé, leaves her for another woman. Krüger is a brilliant inventor, a technician of rare theoretical talent and even rarer personal immaturity. Determined to keep him, Regina decides that she must impress him intellectually: she applies for a course of study that would result in an engineering degree in six years of further evening study. All the functionaries in the factory try to talk her out of her decision—some from a "male chauvinist" position, and others because they suspect her true motivation:

> KLOPFER: I suspect she wants to compensate for an experience which has undermined her self-confidence.
> KLARMANN: What does that mean?
> KLOPFER: When a decision is motivated like that, it's easy to overestimate one's own strength. The result: One fails to achieve the great goal. The feeling gets stronger: You are a failure.
> KLARMANN: Well, we'd better talk her out of it then.[6]

Klopfer, the plant psychologist, has reasoned correctly. This is coupled with the fact that Regina's socialist perspective does not go beyond her job and her objective of gaining material security for her children: "Sure she has 'qualified' herself on the job, but how? She hasn't the faintest idea of today's problems, economically. She does her job as if the factory still belonged to old Frick."[7] When Krüger also approaches her and tells her to drop her "silly idea," she drops her resolute bearing and, seeing that she has lost Krüger, engineering school or no engineering school, she withdraws her application. But a discussion of the objective difficulties of the plant with Dieter Erfurth, who has just been promoted to plant manager, leads her to a basic discovery about the woman's role in the GDR society. It is essentially the same as that of a man, but it is harder to sustain:

> REGINA: I'm not surprised at all that so few women play first fiddle in our plant— and even further, in the government.
> ERFURTH: Why do you suppose that is?
> REGINA: You demand too much. Women must be as productive as men, achieve the same results with their personnel—and be charming in the process. If I go to our supervisor and say "Be charming," he'll throw me out.[8]

Through Erfurth's arguments she realizes that life is made better by the individuals who accept its challenges. The socialist system, according to Erfurth, does not need another housewife; but it does need another engineer. Regina Bayer needs a challenge in order to live a meaningful life in her society. Thus she

[6] Siegfried Pfaff. *Regina B.: Ein Tag in ihrem Leben,* in *Neue Stücke,* p. 120.
[7] *Ibid.,* p. 113.
[8] *Ibid.,* p. 158.

accepts the challenge to become a wheel rather than a cog in the further development of a world that has nurtured her development from the position of a Marie
Hedder—the sexually and economically exploited female—into that of a woman
on the verge of realizing her fullest social and personal potential. If the contemporary topical drama does indeed hold a mirror in front of its society, the transformation, over twelve years, of Marie Hedder into Regina Bayer reflects
admirably on the German Democratic Republic.

Although the cultural political emphasis has shifted considerably since 1971,
the GDR drama, except for some notable exceptions to be discussed later, has
remained consistent. Thus these four plays of 1967 and 1968 are representative of
the recent developments in the GDR theater. They exhibit some common
weaknesses—the main one being schematic characterization, and common strong
points—they are entertaining and directly communicative, and they try to clarify
for their audience new approaches to common problems which have arisen in the
GDR society. Some critics belittle these plays as "consumer drama"[9] and "Polly-
anna pieces,"[10] unaware that their negative critiques only attest to the success of
such drama, since they reflect the precise intentions of the authors and the pre-
determined scope of modern topical theater in the GDR. If we insist on deriding
the "functional" emphasis simply because it does not correspond to the recognized function of art in our society, we can never come to rational historical
conclusions about the GDR drama. When dealing with this drama, we cannot
seek some aesthetic pie in the German sky which would give a play an intrinsic
value outside of the content of the social structure to which it *must* relate. The sky,
as is historically and politically evident, has been divided. The aesthetic pie, the
dessert of the "bourgeois intellectuals," has been taken down to earth in the GDR
and rebaked into solid cultural-political bread, a staple in the diet of that socialist
society.

Subsequent contemporary topical plays operate well within the framework
of the Planned Perspective Until 1970, which was announced in 1965. The
primary emphasis remains on the drama's cognitive task of inculcating the
necessity for further integration of all segments of GDR society into the overall
collective of the Socialist Brotherhood. The topics already developed in the plays
discussed above receive further examination. Arne Leonhardt's *The Graduate*
(*Der Abiturmann* [1969]) and Paul Gratzik's *Detours* (*Umwege* [1970]) cite the need
for the progressive utilization of youthpower in the society, while the further
development of the socialist economic system through the scientific/technologi-
cal revolution and the corresponding revolution in individual and social attitudes
surfaces as the primary concern in Helmut Baierl's *St. Joan of Döbeln* (*Johanna von*

---

[9] Fritz J. Raddatz, *Traditionen und Tendenzen: Materialen zur Literatur der DDR* (Frankfurt am
Main: Suhrkamp, 1972), p. 587.

[10] *Ibid.*, p. 410.

Döbeln [1969]) and in Hans Lucke's *Moderation, the Root of All Evil (Mäßigung ist aller Laster Anfang* [1969]), which deals with the reconstruction of the Berlin Alexanderplatz, the central cultural and business district of East Berlin.

Of these new dramatists Hans Lucke, born in 1927, was the only one to actively experience the war, having been drafted in 1945. Lucke returned from a Soviet POW camp in 1946 and has been an actor and director ever since; he has worked on practically every stage in the GDR. He has been prolific and successful with a myriad of entertaining histories, mysteries and farces, but has only recently turned to contemporary topics. His drama develops organically from his work in the theater. Today he is a leading actor, director and playwright at the Deutsches Theater in Berlin.

Arne Leonhardt, born in 1931, and Paul Gratzik, born in 1935, have almost no literary, and certainly no theatrical background. Leonhardt was a construction worker turned teacher turned novelist; Gratzik was a carpenter turned social worker and correctional worker with juveniles. The experiences of these dramatists in working with the youth of the new socialist state impressed upon them the need for a more sensitive treatment of the GDR's young people. After all, not everyone was a Free German Youth agitator. In their plays, Leonhardt and Gratzik try to demonstrate the conflict between the needs for youthful individualism and societal conformity. The solutions they offer may well be the product of wishful thinking, but they have broken a GDR taboo by presenting this conflict in the first place, and this is in itself commendable.

The most interesting contemporary question for the GDR "How do we retain our revolutionary perspective in a finalized society?" was treated in *Stimulus, or What Is Revolutionary Today? (Anregung, oder Was ist heute revolutionär?* [1969]). This experimental drama, under the direction of Horst Schönemann, currently the best of all GDR directors, used a cabaret-like structure to develop the answers that Claus Hammel's *The Chimney Sweep Comes Tomorrow* had already brought forth in 1967. We must remember that SED dialectics have, in effect, revised the Marxist/Leninist definition of revolution; the SED's objective has become the conservation of a system rather than its upheaval.

By 1968, the GDR stage, as represented by the contemporary topical drama, had become that "moral institution" envisioned by the SED, which resembled German classicism of the late eighteenth century. But as it fulfilled its social-political role to the greatest extent, it also confronted its greatest crisis. For by 1968, there was a dearth of plays, a dearth of authors, and even more critical, a waning audience. Statistics show that GDR theater attendance for nonmusical or operatic works was cut almost in half from a modern high of 6,974,000 visitors in the 1959–60 season to an all-time low of 3,743,800 in the 1967–68 season.[11]

---

[11] Cf. *Statistisches Jahrbuch der Deutschen Demokratischen Republik 1969* (Berlin: Staatsverlag der DDR, 1969), p. 394.

One possible reason for this was suggested by a member of the audience that attended the premiere of *Stimulus*: "[*Stimulus*] is an unreasonable demand on a theatergoer who lives in a culturally and economically well-developed socialist state. Every worker has attained a higher level in the content and form of his life-style than what we are presented with here."[12] If indeed the consciousness of the average GDR citizen has risen to a higher level than that of the contemporary topical socialist drama, then the drama's cultural-political role as a formative tool of that society has been realized; it has been synthesized into planned obsolescence. But even if that state of consciousness postulated by our theatergoer is not yet a reality, it is clear that it cannot be far away. Indications are that the current crisis in which the theater depends more and more on adaptations from other sources— such as stage versions of novels like Hermann Kant's *The Auditorium* (*Die Aula*), which Horst Schönemann turned into the longest-running contemporary topical play in GDR history, and Helmut Sakowski's plays (all of which are adapted from television plays)—can be traced to a change of emphasis already indicated in Walter Ulbricht's Planned Perspective Until 1970.

In his prognosis, Ulbricht defined artistic products as the material for recreational activity: "Naturally we give the greatest consideration of all the possible recreational activities [*Freizeitbeschäftigung*] to the involvement with art and literature."[13] This raises the question of whether going to the theater, with its traditional formal trappings, is still a viable recreational activity in GDR society. Theater, we must remember, necessitates the collection of a large number of people in one location to experience a single cultural act which demands a great amount of time, effort, and expense both from the artists on the stage and from the audience. (No German proletarian would be caught dead in a theater without his dark but proletarian suit.) Furthermore, in the GDR the work week still consists of five and one-half days for most working people, plus semi-mandatory evening courses for technical advancement, plus mandatory involvement in social action groups which further limit free time.

It is, of course, also a foregone conclusion that television has relieved the contemporary topical drama of the cultural-political role as a communication tool it had just realized under the theater policy of the GDR. There are no more than five or six dramatists who write for the stage today in the GDR. Most of these are young and inexperienced, and those who have two or three plays under their belts—Hammel, Kleineidam, Salomon, and Sakowski—are not producing in any significant quantity. The tremendous success and audience approval of television play cycles (the GDR version of TV series as we know them) like Bernhard Seeger's *The Heirs of the Manifesto* (*Die Erben des Manifests* [1968]), Helmut

[12] Horst Schönemann, *Anregung oder Was ist heute revolutionär?* ed. Christoph Funke and Peter Ullrich (Berlin: Buchverlag der Morgen, 1970), p. 138.

[13] Ulbricht, *Neues Deutschland*, 18 December 1965.

Sakowski's *Country Roads* (*Wege übers Land* [1969]) and Benito Wogatski's *Time Is Happiness* (*Zeit ist Glück* [1970]) have put the monkey on the theater's back. The contemporary topical television play has become the incarnation of straight-forward, people-oriented, dramatic socialist realism. There is no doubt that the eye of the camera can add new depth to the characterizations in that genre, characterizations that audiences had never quite come to appreciate on the stage. Also, the television plays reach—and thus can potentially influence—a far wider audience; and television productions are more conducive to the collective artistic production process favored by the SED. A television play is seldom the product of one author and one producer; it is usually a collaboration of authors and producers with a large number of additional artist-technicians, each of whom influences the final artistic product. It is hardly surprising that the GDR consumer of drama seems more disposed to partake of a dramatic "slice of life" from within his own environment, his easy chair, than in the artificial, tradition-bound environment of the theater seat.

2. DEVELOPMENTS SINCE THE EIGHTH PARTY CONGRESS OF 1971

Thus in 1971, when the GDR had developed politically and economically into a socialist bulwark jutting into Western Europe, GDR drama had reached a low ebb. For five years, dramatists had been laboring under the ideological postulate of the Socialist Brotherhood, Walter Ulbricht's attempt to cover the nation and all its internal differences with a harmonious security blanket of socialist humanism. But this rosy view of GDR society had only spawned dis-interest in the theater: there were too few exciting playwrights, and all addressed themselves to familiar topics. But the contemporary drama was not the only cultural area affected. All of GDR literature had suffered, since the postulation of the Socialist Brotherhood had effectively precluded any critical examination of conflicts or contradictions—social, individual, political or otherwise—from literary treatments of life in the GDR.

The Eighth Party Congress of 1971 had brought new, younger faces into the GDR leadership. The last of the old guard, Walter Ulbricht, had been retired, and a new generation of political "technocrats" led by Erich Honecker assumed the leadership. Thus 1971 brought with it hopes for a new liberalization in domestic and cultural policies. At first it seemed that there would indeed be another so-called "thaw." In December 1971 the Fourth Conference of the Central Com-mittee of the SED officially criticized Ulbricht's concept of the Socialist Brother-hood for failing to encompass the full range of individual, social and political life in the GDR. Specifically, the Central Committee found fault with the concept because it did not reflect reality adequately, "obscured class differences which still exist in reality, and overestimated the real progress toward overcoming differences between classes and strata."[14]

With this self-criticism, the party officially admitted a mistake, a rarity indeed. In analyzing and correcting their error, party leaders theorized that the 1967 postulation of an ideal future state of affairs as a *fait accompli* had actually prevented the removal of those last vestiges of class differences, bourgeois attitudes, and transitional conflicts that still remained as real forces in everyday GDR life. The purveyors of the smug Brotherhood view had swept the GDR's problems under the rug instead of bringing them out into the open to be overcome through conscious confrontation. At the Fourth Conference the party admitted that the suppression of "contradictory" critical opinions had consumed time and energy that should have been channelled into the GDR's development as a socialist nation.

A new, more liberal "Honecker era" became a distinct possibility in view of Honecker's statements at the Fourth Conference: "In practice there is nothing which restricts the creative activity of our artists."[15] Becoming more specific, he continued: "If one proceeds from solid premises of socialism, there can, in my opinion, be no taboos in the realm of art and literature."[16] In this connection, the West German cultural critic Gerd Hennig significantly notes that "Honecker spoke out only about socialist literature and art and never mentioned the artistic doctrine of socialist realism."[17] Naturally, this was interpreted by GDR writers as the lifting of the aesthetic restrictions that had been imposed during the formalism debate of the early fifties.

For some time after the Fourth Conference in December 1971, party policies were consistent with the views expressed in its discussions. GDR literature very quickly turned to crucial contemporary problems. The party actually invited open discussions and criticism, as was indicated by the appearance of new printings of works critical of the GDR system, especially in their depiction of individuals at odds with the social structure instead of in harmony with it. These works included Ulrich Plenzdorf's *The New Sorrows of Young W.* (*Die neuen Leiden des jungen W.*), Hermann Kant's *The Imprint* (*Das Impressum*), and Christa Wolf's *The Quest for Christa T.* (*Nachdenken über Christa T.*).[18]

The importance of this development for the drama is not as crucial as we

---

[14] Kurt Hager, "Die entwickelte sozialistische Gesellschaft: Aufgaben der Gesellschaftswissenschaften nach dem VIII Parteitag der SED," *Einheit*, XXVI/11 (1971), 1212.

[15] Erich Honecker, Address at the Fourth Plenary Conference of the Central Committee of the SED, *Neues Deutschland*, 18 December 1971.

[16] *Ibid.*

[17] Hennig, "Mass Cultural Activity in the GDR: On Cultural Politics in Bureaucratically Deformed Transitional Societies," *New German Critique*, 2 (1974), 50.

[18] *Ibid.*, 51.

might think however. More plays are simply not being written; new dramatists do not break onto the scene. If anything, the relative stagnation of contemporary drama seen at the turn of this decade seems to continue. This is indicated by the fact that the two most significant theater productions since 1971 are also adaptations from other sources. They are the stage version of Plenzdorf's *The New Sorrows of Young W.* and Heiner Müller's dramatic adaptation of one of the great Soviet novels of the postrevolutionary era, Gladkov's *Cement* (*Zement*). Müller's adaptation is unmistakable in its reference to the contemporary GDR, and is overtly critical of complacent bureaucratic socialists. This play, basically the story of a young woman's struggle in post-revolutionary Russia, was the most controversial offering of the Berliner Ensemble in the 1973–74 season. Again Müller confronts the GDR with uncomfortable questions about the development of its society and the true nature of the dialectics of individual and society in a Communist system. The fact that Müller, a virtual persona non grata during the era of the Socialist Brotherhood, is again one of the leading GDR theater artists today in his role as dramaturge at the renowned Berliner Ensemble testifies to a marked shift in the prevalent cultural policy.

The most popular dramatist in the last two years, however, has been Ulrich Plenzdorf, whose stage version of the novel *The New Sorrows of Young W.* has taken the GDR by storm. Born in Berlin in 1934, Plenzdorf studied philosophy in Leipzig before graduating from the GDR Film Academy. Thus he is another of the newer dramatists whose roots are not in the theater, but in the rapidly developing electronic "media arts" of television and film. Since 1963 he has been a screenwriter for Deutsche Film-Aktiengesellschaft (DEFA), the GDR's film production organization.

This may indicate that one of the reasons for the relative decline of GDR drama might be the reorientation of the GDR's younger talents to the specifically "twentieth-century" artistic media of television and film. This seems to be only a natural development in a society which has, in the past decade, overtly propagated the so-called "scientific/technical" revolution in all facets of life from industrial and agricultural production to literature. Thus Marshall McLuhan's vision of the electronically oriented and dominated society has extended itself even to the GDR. Here it is regarded positively, however, as the logical coproduct of the GDR's version of socialism, which is officially seen as the necessary corresponding political system of this "scientific technical" age. It should not come as a surprise, then, that such traditional cultural forms as the theater, with all of its old-fashioned trappings of the cultural heritage, are losing their regenerative lifeblood, the young, talented authors. But judging by the success of *The New Sorrows of Young W.* on the stages of the GDR, the old universal fear that the theater may already have died—even in the GDR—is unfounded. Naturally there has been a change. Although, due to our experience in our own society, we expect plays to generate films and television productions, the process may be undergoing a reversal in the GDR. And perhaps this is a logical reversal in a situation in which the most important artistic "moral institution" is no longer the theater, but instead the electronic media.

Plenzdorf's young protagonist Wibeau drops out of the "scientific technical" revolution of the GDR. He opts for rock music, blue jeans, and a lifestyle which could be categorized as a tame version of early Haight-Ashbury. He shows signs of classic postadolescent behavior patterns rejective of the social structure around him, patterns that have been treated in literature ever since individual psychology became the focus of literary attention—from Goethe's *The Sorrows of Young Werther* (to which the title obviously alludes) to Salinger's *Catcher in the Rye*, which Wibeau considers the zenith of literature. Thus he is not unlike Harald Schmieder in Salomon's *Ein Lorbaß*, except that his doubts and fears are not overcome, and he is not reintegrated into the Socialist Brotherhood at the end of the play. Wibeau dies conveniently and ambiguously in an accident—or by suicide, depending on the interpretation. The play found its greatest acceptance with the GDR's young people. Wibeau's rejection of the impersonal bureaucracy, his quest for impossible individual relationships with his parents, teachers, and even his peers, must have struck a resonant chord with Plenzdorf's youthful audience.

The play created an open controversy in the GDR press and at seminars, conferences and discussions, a rare phenomenon in the GDR. It was defended as "the greatest" and condemned as "trash" at the same time. It found favor with some party leaders and was violently denounced by others as an attack on the socialist way of life. The basic criticism in this discussion of the newest trends in GDR literature was voiced by Hans Koch, one of the leading cultural ideologists of the party. He considered the major fault that "the individual's self-realization is sought outside the social situation. . . . Ideals of personality are postulated which are different from ideals of the society and therefore have nothing to do with them anymore."[19] Previously such criticism from official sources would have meant the removal of the offending literature from the public domain. But the discussion is still going on today, and *The New Sorrows of Young W.* is still playing to packed houses all over the GDR—and in the Federal Republic as well. The social criticism inherent in this play, Müller's *Cement*, and other literature of this new "Honecker era" is not anti-Communist in nature. It is rather a criticism which the West German critic Gerd Hennig correctly identifies as "a criticism based upon solidarity which contrasted the existing reality in the GDR with the concept of socialist humanism."[20]

Thus, if the new, more liberal "Honecker era" has had an effect, its major

[19] Koch, "Weite Vielfalt und Widersprüche unserer Kunstentwicklung," *Einheit*, XXVIII/7 (1973), 802.

[20] Hennig, "Mass Cultural Activity in the GDR," 52.

impetus is that today even doctrinaire party line statements such as Koch's are no longer the last word. There seems to be a new dialogue, a give and take among the party, their authors, and the public, the extent of which is quite novel in the GDR. The final returns are not yet in, but barring any radical change in cultural policy, at least from our perspective the prognosis looks positive for the GDR's cultural development during the seventies. The summer of '74 brought a festival of Rumanian art, a festival of Soviet film, and a celebration of Bulgarian culture to the GDR—and the American films *Oklahoma Crude* and *Klute* played in the GDR's largest movie houses. Thus, if recent events are any indication, the dialogue continues. For the GDR dramatists and GDR drama as a whole, this can provide a new base of operation—for where there is dialogue, drama is already half written.

Bibliography

Plays

Baierl, Helmut. *Stücke*. Berlin: Henschel, 1969. [Contents: *Die Feststellung; Frau Flinz; Der Dreizehnte; Johanna von Döbeln*.]

Bauer, Friedhold. *Baran und die Leute im Dorf*. Berlin: Henschel, 1968.

Braun, Volker. *Die Kipper*. *Sinn und Form*, XXIV/1 (1972).

———. *Kipper Paul Bauch*. *Deutsches Theater der Gegenwart*. Vol. II. Ed. Karlheinz Braun. Frankfurt am Main: Suhrkamp, 1967.

Brecht, Bertolt. *Gesammelte Werke*. 20 vols. Frankfurt am Main: Suhrkamp, 1967.

Dudow, Slatan, and Tschesno-Hell, Michael. "Der Hauptmann von Köln." MS. Berlin: Henschelverlag Abteilung Bühnenvertrieb, 1959.

Freitag, Manfred, and Nestler, Jochen. *Seemannsliebe*. Berlin: Henschel, 1968.

Freyer, Paul Herbert. "Der Dämpfer." MS. Berlin: Henschelverlag Abteilung Bühnenvertrieb, 1953.

———. "Kornblumen." MS. Berlin: Henschelverlag Abteilung Bühnenvertrieb, 1954.

———. "Die Straße hinauf." MS. Berlin: Henschelverlag Abteilung Bühnenvertrieb, 1955.

Grosz, Helmut. *Porträt eines Helden*. Leipzig: Zentralhaus für Kulturarbeit, 1968.

Grubert, Peter O., and Behrens, Klaus. *Bewährungsfrist: Eine Dokumentation über die Arbeit an "Bewährungsfrist" durch das Arbeitertheater des Kabelwerks Oberspree*. Berlin: Henschel, 1962.

Grünberg, Karl. *Golden fließt der Stahl*. Berlin: Neues Leben, 1950.

Hacks, Peter. *Vier Komödien*. Frankfurt am Main: Suhrkamp, 1971.

———. *Fünf Stücke*. Frankfurt am Main: Suhrkamp, 1965.

Hammel, Claus. *Komödien*. Berlin: Aufbau, 1969.

Hauser, Harald. "Barbara." MS. Berlin: Henschelverlag Abteilung Bühnenvertrieb, 1968.

———. *Weißes Blut*. Berlin: Henschel, 1961.

Hörspiele 8. Ed. Staatliches Rundfunkkomitee der Deutschen Demokratischen Republik. Berlin: Henschel, 1968.

Kant, Hermann. "Die Aula." MS. Berlin: Henschelverlag Abteilung Bühnenvertrieb, 1968.

Kerndl, Rainer. "Schatten eines Mädchens." MS. Berlin: Henschelverlag Abteilung Bühnenvertrieb, 1965.

———. "Die seltsame Reise des Alois Fingerlein." MS. Berlin: Henschelverlag Abteilung Bühnenvertrieb, 1968.

———. *Stücke*. Berlin: Henschel, 1972.

Kipphardt, Heinar. *Shakespeare dringend gesucht*. Berlin: Henschel, 1954.

Kleineidam, Horst. "Der Millionschmidt." MS. Berlin: Henschelverlag Abteilung Bühnenvertrieb, 1963.

Knauth, Joachim. *Stücke*. Berlin: Henschel, 1973.

Lange, Hans. *Die Schwitzkur und andere Szenen für Kinder*. Leipzig: Zentralhaus für Kulturarbeit, 1971.

Lange, Hartmut. *Marski: Eine Komödie*. Frankfurt am Main: Suhrkamp, 1965.

———. *Senftenberger Erzählungen oder Die Enteignung*. *Deutsches Theater der Gegenwart*. Vol. II. Ed. Karlheinz Braun. Frankfurt am Main: Suhrkamp, 1967.

Lucke, Hans. "Mäßigung ist aller Laster Anfang." MS. Berlin: Henschelverlag Abteilung Bühnenvertrieb, 1969.

Matusche, Alfred. *Dramen*. Berlin: Henschel, 1971.

Müller, Heiner. *Der Bau*. Sinn und Form, XVII/1 (1965).

———. "Klettwitzer Bericht 1958." MS. Berlin: Henschelverlag Abteilung Bühnenvertrieb, 1970.

———. *Der Lohndrücker*. Neue Deutsche Literatur, V/5 (1957).

———. *Die Korrektur*. Neue Deutsche Literatur, VI/5 (1958).

Neue Stücke: Autoren der Deutschen Demokratischen Republik. Ed. Manfred Hocke. Berlin: Henschel, 1971. [Contents: Günter Rücker, *Der Herr Schmidt*; Helmut Baierl, *Der lange Weg zu Lenin*; Siegfried Pfaff, *Regina B.—ein Tag in ihrem Leben*; Armin Stolper, *Zeitgenossen*; Claus Hammel, *Morgen kommt der Schornsteinfeger*; Rainer Kerndl, *Ich bin einem Mädchen begegnet*; Volker Braun, *Freunde*; Horst Salomon, *Ein Lorbaß*; Arne Leonhardt, *Der Abiturmann*; Paul Gratzki, *Umwege*.]

Plenzdorf, Ulrich. *Die neuen Leiden des jungen W.* [Erzählung]. Frankfurt am Main: Suhrkamp, 1973.

Pons, Peter. *Feuer im Dorf*. Leipzig: Hofmeister, 1961.

Reichwald, Fred. "Das Wagnis der Maria Diehl." MS. Berlin: Henschelverlag Abteilung Bühnenvertrieb, 1959.

Ret, Joachim. "Die Zange." MS. Leipzig: Hofmeister, 1959.

Sakowski, Helmut. *Die Entscheidung der Lene Mattke*. Berlin: Henschel, 1967.

————. *Die Säge im Langenmoor*. Berlin: Aufbau, 1960.

————. *Sommer in Heidkau*. *Volksstück*. Berlin: Henschel, 1967.

————. *Steine im Weg*. *Sozialistische Dramatik: Autoren der Deutschen Demokratischen Republik*. Berlin: Henschel, 1968.

————. *Wege übers Land*. *Fernsehroman*. Halle: Mitteldeutscher Verlag, 1969.

Salomon, Horst. "Katzengold." MS. Berlin: Henschelverlag Abteilung Bühnenvertrieb, 1964.

Schmidt, Hans-Dieter. "3 X klingeln." MS. Berlin: Henschelverlag Abteilung Bühnenvertrieb, 1968.

Schneider, Rolf. *Einzug ins Schloß*. Berlin: Henschel, 1972.

————. *Stücke*. Berlin: Henschel, 1970.

Seeger, Bernhard. *Hannes Trostberg: Die Erben des Manifests*. *Fernsehspiele*. Halle: Mitteldeutscher Verlag, 1968.

Strittmatter, Erwin. *Katzgraben/Die Holländerbraut*. Berlin: Aufbau, 1967.

Stücke gegen den Faschismus: Deutschsprachige Autoren. Ed. Christoph Trilse. Berlin: Henschel, 1970.

Tuschel, Karl Heinz. *Ein guter Rat*. *Gedichte, Szenen, Songs für Agitprop*. Leipzig: Hofmeister, 1961.

Wangenheim, Gustav von. *Mit der Zeit werden wir fertig: Eine Studentenkomödie*. Berlin: Neues Leben, 1958.

Waterstradt, Berta. "Ehesache Lorenz." MS. Berlin: Henschelverlag Abteilung Bühnenvertrieb, 1963.

Wogatzki, Benito. *Die Geduld der Kühnen | Zeit ist Glück | Die Zeichen der Ersten*. Berlin: Henschel, 1969.

Wolf, Friedrich. *Gesammelte Werke*. 16 vols. Berlin: Aufbau, 1960.

Zinner, Hedda. "Was wäre wenn—?" MS. Berlin: Henschelverlag Abteilung Bühnenvertrieb, 1959.

Secondary Literature

A bis Z: Ein Taschen- und Nachschlagebuch über den anderen Teil Deutschlands. Ed. Bundesministerium für gesamtdeutsche Fragen. Bonn: Deutscher Bundesverlag, 1969.

Abusch, Alexander. Address at the Cultural Conference of the SED, 23 October 1957. *Zur sozialistischen Kulturrevolution: Dokumente*. Berlin: Dietz, 1960.

————. "Aktuelle Fragen unserere Kunstpolitik." *Sonntag*, 25 March 1956.

————. *Kulturelle Probleme des Sozialistischen Humanismus: Beiträge zur deutschen Kulturpolitik 1946–1967*. Berlin: Aufbau, 1967.

————. *Literatur im Zeitalter des Sozialismus: Beiträge zur Literaturgeschichte 1921–1966*. Berlin: Aufbau, 1967.

Agde, Günter. "Fernsehdramatik als Lesestoff." *Neue Deutsche Literatur*, 1970.

Arbeiterklasse und kulturelles Lebensniveau. Ed. ZK der SED. Berlin: Dietz, 1973.

Ballusek, Lothar von. *Dichter im Dienst: Der sozialistische Realismus in der deutschen Literatur*. Wiesbaden: Limes, 1963.

Becher, Johannes R. "Programmerklärung des Ministeriums für Kultur über den Aufbau einer Volkskultur in der Deutschen Demokratischen Republik." *Sonntag*, 17 October 1954.

Bestandesaufnahme: Eine deutsche Bilanz 1962. Ed. Hans Werner Richter. München: Desch, 1962.

Bilke, Jörg Bernhard. "Planziel Literaturgesellschaft oder Gibt es zwei deutsche Literaturen?" Supplement to *Das Parlament*, No. 51 (18 December 1971).

Brown, Edward J. *Russian Literature Since the Revolution*. London: Collier, 1969.

Die deutsche Literatur der Gegenwart. Ed. Manfred Durzak. Stuttgart: Reclam, 1971.

Deutscher Schriftstellerverband. "Abschließende Stellungnahme des Sekretariats des Deutschen Schriftstellerverbandes zu *Die Sorgen und die Macht*." *Neue Deutsche Literatur*, XI/3 (1963).

Doernberg, Stefan. *Kurze Geschichte der DDR*. Berlin: Dietz, 1969.

Dokumente des VIII Parteitages der SED. Berlin: Dietz, 1971.

Dokumente zur Kunst-, Literatur- und Kulturpolitik der SED. Ed. Elimar Schubbe. Stuttgart: Seewald, 1972.

Dymshits, Alexander. "The Literature of Democratic Germany." *Soviet Literature*, XIX/2 (1950).

"Eine Aussprache mit Theaterintendanten." *Neues Deutschland*, 4 May 1956.

Einführung in Theorie, Geschichte und Funktion der DDR Literatur. Ed. Hans-Jürgen Schmitt. Literaturwissenschaft und Sozialwissenschaften, 6. Stuttgart: Metzler, 1975.

Fehervary, Helen. "Heiner Müllers Brigadenstücke." *Basis: Jahrbuch für deutsche Gegenwartsliteratur*, II (1971), 103–140.

Franke, Konrad. *Die Literatur der Deutschen Demokratischen Republik*. München: Kindler, 1971.

Fuegi, John. "The Exile's Choice: Brecht and the Soviet Union." MS. of Lecture, Kentucky Foreign Language Conference, 1971.

Funke, Christoph. *Der Regisseur Horst Schönemann. Bericht. Analyse. Dokumentation*. Berlin: Henschel, 1971.

"Für eine sozialistische Kultur: Die Entwicklung der sozialistischen Kultur in der Zeit des zweiten Fünfjahresplanes." *Neues Deutschland*, 7 December 1957.

Glenn, Jerry. *Deutsches Schrifttum der Gegenwart (ab 1945). Handbuch der Deutschen Literaturgeschichte*. München: Francke, 1971.

Hacks, Peter. "Das realistische Theaterstück." *Neue Deutsche Literatur*, V/10 (1957).

Hager, Kurt. "Die entwickelte sozialistische Gesellschaft: Aufgaben der Gesellschaftswissenschaften nach dem VIII. Parteitag der SED." *Einheit*, XXVI/11 (1971).

Hennig, Gerd. "Mass Cultural Activity in the GDR: On Cultural Politics in Bureaucratically Deformed Transitional Societies." *New German Critique*, 2 (1974).

Hofmann, Heinz. "Blick auf die neue Dramatik." *Neue Deutsche Literatur*, III/3 (1955).

Hörz, Helga. *Die Frau als Persönlichkeit: Philosophische Probleme einer Geschlechterpsychologie.* Berlin: Deutscher Verlag der Wissenschaften, 1971.

Jarmatz, Klaus. "Die literarische Entwicklung in der Deutschen Demokratischen Republik." *Weimarer Beiträge*, X/5 (1964).

————. "Literaturpolitische Probleme der 2. Bitterfelder Konferenz." *Weimarer Beiträge*, XIV/3 (1968).

John, Erhard; Lippold, Eberhard; and Rammler, Michael. *Kunst und sozialistische Bewusstseinsbildung.* Berlin: Dietz, 1974.

Kähler, Hermann. *Gegenwart auf der Bühne: Die sozialistische Wirklichkeit in den Bühnenstücken der DDR von 1956–1963/64.* Berlin: Henschel, 1966.

Karau, Gisela. *Sozialistischer Alltag in der DDR.* Berlin: Aus erster Hand, 1971.

Kritik in der Zeit: Der Sozialismus—seine Literatur—ihre Entwicklung. Ed. Klaus Jarmatz et al. Halle: Mitteldeutscher Verlag, 1970.

Kulturkonferenz 1960. Ed. ZK der SED. Berlin: Dietz, 1960.

Kulturpolitisches Wörterbuch. Ed. Harald Bühl et al. Berlin: Dietz, 1970.

Kulturwissenschaft und Arbeiterklasse. Ed. Gudrun Freitag et al. Berlin: Dietz, 1968.

Mäde, Hans-Dieter, and Püschel, Ursula. *Dramaturgie des Positiven.* Berlin: Henschelverlag, 1973.

Marx, Karl, and Engels, Friedrich. *Über Kunst und Literatur.* 2 vols. Berlin: Dietz, 1968.

Marx, Karl; Engels, Friedrich; and Lenin, Wladimir Iljitsch. *Über Kultur, Ästhetik, Literatur.* Ed. Hans Koch. Leipzig: Reclam, 1971.

Mayer, Hans. *Deutsche Literatur seit Thomas Mann.* Reinbek bei Hamburg: rororo, 1968.

————. "Literature and Daily Life: Everyman in the Soviet Union and the United States." *Steppenwolf and Everyman: Outsiders and Conformists in Contemporary Literature.* Trans. Jack D. Zipes. New York: Thomas Y. Crowell Co., 1971.

Mittenzwei, Werner. *Gestaltung und Gestalten im modernen Drama.* Berlin: Aufbau, 1965.

Münz-Koenen, Ingeborg. *Fernsehdramatik: Experimente—Methoden—Tendenzen.* Berlin: Akademie, 1974.

"Nachterstedter Brief." *Tribüne*, 27 January 1955.

Nelson, Walter Henry. *The Berliners. Their Saga and Their City.* New York: David McKay Co., 1969.

Nettl, Joseph P., *The Eastern Zone and Soviet Policy in Germany 1945–50.* London: Oxford, 1951.

Neubert, Werner. "Unsere Konflikte in unserer Literatur." *Neue Deutsche*

Literatur, XVIII/3 1970.

Oelßner, Fred. *Kampf gegen den Formalismus in Kunst und Literatur*. Berlin: Dietz, 1951.

Politische Ökonomie des Sozialismus und ihre Anwendung in der DDR. Ed. ZK der SED. Berlin: Dietz, 1969.

Positionen: Beiträge zur marxistischen Literaturtheorie in der DDR. Ed. Werner Mittenzwei. Leipzig: Reclam, 1971.

Raddatz, Fritz J. *Traditionen und Tendenzen: Materialen zur Literatur der DDR*. Frankfurt am Main: Suhrkamp, 1972.

Revolution und Literatur: Zum Verhältnis von Erbe, Revolution und Literatur. Ed. Werner Mittenzwei and Reinhard Weisbach. Leipzig: Reclam, 1971.

Rühle, Jürgen. *Das gefesselte Theater: Vom Revolutionstheater zum Sozialistischen Realismus*. Köln: Kiepenheuer & Witsch, 1957.

Rülicke-Weiler, Käthe. *Die Dramaturgie Brechts: Theater als Mittel der Veränderung*. Berlin: Henschel, 1968.

SBZ von A bis Z: Ein Taschen- und Nachschlagebuch über die Sowjetische Besatzungszone Deutschlands. Ed. Bundesministerium für gesamtdeutsche Fragen. Bonn: Bundesverlag, 1966.

Schauspielführer. Vol. II. Ed. Karl Heinz Berger et al. Berlin: Henschel, 1968, 1972.

Schönemann, Horst. *Anregung oder Was ist heute revolutionär?* Ed. Christoph Funke and Peter Ullrich. Berlin: Buchverlag der Morgen, 1970.

Slonim, Marc. *Russian Theater from the Empire to the Soviets*. New York: Collier, 1962.

"So denken wir darüber." *Theater der Zeit*, 3, 1957.

Statistisches Jahrbuch der Deutschen Demokratischen Republik 1969. Berlin: Staatsverlag der DDR, 1969. [Also 1970, 1971, 1972, 1973.]

Stephan, Alexander. *Christa Wolf*. München: Beck and *Text + Kritik*, 1976.

Theaterarbeit: 6 Aufführungen des Berliner Ensembles. Ed. Berliner Ensemble and Helene Weigel. Berlin: Henschel, 1967.

Theater Bilanz: Bühnen der DDR: Eine Bilddokumentation 1945–1969. Ed. Christoph Funke et al. Berlin: Henschel, 1971.

"Das Theater der Gegenwart: Eine Rundfrage." *Neue Deutsche Literatur*, V/4 (1957).

Theater hier und heute. Ed. Rolf Rohmer et al. Berlin: Henschel, 1968.

Theater hinter dem "Eisernen Vorhang." Ed. Reinhold Grimm et al. Hamburg: Basilius, 1964.

Thomas, Rüdiger. *Modell DDR: Die kalkulierte Emanzipation*. 4th ed. München: Hanser, 1974.

Träger, Klaus. *Studien zur Literaturtheorie und Literaturgeschichte*. Leipzig: Reclam, 1970.

Träger, Klaus. *Studien zur Realismustheorie und Methodologie der Literaturwissenschaft*. Leipzig: Reclam, 1972.

Trommler, Frank. "Der 'Nullpunkt 1945' und seine Verbindlichkeit für die Literaturgeschichte." *Basis: Jahrbuch für deutsche Gegenwartsliteratur*, I (1970), 9–25.

———. "Von Stalin zu Hölderlin: Über den Entwicklungsroman in der DDR." *Basis: Jahrbuch für deutsche Gegenwartsliteratur*, II (1971), 141–90.

———. "Der zögernde Nachwuchs: Entwicklungsprobleme der Nachkriegsliteratur in West und Ost." *Tendenzen der deutschen Literatur seit 1945*. Ed. Thomas Koebner. Stuttgart: Kröner, 1971.

Ulbricht, Walter. *Die Bedeutung des Werkes Das Kapital von Karl Marx für die Schaffung des entwickelten gesellschaftlichen Systems des Sozialismus in der DDR und den Kampf gegen das staatsmonopolistische Herrschaftssystem in Westdeutschland*. Berlin: Dietz, 1967.

———. "Fragen der deutschen Nationalliteratur." *Neues Deutschland*, 17 January 1956.

———. *Die historische Mission der Sozialistischen Einheitspartei Deutschlands: Sechs Reden und Aufsätze*. Berlin: Dietz, 1971.

Der Weg zur Sicherung des Friedens und zur Erhöhung der materiellen und kulturellen Lebensbedingungen des Volkes. Ed. ZK der SED. Berlin: Dietz, 1959.

Wekwerth, Manfred. *Theater und Wissenschaft: Überlegungen für das Theater von heute und morgen*. München: Hanser, 1974.

Wolf, Friedrich, and Wischnewski, Wsewolod. *Friedrich Wolf/Wsewolod Wischnewski: Eine Auswahl aus ihrem Briefwechsel*. Ed. Gudrun Düwel. Berlin: Deutsche Akademie der Künste, 1965.

Zur sozialistischen Kulturrevolution: Dokumente. Ed. ZK der SED. Vol. II. Berlin: Dietz, 1960.

Zur Theorie des Sozialistischen Realismus. Ed. Hans Koch. Berlin: Dietz, 1974.

Zweite Bitterfelder Konferenz 1964: Protokoll der von der Ideologischen Kommission beim Politbüro des ZK der SED und dem Ministerium für Kultur am 24. und 25. April im Kulturpalast des Elektrochemischen Kombinats Bitterfeld abgehaltenen Konferenz. Ed. ZK der SED. Berlin: Dietz, 1964.

Index

UNIVERSITY OF NORTH CAROLINA
STUDIES IN THE GERMANIC LANGUAGES
AND LITERATURES

For other volumes in the "Studies" see page ii and following pages.

Send orders to: (U.S. and Canada)
The University of North Carolina Press, P.O. Box 2288
Chapel Hill, N.iC. 27514
(All other countries) Feffer and Simons, Inc., 31 Union Square, New York, N. Y. 10003

UNIVERSITY OF NORTH CAROLINA
STUDIES IN THE GERMANIC LANGUAGES
AND LITERATURES

73. Donald G. Daviau and Jorun B. Johns, eds. THE CORRESPONDENCE OF ARTHUR SCHNITZLER AND RAOUL AUERNHEIMER WITH RAOUL AUERNHEIMER'S APHORISMS. 1972. Pp. xii, 161. Cloth $7.50.
74. A. Margaret Arent Madelung. THE LAXDOELA SAGA: ITS STRUCTURAL PATTERNS: 1972. Pp. xiv, 261. Cloth $9.25.
75. Jeffrey L. Sammons. SIX ESSAYS ON THE YOUNG GERMAN NOVEL. 1972. 2nd ed. 1975. Pp. xiv, 187. Cloth $8.00.
76. Donald H. Crosby and George C. Schoolfield, eds. STUDIES IN THE GERMAN DRAMA. A *FESTSCHRIFT* IN HONOR OF WALTER SILZ. 1974. Pp. xxvi, 255. Cloth $10.75.

For other volumes in the "Studies" see p. ii.

Send orders to: (U.S. and Canada)
The University of North Carolina Press, P.O. Box 2288
Chapel Hill, N.iC. 27514
(All other countries) Feffer and Simons, Inc., 31 Union Square, New York, N. Y. 10003

UNIVERSITY OF NORTH CAROLINA
STUDIES IN THE GERMANIC LANGUAGES
AND LITERATURES

Vols. 1-44 and 46-49 of the "Studies"
have been reprinted and may be ordered from:
AMS Press, Inc., 56 E. 13th Street, New York, N. Y. 10003

For a complete list of reprinted titles write to:
Editor, UNCSGL&L, 442 Dey Hall 014 A, UNC, Chapel Hill, N. C. 27514

For other volumes in the "Studies" see preceding pages and p. ii.